# TRIUMVIRATE

★ ★ ★

*The Story of*

THE UNLIKELY ALLIANCE THAT

SAVED THE CONSTITUTION AND

UNITED THE NATION

BRUCE CHADWICK

SOURCEBOOKS, INC.
NAPERVILLE, ILLINOIS

Published by Sourcebooks, Inc.
P.O. Box 4410, Naperville, Illinois 60567-4410
(630) 961-3900
Fax: (630) 961-2168
www.sourcebooks.com

Library of Congress Cataloging-in-Publication Data
Chadwick, Bruce.
   Triumvirate : the story of the unlikely alliance that saved the Constitution and
united the nation / Bruce Chadwick.
      p. cm.
   Includes bibliographical references and index.
   1.   United States—Politics and government—1783-1789. 2.   Constitutional
history—United States. 3.  Madison, James, 1751-1836. 4.  Hamilton, Alexander,
1757-1804. 5.  Jay, John, 1745-1829. 6.  Alliances—Case studies. 7.  New York
(State)—Politics and government—1775-1865. 8.  Pennsylvania—Politics and government—1775-1865. 9.  Massachusetts—Politics and government—1775-1865.
10.  Virginia—Politics and government—1775-1865.  I. Title.
   E303.C47 2009
   973.3'18—dc22
                                    2008043081

Printed and bound in the United States of America.
BG 10 9 8 7 6 5 4 3 2 1

*For*
*Margie and Rory*

I have seen no other [writings] so well calculated to produce conviction on an unbiased mind as...your Triumvirate.

—George Washington to Alexander Hamilton

on *The Federalist*

# CONTENTS

# ACKNOWLEDGMENTS

I have written a number of books and *Triumvirate* was probably the most difficult. Exhaustive research was necessary in documents concerning the thirteen states and in the constitutional battles in each of them. Putting together the arguments for and against the Constitution, and profiling the Federalists and Anti-Federalists, was not easy. Fortunately, I had help.

I would like to thank Dr. Paul Clemens, at Rutgers University, and Dr. Fran Moran, at New Jersey City University, for reading the manuscript and making very helpful suggestions to improve it.

My journey took me to many libraries, archives, and museums. Many thanks to the librarians at the David Library of the American Revolution, New York Historical Society, New Jersey Historical Society, Massachusetts Historical Society, Virginia Historical Society, the Rockefeller Library at Williamsburg, Virginia, the Virginia State Library, the New Jersey City University Library (and librarian Fred Smith), the Rutgers Library, the Princeton Library, Morris County Library, Randolph Library, and the staff at the Library of Congress.

I want to thank the photo editors at the Independence Hall Historical Park, in Philadelphia, the Rockefeller Library, and the New York Historical Society for their help.

At Sourcebooks, my publisher, I owe much to the extremely talented executive editor, Hillel Black, who has edited this book and others I wrote. Thanks, too, to Steve O'Rear (production editor), Brenda Horrigan (copy editor), and Heather Moore (Sourcebooks publicist).

My agents at McIntosh and Otis, especially Elizabeth Winick and Rebecca Stauss, were instrumental in the development of this book.

Thanks to Jo Bruno, vice president at New Jersey City University, for her help in obtaining grants at the university that helped me conduct my research.

Finally, thanks, as always, to my loving wife Marjorie, for all of her support and help during the time it took me to write this book.

# THE IMPORTANT PLAYERS

## Maryland

### Federalist

Daniel Carroll—Member of the Continental Congress, delegate to the Constitutional Convention, member of the state legislature.

Thomas Johnson—Member of the state legislature, member of the Continental Congress, Revolutionary War governor of Maryland.

### Anti-Federalist

Luther Martin—Officer in the Continental Army, member of the Continental Congress, attorney general of Maryland.

## Massachusetts

### Federalist

Rufus King—Delegate to the Constitutional Convention, member of the Continental Congress.

Benjamin Lincoln—Continental Army general, member of the Continental Congress, secretary of war, and Maine farmer.

### Anti-Federalist

Samuel Adams—Signer of the Declaration of Independence, chief propagandist for the American Revolution, member of the Continental Congress, owner of a Boston beer brewery.

Elbridge Gerry—merchant, member of the Continental Congress, signer of the Declaration of Independence.

### Neutral

John Hancock—Shipping mogul, president of the Continental Congress, signer of the Declaration of Independence, governor of Massachusetts in 1788.

# New York

## *Federalist*

John Jay—President of the Continental Congress, Revolutionary War peace treaty negotiator, secretary of foreign affairs, newspaper columnist "Publius."

Alexander Hamilton—Washington's chief of staff in the American Revolution, member of the Continental Congress, delegate to the Constitutional Convention, newspaper columnist "Publius."

## *Anti-Federalist*

Melancton Smith—Officer in the Continental Army, member of the Continental Congress, president of the New York Manumission (anti-slavery) Society, author of the newspaper series "Letters from a Federal Farmer."

George Clinton—General in the Continental Army, governor of New York, member of the New York State Assembly, member of the Continental Congress, reportedly the newspaper columnist "Cato."

John Lansing Jr.—Secretary to General Philip Schuyler in the American Revolution, speaker of the New York State Assembly, delegate to the Constitutional Convention.

# Pennsylvania

## *Federalist*

Gouverneur Morris—Former New Yorker who was a member of the Continental Congress, delegate to the Constitutional Convention, reportedly the author of the opening line of the Constitution, "We the people…"

James O. Wilson—Member of the Continental Congress.

## South Carolina

### Federalist

John Rutledge—Member of the state legislature, member of the Continental Congress, governor of South Carolina.

### Anti-Federalist

Aedanus Burke—Officer in the Continental Army, member of the state legislature, state circuit court judge.

## Virginia

### Federalist

James Madison—Member of the Continental Congress, member of the state legislature, primary author of the Constitution.

George Wythe—Member of the state legislature, member of the Virginia Supreme Court, mayor of Williamsburg, first law professor in the United States.

Edmund Pendleton—Speaker of the state legislature, member of the Virginia Supreme Court, member of the Continental Congress.

George Washington—former commander in chief of the Continental Army.

### Anti-Federalist

Richard Henry Lee—Member of the state legislature, president of the Continental Congress.

George Mason—Member of the Continental Congress, signer of the Declaration of Independence, member of the state legislature, delegate to the Constitutional Convention.

Patrick Henry—Two-time governor of Virginia, member of the state legislature, renowned public speaker ("Give me liberty or give me death...")

## *Neutral*

Edmund Randolph—Aide to George Washington in the
Revolutionary War, state attorney general, member of the
Continental Congress, delegate to the Constitutional Convention,
mayor of Williamsburg.

# SUMMER 1787, AND THE CONSTITUTIONAL CONVENTION IN PHILADELPHIA

The Constitution of the United States was not written to create a government for the newly independent United States. It was produced to replace the old government, created by the Articles of Confederation during the American Revolution, that failed badly. The government under the old articles had no elected chief executive, no supreme court, one house of congress, and did not have the power to levy taxes. No bill could become law unless all thirteen states approved. By the summer of 1787, the nation was crumbling under it. A Federal Convention (also known as the Constitutional Convention) in Philadelphia, attended by the most prominent men in the country, including George Washington, Benjamin Franklin, Alexander Hamilton, and James Madison, was called to correct the articles.

The delegates quickly abandoned the Articles of Confederation, ignored the current government, and set out to devise a brand-new government, one based on the popular ideas of the era espoused by political philosophers such as John Locke, Voltaire, and Thomas

Paine. It was a government designed to meet the unique needs of America, one that could change as the people changed over the coming years. It was a government, the delegates hoped, that would reflect the will of the people and recognize the rights of the poor and middle class as well as those of the wealthy.

And it would be a government, too, as defined in the debates and disputes of the delegates, that gave certain powers to the national government and other, equally important, powers to the states.

The result was a long summer of deliberations filled with controversies, sectional prejudice, arguments, and compromises. Now, people look back on the Constitution as not only the template for good government, but a document that permitted the United States to be born and flourish as the world's greatest democracy. But at the time of the Constitutional Convention in 1787, no one was certain what the outcome would be.

Everyone realized the importance of the Constitution when the delegates gathered in Philadelphia on May 25, 1787. The *Pennsylvania Journal* wrote, "Upon the event of this great council, indeed, depends everything that can be essential to the dignity and stability of the national character...all the fortunes of the future are involved in this momentous undertaking."[1]

The passage of the Constitution was not easy.

The fifty-five delegates were an elite group. Thirty-five were lawyers, thirteen were tradesmen, and a dozen owned plantations and slaves. Forty-two had served in the Continental Congress and eight had been the governor of their state. Twenty-one were veterans of the Revolutionary War. In an age when very few men even attended college, more than half the delegates were college graduates; nine went to Princeton. They lived at boarding houses near the Pennsylvania State House, where the "secret" sessions were held, or at the homes of Philadelphians they knew. The men worked nearly all day, six days a

week, and retired to the City Tavern at night, exhausted, in an exceedingly hot summer. They represented large states and small, slave states
and free, and states that thrived on diverse businesses, such as fishing, shipping, industry, and farming. All of the states seemed to have
different interests.

The delegates wasted no time. In the first week, Virginia governor Edmund Randolph proposed the Virginia Plan, cobbled together
by James Madison, under which the Confederation government was
abolished and a new government was introduced. Under the plan, the
larger states had more voting power than the smaller ones, the people
would elect a House of Representatives, and the House would elect
the Senate. There was talk, too, of a national executive and a federal
system of courts.

The plan was opposed by delegates who proposed the New Jersey
Plan, under which each state had the same vote in any congressional
decision, with tiny states such as New Jersey and Delaware having the
same power as large ones, such as New York and Pennsylvania. The
delegates from the small states were afraid that the congressmen from a
handful of large states would combine their votes to assist larger states
and ignore the others. The small states also argued for more power
to the people in electing Congress. The compromise, proposed by
Connecticut delegates, was that the people would elect the House of
Representatives and that each state legislature would elect that state's
United States senators.[2]

The decision included a historic move to count each slave as
three-fifths of a white person in the population of slave states, giving the southern states enormous voting power. That prompted
criticism. Northerner Gouverneur Morris spoke for many when he
rose to say, "I never will concur in upholding domestic slavery. It is
a nefarious institution. It is the curse of heaven on the states where
it prevails."[3]

The slavery compromise on state populations passed, but in return the convention outlawed slavery in the Northwest Territories and called for the end of slave trade with Africa by 1807.

The adoption of the Virginia Plan started arguments in the convention that lasted for weeks. Delegates from the smaller states contended that those from the large states had not only pushed through a Constitution that favored the large states, but were creating a huge national government that would replace the states and run the country in oppressive, tyrannical fashion. Many delegates also saw the entire new government as a scheme to give the well-to-do control of the country. One was Benjamin Franklin, who said, "Some of the greatest rogues I was ever acquainted with were the richest rogues."[4] There were arguments that threatened to break up the convention, and some angry delegates even went home over them.

Luther Martin, of Maryland, renowned for his lengthy talks during the deliberations, was livid over the nationalistic Constitution and predicted it would not pass. "I'll be hanged if ever the people of Maryland agree to it," he said. Another delegate jumped to his feet, pointed at Martin, smiled, and told him, "I advise you to stay in Philadelphia lest you should be hanged."[5]

There was some talk of modeling America on the British Parliament. Many opposed that. America had just declared independence from Britain because of the oppression of the British Parliament. Besides, Charles Pinckney of South Carolina told the convention, America was unique. He said, "The people of this country are not only very different from the inhabitants of any state we are acquainted with in the modern world, but I assert that their situation is distinct from either the people of Greece or Rome or of any state we are acquainted with among the ancients."[6]

The arguments in Philadelphia went back and forth. It was agreed that Congress had the power to levy taxes and provide for the common defense of the country. Congress could declare war. It could pass "necessary and proper" new laws to carry out its programs. They agreed that the Constitution could be amended at a later date.

Under it, a chief executive also served as commander in chief of the army. He could propose treaties with foreign countries, but the powers of the office were vague. The creation of the president was the center of great debate and opposed by many who did not want a tyrant such as George III running the country for years.

A Supreme Court was established whose justices the president would nominate and the Senate confirm.

Hot and humid days dragged into weeks and months, and delegates in favor and against the new government became upset that the convention was taking so long. John Rutledge of South Carolina sighed, "The proceedings are becoming very tedious."[7]

Toward the end of the convention, two angry delegates, Elbridge Gerry of Massachusetts and George Mason of Virginia, tried to have a bill of rights passed that protected the rights of the people against the national government—such as guarantees for freedom of religion, speech, and the press; and of the right to jury trials, to lawyers, to carry firearms; and protection from forced quartering of soldiers in private homes, unreasonable search and seizure; plus a guarantee that the states maintained numerous rights. Their efforts were abruptly voted down, a move by the majority that further enraged the dissidents who opposed the Constitution.

The public held its collective breath as the convention continued on through the end of the summer and into the first week of September. A writer for the *Pennsylvania Gazette* wrote, "Every enterprise, public as well as private, in the United States seems suspended till it is known what kind of government we are to receive from our national convention."[8]

The delegates feared state legislatures, which would lose power under its laws, would vote down the Constitution, so they decreed that newly elected state ratification conventions be created for passage. They wanted each state to approve the new government, but that seemed impossible. Rhode Island had refused to send any delegates at all to the convention, two of New York's three delegates had gone home in anger, and Maryland's delegates seemed dead set against it. Instead, the delegates decided that the Constitution could be approved if nine of the thirteen states voted for it at independent ratification conventions.[9]

That decision kicked off a political storm that raged for nearly a year. No one in Philadelphia foresaw the vicious fight that would occur in the ratification conventions, a fight that would determine whether or not there would even be a United States of America.

## Chapter One

# A FIGHT BREWS

*Aboard a sloop anchored in the Hudson River at Albany, New York, evening, late October 1787.*

The slow arrival of the night cast a dusky blanket over the waters of the Hudson River in New York. The lush forests that lined the shores of the river, blindingly beautiful in the autumn when the leaves changed from green into all the blazing colors of a painter's palette, were quiet and still. On board a single-masted sloop moored in the Hudson at Albany, near the mills of his father-in-law, Philip Schuyler, the Revolutionary War general, the light of a candle shone from the window of a cabin.

Inside the dimly lit cabin, Alexander Hamilton began to write quickly across paper that covered a wide wooden desk. Hamilton, thirty-two, had been in Albany on business before the state Supreme Court and to see Schuyler, whose daughter Eliza he had married in 1780. The sandy-haired Hamilton, a gifted political theorist, author, and speaker, was working on the first of what would be eighty-five essays of support for the newly approved U.S. Constitution, the

*Federalist*, that would be published in New York newspapers, and others throughout the nation, during the next eight months, just in time for the delegates to the state conventions called to ratify the Constitution to read them.

Hamilton felt comfortable writing quickly. He had spent nearly five years in the American Revolution as the chief of staff to Commander in Chief George Washington; among his many responsibilities was the production of thousands of pages of letters, reports, and orders. Then, and now, the loquacious, personable Hamilton cut quite a figure. He was about 5 feet 7 inches in height and thin, but stood and walked ramrod straight, chin always tilted up slightly, to give the appearance of a taller man. Hamilton had a thin nose and a square chin that in later years might be called a boxer's jaw. His fair complexioned face was highlighted by a slight smile and dazzling, clear blue eyes that attracted the attention of everyone who met him. He was always well dressed, favoring the most expensive jackets, breeches, and stockings and was sometimes attended by a hairdresser. The former army colonel and congressman was a spry man with a sophisticated demeanor. A man who knew him, Fisher Ames, marveled that he possessed "a degree of refinement and grace which I never witnessed in any other man…it is impossible to conceive a loftier portion of easy, graceful, and polished movements than were exhibited in him."[10]

With the outdoor light dying slowly and the sounds of the river and the port town in the background, he wrote to his countrymen in *The Federalist* No. 1, "After an unequivocal experience of the inefficacy of the subsisting Federal Convention, you are called upon to deliberate on a new Constitution for the United States of America. The subject speaks of its importance comprehending in its consequences nothing less than the existence of the Union, the safety and welfare of the parts of which it is composed, the fate of an empire, in many respects the most interesting in the world…"[11]

Hamilton worked all night and throughout the next days on the essay, one of the many he would write as his contribution with John Jay of New York, the U.S. secretary for foreign affairs, and James Madison, the congressman from Virginia. The essays had to be written quickly, and published as soon as possible, because the Anti-Federalists, the angry group arrayed against the passage of the Constitution, had already managed to publish several stinging columns attacking it in the New York newspapers after succeeding in obtaining publication of similar essays in cities throughout the country.[12]

All writers have different idiosyncrasies that they employ in order to gather their thoughts. Some look out windows and others stare at the paper on their desk. The fidgety Hamilton liked to walk back and forth, whether in his New York City home, his old army quarters, or on ships. He paced on the deck of the ship that night, and throughout the following days before the vessel reached New York City. As he did so, Hamilton had to be astonished by the spectacular scenery the sloop passed on its way south. The wide river's beauty had astonished Henry Hudson, the explorer for whom the waterway was named, and the hundreds of thousands of people who had traveled on it or lived on its banks over the next two hundred years.

The Hudson River and the surrounding valley were majestic, with jagged rock formations, rolling green hills, deep valleys, swift-running creeks, and miles of gorgeous forests. Troops in the Continental Army marching through it during the Revolution often asked their commanders for permission to climb to the tops of hills to get a better view of the river. Hundreds of painters would try to capture its beauty on their canvasses. Novelist F. Scott Fitzgerald would portray it better than anyone when he wrote of the river in *The Great Gatsby*: "For a transitory moment, man must have held his breath in the presence of this continent, compelled into an aesthetic contemplation he neither understood nor desired, face to face for the last time in history with something commensurate to his capacity for wonder."[13]

The voyage down the Hudson was a repetition of previous memorable journeys for Hamilton, too. The ship passed Kingston, a river town that the British nearly leveled when their navy bombarded it. There were the shores of Westchester County, near White Plains, where the British had defeated the Americans in the fall of 1776. The sloop drifted past West Point, an American fortress on the river that was the scene of Benedict Arnold's betrayal, and finally past Fort Washington, on the northwest corner of Manhattan Island, where three thousand American were captured when it fell in 1776. And, finally, there was New York City, which George Washington had wanted so desperately to capture during the war and finally rode through in triumph when the peace treaty was signed in 1783.

Hamilton wrote as rapidly as he could because he had to convey the finished letter to Thomas Greenleaf, the publisher of New York's *Independent Journal,* who had promised to print all of the essays to help Hamilton get the Constitution ratified in his home state of New York and, indirectly, in the others. The sloop and Hamilton were in a race against time; Greenleaf had to have the initial letter on October 26 so that it could appear in print the next day. He was holding up an entire page of space and type for the arrival of the essay. Although Hamilton did not think about it at the time, the need for speed in writing *The Federalist* that drove all three authors at a frantic pace probably enabled them to frame their ideas more clearly and to write with great eloquence, organization, and discipline, something that might not have been possible if they had time to complete and revise several drafts of their letters before publishing them.

Writing quickly, Hamilton managed to finish the essay just before the sloop docked in New York. It landed at a wharf on the west side of New York and Hamilton disembarked and traveled by carriage over bumpy dirt roads to his home at 57 Wall Street. Nervously waiting for him at the residence was a teenage apprentice printer sent by editor Greenleaf. Hamilton handed the boy the essay and the courier left, headed for the office of the *Independent Journal*, a few blocks away.[14]

The following morning Hamilton, and the rest of New York City, read letter number one of *The Federalist*, signed by the nom de plume "Publius," a Latin word meaning "to proclaim" or "to bring before the public" that the trio had agreed to use to both hide their identities and to write as one voice.[15] He took great satisfaction in seeing the essay in print in the narrow columns of the newspaper and in watching others read his ideas, laid out brilliantly in the text. Hamilton was so pleased that he mailed a copy of the newspaper to George Washington at Mount Vernon. Washington was astonished by the force and beauty of the essay, and all the others that followed, and told Hamilton later that when the Constitutional Convention and the beginnings of the American government were long forgotten, the world would still remember the power of the ideas concerning democracy expressed in the essays themselves and later as the book *The Federalist*.[16]

Hamilton was certain that the essay, and the others that would soon be printed, would furnish the public, and history, with a crystal clear explanation of the new democracy proposed in the Constitution and the need for the states to approve it.

Alexander Hamilton knew, too, that the initial letter was just the first step in the fierce battle to get the Constitution ratified, a long political drama that would unfold, state by state, month by month, over the following year. It would include speeches by the fiery orator Patrick Henry in Virginia and angry newspaper columns by New York governor George Clinton, both dead set against it, by arm twisting in Massachusetts, feuds in Pennsylvania, arguments in New Hampshire, corruption and chicanery in the elections of delegates, vitriolic denunciations by politicians of each other, deception, duplicity, duels, fist fights, riots, and a nasty, blistering war of words in the American press.

Alexander Hamilton, James Madison, and John Jay led the ratification fight. They were among the most experienced public figures in the country, heroes of the Revolution, and brilliant. None of that would matter much in the ratification battle, though, where they would have to take off their fancy coats and engage in rough-and-tumble bareknuckle politics, backroom intrigue, endless cajoling, brassy electioneering, and sheer intimidation to get the Constitution approved.

Hamilton, Madison, and Jay were an unlikely trio, men with very different interests, backgrounds, and personalities, and now they had come together to take on a screaming horde of politicians who opposed the proposed nationalistic federal government, afraid it would swallow up the thirteen states and quash all of the individual liberties that 240,000 men had fought for—and 20,000 had died for—in the Revolution.

It would be a battle that would determine the future course of the United States and, with it, perhaps, the world.

# THE ARRIVAL OF JAMES MADISON IN A TURBULENT NEW YORK CITY

*Autumn 1787*

It is contended that the present confederation is utterly inefficient, and that if it remains much longer in its present state of imbecility, we shall be one of the most contemptible nations on the face of the earth.

—William Grayson of Virginia
to James Madison.[17]

By 1786, numerous congressmen openly complained about the weakness of the national government under the Articles of Confederation, adopted in 1780. They had begun to discuss plans to call a convention to create a new government. Samuel Otis, a congressman from Massachusetts, outlined the many weaknesses of the Confederation government, from its inability to collect taxes to conduct foreign affairs and lamented "can it be wondered at that a government [like that] should be viewed in a ridiculous light by her own citizens, and a contemptible one by other nations? Every good citizen feels himself hurt by the indignities his country is liable to in this humiliating predicament both at home and abroad."[18]

Benjamin Lincoln, the Revolutionary War general, agreed. He wrote at the beginning of 1786, "The United States, as they are called, seem to be little more than a name."[19]

The country was a mess. The powerless national government, with a figurehead president and no judiciary, tottered on the brink of collapse. Foreign affairs were chaotic. Morocco and other countries had seized U.S. merchant ships and stolen their cargo, sometimes selling American sailors into slavery, knowing that the Confederation government had no way to punish them for doing so. Many European banks, wary of the shaky American economy, then in deep recession, insisted on charging the United States much higher interest rates on loans than anyone else. Great Britain refused to withdraw its army from the Northwest Territories, as it had promised in the peace treaty of 1783. From time to time, Spain closed the Mississippi River to navigation in political disputes.

Domestically, the situation was just as chaotic. States and counties feuded with each other and oversized state assemblies, some with more than four hundred members, were unable to pass legislation. Legislators in all the states seemed to value their personal agendas over that of the people and the country. Large and unruly crowds of citizens marched on the homes of state legislators, demanding passage of pet bills. Mob activity sometimes closed statehouses, city halls, and courthouses. Political groups, who saw legislators as merely their tools, staged riots to get their way, crippling city and state governments. These "Regulators," as they were called, threatened to create anarchy in all the villages in the country. By the mid-1780s, the national army disbanded, many congressmen left office, and the Confederation government of the United States, it seemed, had no power to do anything.[20]

The country had plunged into an economic depression when the war ended. After an eight-year business lull caused by the war, foreign ships now flooded American ports, overselling products such as clothing, books, and household wares to retailers who tried to then distribute the goods to a public that did not have the money to buy them. Prices plunged as the shiploads full of commercial cargo sat on the docks; the low foreign prices drove down American prices for the same goods. American farmers produced more food for the country, but the people had no money to buy it and it was sold cheaply or rotted.

Foreign markets dried up as quickly as the American. New England cod fishermen sold 25,630 tons of fish in 1775, but just 19,185 in 1788. Total New England shipping revenue from sales to the West Indies was $448,000 in 1775, but just $284,000 in 1788. New Englanders had 150 merchant ships on the seas before the war but only 32 in 1788. The price of a hogshead of tobacco from southern slave plantations dropped by nearly 30 percent from 1772 to 1787. One study showed that the prices of all the goods sold in Charleston, South Carolina, fell by a third from the year before the war to 1787. The depression also meant that thousands of men and women were out of work and had no money to buy anything, driving prices downward even farther.[21]

The Confederation government had no mechanism to combat the depression and the people fumed while their representatives did nothing.[22]

Everything that was wrong came to a head in 1786, when Daniel Shays, a Massachusetts army veteran, gathered together a thousand men, closed a courthouse, and seized a federal arsenal to protest high taxes. Shays's Rebellion only ended when a federal armed force was sent and forced Shays and his rebels to quit, amid much international news coverage. It was a jarring example to all that the government was unable to run the country.

The Continental Congress, whose attendance was always low, accomplished little. One congressman lamented in the spring of 1786 that the only bill the members managed to pass during the entire year would do no more than establish the salary of the Treasury Department's secretary.[23]

Many political leaders wanted a new government. None described the need for a constitution and a new government with more clarity and force than James Madison. He wrote in the winter of 1787 that "the present system neither has or deserves advocates; and if some very strong props are not applied will quickly tumble to the ground. No money is paid into the public treasury; no respect is paid to the federal authority. Not a single state complies with the requisitions, several pass over them in silence and some positively reject them...It is not possible that a government can last long under these circumstances..."[24]

What was necessary, Madison said, was a representative government elected by the people with some sort of system of checks and balances to prevent injustices and corruption. He wrote, "From the first moment that my mind was capable of contemplating political subjects, I never, till this moment, ceased wishing success to well regulated republican government."[25]

The chronic failures of the Confederation brought about the Constitutional Convention in Philadelphia in 1787 and the controversial framework for a brand-new government with executive, judicial, and legislative branches, led by an independent president, unprecedented in the world. The Constitution now had to be ratified by nine of the thirteen colonies in order to be formed. It was a decisive moment in American history.

The Constitutional Convention delegates needed the approval of the country for the new government. They shrewdly realized, too, that if the state legislatures were involved, the public might have seen all the politicians in "league" with each other.[26]

The debates over the Constitution began to reach feverish heights as the convention delegates arrived back in their hometowns after most had signed it.

In late September of 1787, Madison, exhausted, unpacked his bags in New York City after his journey following the end of the Convention in Philadelphia to rejoin the Continental Congress that continued to operate under the Articles of Confederation. There, he found that the Constitution was all anybody talked about. "[It] engrosses almost the whole political attention of America," he wrote.

And the constitution was already in deep trouble.[27]

Madison was its chief architect. His hopes for its passage and the creation of a new government had been buoyed when America's sage, Benjamin Franklin, surprised many when he announced that he favored it, adding with great solemnity that it would produce a successful government. He signed the document, he said, because "...I expect no better and because I am not sure that it is not the best." The highly respected Franklin had been opposed to the Constitution for weeks and only at the last minute changed his mind about it. Later, despite some objections, Thomas Jefferson would write Madison from Paris that, in general, he liked it, too. Jefferson was serving as America's diplomat to France at the time and would not return until 1789. The Constitution also had the backing of George Washington, the most important man in the country, although he worried about its passage.[28] He had prophetically called the document "a child of fortune" when it was approved, but wondered, like everyone else, what would happen to it.[29]

Madison was proud of the Constitution. He reminded all of the critics of the Constitution that he so despised that there was no perfect government. This one was good and ought to be adopted. He wrote, "It is a wonder and regret that those who raise so many objections against the new constitution, should never call to mind the defects of that which is to be exchanged for it. It is not necessary that the former should be perfect; it is sufficient that the latter is more imperfect."[30]

And it was simple. It was a republican, peoples' government, not complicated, and could be understood by anyone.[31]

Madison's joy was short-lived, though; nineteen of the fifty-five delegates to the convention refused to sign the Constitution, a clear warning that it would be difficult to have it ratified by the states. Some of the most influential men in the key states had come out against it—Samuel Adams and John Hancock in Massachusetts and Governor George Clinton of New York. Numerous politicians in Pennsylvania, particularly those from the frontier sections of the western part of the state, vowed to vote it down at their state's convention.

Even more troublesome to Madison was that several who refused to sign it were powerful Virginians—the current governor, Edmund Randolph, and longtime state legislator George Mason. Randolph was so strenuously opposed that he called for a second Constitutional Convention to right the wrongs of the first one. James Monroe, a close friend of Jefferson and a rising political star in Virginia, was against it, as was Madison's cousin, the president of William and Mary College, one of the most prestigious institutions of higher education in America and the school where most of Virginia's leaders were educated. A majority of the judges in Virginia opposed the new federal government. Former Governor Patrick Henry was one of the most influential and popular men in the state, and in the country. His dramatic "Give me liberty or give me death!" speech prior to the Revolution was hailed throughout America. Henry also was opposed to the Constitution. He so loathed the idea of a national government that he had even refused to go to Philadelphia as a delegate to the Convention (as early as March 1787, Madison had been telling everyone that Patrick Henry was staying home on purpose so that he could be the kingmaker who would make or break the Constitution).

Patrick Henry's role in the fight over the Constitution was critical and everyone knew it. A powerful Richmond, Virginia, politician named Edward Carrington warned that "much will depend on" the influential Henry, who had many followers. Henry Knox, in Massachusetts, was blunter, calling Henry "that overwhelming torrent."[32]

The main reason the nineteen delegates refused to sign the Constitution was that it contained no bill of rights to protect ordinary citizens against a government that they saw as too nationalistic and too powerful. John Dickenson argued that all of the state constitutions had clauses to protect the people and the national government had to have them, too. A big government, argued Congressman Fisher Ames, meant big despotism and the crushing of the people. All that would be left to watch in America, he complained, would be "the velocity of its fall."[33]

George Mason was one of the strongest proponents of the bill of rights, as was Edmund Randolph. They were stunned when a bill of personal rights was voted down unanimously toward the end of the Philadelphia proceedings; those who defeated it contended that personal guarantees of liberty were "understood" in the Constitution.[34] The pair then quickly moved to have a second Constitutional Convention called expressly to pass some kind of bill of rights. That, too, was voted down. The two men felt that they had been ignored and that the delegates were in such a hurry to go home that they had no time for what the pair considered vitally important legislation. Mason had even told the convention that he could write the whole bill in an afternoon and was certain the entire debate over it would take just a few hours.

He certainly could have. All admired Mason's ability to get things done. One man from Georgia wrote, "Mr. Mason is a gentleman of remarkable strong powers and possesses a clear and copious understanding. He is able and convincing in debate, steady and firm, in his principles."[35]

If the Convention had simply passed the Bill of Rights then, the pro-Constitution forces would have muted the greatest argument against the new government and opposition throughout the country would have been minor.[36]

The turndown hurt Mason and Randolph, who believed that the pro-Constitution delegates also voted it down out of personal disrespect to them. Their anger grew. A friend wrote, "Mason would sooner chop off his right hand than put it to the Constitution as it now stands."

Their fellow Virginian, Richard Henry Lee, not at the convention, expressed their feelings when he denounced the proposed federal government to Samuel Adams as an "oligarchy" and "elective despotism." He wrote heatedly of the votes against the bill of rights and a second convention that "violence has been practiced by the agitators of this new system in Philadelphia to drive on for its immediate adoption as if the subject of government were a business of passion instead of cool, sober, and intense consideration." He was so upset about it, he told George Washington, that he ranked it "among the first distresses that have happened to me in my life."[37]

Madison had become nervous about passage of the Constitution even before the vote in Philadelphia, writing Jefferson in Paris on September 6 that "all the prepossessions are on the right side, but it may well be expected that certain characters will wage war against any reform whatever." He told Jefferson that he was certain that the need for a more stable government would bring about acceptance by the public and ratification, but feared individual opposition would sink it. He lamented, "If the present moment be lost, it is hard to say what may be our fate."[38]

Madison had been deluged with letters from Federalists fearful that the Constitution would not pass. During the first days he returned to Mrs. Elsworth's boarding house, he received a letter telling him that New York politicians were already trying to dismantle it.[39]

He knew, too, that much of Virginia had slid into ferment over the past year, as had so many regions of the new United States. "Our information from Virginia is far from being agreeable," Madison wrote in the fall of 1787. A bad drought, "severest that ever was experienced," according to Washington,[40] had ruined the corn crop in several counties. Residents wanted paper money, issued by their state, and not hard currency so that they had plenty of money, regardless of its cost, to pay bills. Debts and taxes went unpaid by farmers, especially those in the western areas of states, far from the cities, who were practically penniless, and saw small, and cheap, government as far preferable to a large, federal government. Angry residents in several counties burned down jails, courthouses, and county offices. The rapid growth in cities such as Richmond and Norfolk brought a significant increase in crime that frightened their residents.

Many applauded the Constitution because it supported the federal assumption of state debts, but others, primarily farmers, and in Virginia there were many, opposed it because it also supported manufacturers over farmers. Some Virginians favored it to protect slavery, but others worried that it opened the door for the federal government to end the institution. Virginians were still recovering from a series of smallpox epidemics that had ravaged parts of the state during the last decade. Madison feared, too, that Virginia's continued refusal to pay taxes to the federal government would result in the disbanding of the federal military force that protected the western regions of the state against Indian attacks and might even be a signal to England to start another war. Exasperated, he wrote that autumn that the members of the Virginia General Assembly were "engaged in mad freaks."[41]

Madison was shaken by a letter from Monroe in which he warned him that some of the most influential men in the state were against it.[42]

In just about every newspaper he picked up, Madison found stories warning that many of the delegates already elected to state constitution conventions were against it.[43]

In New York, many members of the Continental Congress were opposed. Rumors had flown up and down the east coast that the Constitution was going to be forced upon the people and that the leaders of the Philadelphia Convention had formed an army to strong arm state leaders into adopting it. One member wrote friends that the Convention delegates were going to insist on a king and another said he heard that a relative of King George III would be asked to be the American monarch. One rumor threatened that all of the delegates from the southern states would bolt and form a new confederation of slave states. Yet another declared that the delegates secretly planned to carve up the United States into three separate confederations.[44]

The opposition to the Constitution was strong in the largest and most important states: Massachusetts, New York, Virginia, and Pennsylvania. Gouverneur Morris said that he seriously doubted it would be ratified in Pennsylvania because of patronage and local infighting. He wrote, "True it is that the city and its neighborhood are enthusiastic in the cause, but I dread the cold and sour temper of the back counties and still more the wicked industry of those who have long habituated themselves to live on the public, and cannot bear the idea of being removed from the power and profit of state government which has been and still is the means of supporting themselves, their families, and dependents."[45]

Madison, who always knew what way the political winds blew, understood that the Constitution was losing ground and fast and told George Washington that just one week after he returned to New York.[46]

The greatest enemy to the Constitution in Congress was Richard Henry Lee. He let everyone in Congress know of his opposition. He did not mince his words. "I find it impossible for me to doubt that in its present state, unamended, the adoption of it will put civil liberty and the happiness of the people at the mercy of rulers who may possess...great unguarded powers," he said.[47]

Madison chafed that Richard Henry Lee and others were already busy laboring to wreck the Constitution. Lee complained to Mason that not only was the Constitution not workable, but it was a harbinger for disaster. "[It] produces a coalition of monarchy men, military men, aristocrats, and drones whose noise, impudence, and zeal exceeds all belief," he wrote on October 1, adding that if it was ratified "either a tyranny will result from it or it will be prevented by a civil war..." His pledge to vote it down was not idle, Madison learned from friends in Virginia. "The same schism that unfortunately happened to our state in Philadelphia threatens us here also," wrote Carrington, who added that the prospects for passage looked bleak in New York also.[48]

Madison may have seen Lee as an enemy of the Constitution, but Lee saw himself as its champion, once it was amended. He told everyone that, in general, it was a framework for a workable form of government, but only if it had a bill of rights to protect the individual. "This Constitution abounds with useful regulations at the same time that it is liable to strong and fundamental objections," he wrote Edmund Randolph, and added that with amendments "...I see no well founded objection but great safety and much good to be the probable result."

And he, like all the Anti-Federalists, resented the view of the Constitution's supporters that any critics of the new government were anti-American. If anything, Lee and the others said, their insistence on a bill of rights made them greater patriots than the supporters. Throughout the ratification process, the Anti-Federalists would fume, like Lee, that the Federalists had set them up as villains, and they were not.[49]

And if all of that was not enough to sour the Anti-Federalist Virginians, Mason was severely injured on his way home when his carriage overturned and he and a companion were tossed out of it onto the dirt highway. Mason was bloodied and complained that "I got very much hurt in my neck and head…at times [it] still [feels] uneasy to me."[50]

Would his own state of Virginia wreck Madison's work and the brilliant future he saw for America? He thought that residents of New York approved of it and word had reached him that the Constitution was favored in both Massachusetts and Connecticut. But he had great trepidations about Virginia. He told Washington, "I am waiting with anxiety for the echo from Virginia, but with very faint hopes of its corresponding with my wishes."[51]

Madison also realized that he and his allies were in a race against time. The crucial Virginia and New York conventions were, on the calendar, a very long nine months away, but the first two conventions, in Delaware and Pennsylvania, were to be held in just weeks. If the Constitution was defeated in any one convention in the nine months prior to June, when Virginia and New York met, it would probably mean the collapse of the entire project. Federalists would be running against the clock from the end of September through the last days of June, constantly trying to develop strategies for passage in each individual state and continually avoiding setbacks that would mean defeat in all of them.

Madison was an easily recognizable figure as he scurried about New York trying to shore up support for the Constitution. He was an average-size man, barely 5 foot 6 inches tall, with dark brown hair and dull blue eyes. Madison, who favored highly fashionable coats, was called "Little Jeremy" by many and would later be referred to by his wife Dolley as "the great little Madison." He possessed a soft voice and had trouble being seen or heard in a large crowd. Madison's speeches were not stirring, like those of Patrick Henry, Richard Henry Lee, or other Revolutionary figures, whose talks were full of literary touches and soaring oratory. His public pronouncements seemed irregular. One man who heard him remembered that he addressed the crowd "as if with a view of expressing some thought that had casually occurred to him, with his hat in his hand and with his notes in his hat and the warmest excitement of debate was visible in him only by a more or less rapid back-and-forward seesaw motion of his body."[52]

Henry Adams wrote, "An imposing personality had much to do with political influence and Madison labored under serious disadvantage." But John Marshall, who knew him well, wrote that "Mr. Madison was the most eloquent man I ever heard." Those who listened to him remembered that his arguments were logical, to the point, full of facts and figures and, when examined, made great sense.[53]

Madison, a bachelor, always seemed sick. Despite all of the sun he was exposed to in Virginia in the summertime, his skin remained pale and his entire physical appearance was frail. He often dressed in black, with black stockings, too, and that exacerbated his undernourished appearance. Friends said that Madison was a hypochondriac whose illnesses were in his head and not his body.[54]

Those who met him at first glance saw him as an aloof, rather dour man who lacked any interest in the finer things in life or exhibited any trace of humor. One woman called him a "gloomy, stiff creature" and another described him as "mute, cold and repulsive" in a crowd of people at a reception.[55]

People who knew him better said that he could be a charming man, especially in a room with just a handful of people that he knew, where he did not feel overwhelmed. Congressmen and foreign diplomats with whom he socialized during the war and in the first few years afterward were all impressed by his political skills and found him engaging. One diplomat wrote that he was "the man of soundest judgment in Congress...He speaks nearly always with fairness and wins the approval of his colleagues." A French journalist wrote of Madison that when he met him in 1788 he looked very tired and that although "his expression was that of a stern censor," Madison's "conversation disclosed a man of learning and his countenance...that of a person conscious of his talents and of his duties."[56]

He had no luck with women as a young man. He did not pursue women in Virginia's high society, and none pursued him. He was engaged to one woman for several years, but she ended the relationship. Ironically, the cold, stiff, socially awkward Madison would later marry one of the most vivacious women in American history, Dolley Payne Todd.

And so the diminutive Madison found himself a bit overwhelmed in the autumn of 1787 when he moved back to Mrs. Elsworth's boarding house at 19 Maiden Lane in New York City. The urban mecca itself was a far cry from the rolling hills and lush countryside of his beloved plantation at Montpelier. New York's population had exploded following the end of the war, despite the departure of many Loyalists, and Manhattan island, with its narrow, twisting lanes, was ringed with hundreds of the large, gorgeous tri-masted sailing ships that anchored there.

Many of the congressmen in the city from around the country loathed New York and wished they were home. The British had occupied it throughout most of the Revolution and they had left it in shambles. Now its residents watched as professional gamblers, prostitutes, and criminals arrived to earn their money off the residents, old and new, as the city grew.

It was a city that embraced a rapidly growing number of residents, transient sailors, and a growing army of shiftless people looking for housing and work. It was freezing cold in the winter and oppressively hot in the summer. Everything always seemed in disorder. Congressmen arriving from Philadelphia and the convention, such as Virginian John Page, yearned to go back. He wrote that "[New York] is not half so large as Philadelphia, nor in any way to be compared to it for beauty and elegance. The New York streets are badly paved, dirty, and narrow as well as crooked." A Massachusetts congressman wrote of New York that "while I am shut up here in this pigsty, smelling perfumes from wharves and the rakings of gutters, I long for the air and company of Springfield."[57]

Madison was always prepared for whatever task he had been assigned, whether writing a nation's constitution or voting on road bills in the Virginia legislature. Jefferson may have purchased more books than Madison, but Madison must have read more books than anyone. His library at his vast plantation at Montpelier, in rural Virginia, overflowed with volumes on history, politics, mathematics, literature, and geography. He had read and reread them all, and perhaps there was no one in the world who had read more and understood the history of politics, from the Greece of Pericles to the England of George III, better than Madison.[58]

Those who favored the Constitution feared trouble. James White recognized that and wrote "these states are now tottering on the brink of anarchy." In the North, many agreed. Nicholas Gilman of New Hampshire predicted civil war and wrote that "if they [Anti-Federalists] succeed, I fear the sword will soon be drawn."[59]

At Mount Vernon, George Washington's anger at the Anti-Federalist opposition grew daily and he finally exploded. He wrote in a letter reprinted in newspapers throughout the country that he believed the "government is now suspended by a thread, and I might go so far as to say it is really at an end..." and insisted that "there is no alternative between the adoption of [the Constitution] and anarchy."[60]

Many other supporters of the Constitution agreed. One man said it was needed to save the nation "from absolute ruin."[61]

Madison worried that any assessment of the friends and foes of the Constitution and proposed new government showed an even split. He wrote a Virginia friend, "Nothing is more common here and I presume the case must be the same with you than to see companies of intelligent people equally divided and equally earnest in maintaining on one side that the general government will overwhelm the state government and on the other hand that it will be a prey to their encroachments; on one side that the structure of the government is too firm and too strong and on the other that it partakes too much of the weakness and instability of the governments of the particular state."[62]

This depressed the congressman from Virginia. He had returned to New York. He settled back into his room at Mrs. Elsworth's boarding house, a few blocks from Hamilton's home on Wall Street, very distressed. There, surrounded by his books, copies of New York newspapers, and stacks of letters that had arrived from around the country, he decided that he was the one who had to lead the campaign to get the Constitution ratified. It was his fight because it was, all agreed, his Constitution.

And there was no one better equipped to defend it, and to sway those with mixed feelings about it, than the Virginian. Throughout the war and the intervening years and the Constitutional Convention, he had impressed all with his knowledge of governments around the world, past and present, his sheer brilliance, and his personal demeanor. Major William Pierce, a delegate from Georgia and former aide to General Nathanael Greene in the war, who met him at the Constitutional Convention, wrote that "every person seems to acknowledge his greatness. He blends together the profound politician with the scholar…he is a most agreeable, eloquent, and convincing speaker…he always comes forward the best informed man of any point in debate. In the affairs of the United States, he perhaps has the most correct knowledge of as any man in the Union." All admired

Madison, Pierce wrote. "[He] was always thought one of the ablest members that ever sat in [Congress]. He is a man of great modesty— with a remarkable sweet temper. [He] has a most agreeable style of conversation."[63]

Samuel Otis wrote of him that he had "the endowments of a great statesman and a fine scholar, in the study of men and books, possesses a cool, deliberate, cautious judgment [and] writes his friends in Congress in terms very encouraging…"[64]

Sometime in late September or early October, Madison decided that the crusade would be too enormous for one man to handle and it would require people around the country, not just in Virginia. He recruited about a dozen leading supporters of a strong federal government, several from each of the key states in the ratification fight, to join him in the battle. These men included Gouverneur Morris of Pennsylvania, Rufus King of Massachusetts, Thomas Johnson of Maryland, and William Duer and Robert Livingston of New York. They then recruited other politicians to work with them. His colleagues worked with him from early October until the commencement of the state conventions, lobbying delegates in person or via letter. They used their influence and press friendships to get pro-Federalist essays published in their home state newspapers. They each led Federalist forces at their home state conventions as those convened.

It remains uncertain how the national Triumvirate that oversaw the work of all those men came to be, but Madison was happy that he formed the Triumvirate with John Jay and Alexander Hamilton. He felt that way for two reasons. The first was that Madison had to be in Virginia to lead the battle at his state's convention and could not attend the one in New York, held at the same time. He needed someone to spearhead the fight in New York, coordinating the work of Duer, Livingston, and other Federalists. Who better than Hamilton and Jay, two of New York's shrewdest politicians, staunch defenders of the Constitution and federal government, and two men whom he had known for years through his friendship with George Washington?

Second, he needed allies with literary skills who could rebut the writing of the Anti-Federalists that had begun to appear in newspaper columns and in pamphlets that seemed to fly off the presses. Jay and, especially, Hamilton were superb writers and had connections with editors in the New York press to get a defense of the Constitution published in different newspapers. Both lived in New York, the city that seemed to be the epicenter of the political world after the Philadelphia Convention ended. It was the home of Congress and most of the important politicians who favored the Constitution were congressmen and present for the session of Congress and could be pressed into service. Between them, Jay, Madison, and Hamilton knew every one of them. The three men also lived within several blocks of each other in Manhattan; instant communication would be rather easy.[65]

Madison also realized that the states had chosen to host ratifying conventions in such a chronological way that the two most important states, and where the vote seemed closest, New York and Virginia, would vote last. The prospect loomed that only seven of the needed nine states would have ratified by the time New York and Virginia held their conventions in late June 1788, and that a defeat in either would kill the Constitution and the new government. Those two states had to be carried.

The Triumvirate of Madison, Hamilton, and Jay would need many supporters who could provide assistance because the fight ahead would be a tough one. Richard Henry Lee mobilized a small group of Anti-Federalists in New York in late September. These men included John Lamb and Melancton Smith of New York, whom Lee believed he could count on to block the Constitution in that state. Lee met with congressmen from around the country in New York who were opposed to the Constitution. He used the recent writings of Thomas Paine, whose pamphlets and their elegant lines, such as "These are the times that try men's souls," had done so much to garner support for the American Revolution. Paine had become an Anti-Federalist after the war. He was tired of the pleas of Hamilton, Jay, and Madison that different kinds of democracies had thrived throughout history; he demanded a nonintrusive government for the modern era. "It is the living, and not the dead, that are to be accommodated," he wrote. He also provided the Antis with a new catchy phrase, "The government is best which governs least."[66]

The Anti-Federalists called themselves the Federal Republicans. The incensed Lee, a states' rights supporter who feared a federal government, then returned home to his Virginia plantation, Chantilly, and began a series of meetings with Virginian Anti-Federalists, certain that alliance could defeat the new government in Virginia. He told the Virginians that he was seeking more assistance from political leaders in Maryland and in South Carolina to stop the Constitution. He told all of them the same thing, that the Constitution was a good one, but had to include protection for the personal rights of the people. He said to everyone, "If it could be reasonably amended it would be a fine system."[67]

Richard Henry Lee's group then went to work drafting newspaper essays and harnessing their skills into a widespread letter-writing campaign, a campaign that started in early October. Antis such as David Redick wrote friends that, "the day on which we adopt the proposed plan of government, from that moment we may justly date the loss of American liberty..."[68]

Redick's fears were shared by many. A group of Pennsylvania dissenters argued that under the proposed government, the Americans were going to lose all the liberties they had gained during the American

Revolution. The new Federalists, they argued, were simply usurping the powers of Great Britain for themselves. Nothing had changed.[69]

The Anti-Federalists insisted that many of the problems of the Confederation government were caused by the corruption of its members and not the structure of the national government itself. Some people had lost their virtue, one of the planks of the American Revolution, and that loss weakened the Confederation government. With Revolution over, the Anti-Federalists charged, many Americans had become self-centered, materialistic, and greedy. The new national government, they feared, might become corrupt, too, and even more chaotic.

The Anti-Federalists were afraid that the great democracy that the Federalists promised might bring about too much democracy. The Federalists had contended that the state legislatures were too large to function and now they wanted a national legislature whose House of Representatives population-proportionate plan threatened to have hundreds of members some day. The Confederation had been one simple assembly, and the proposed new government was three branches of government, with three times as many people and three times as much chance for trouble.

Richard Henry Lee and his colleagues noted, too, that the postwar 1780s were a very difficult era in which to govern. In addition to the establishment of state governments and the Confederation national government, the people had to deal with an economic depression and adjust to new lives after the peace treaty. The Confederation government, they suggested, did the best it could in tough times.

Furthermore, many critics of the Constitution said, the Confederation might have had its problems, but its members had done a good job. Many believed that it functioned rather well, in fact. It needed to be improved, not shelved, as the Federalists proposed.

The arguments between the Federalists and Anti-Federalists

over the role of the federal government versus that of the states has continued for more than two hundred years, instigated numerous constitutional battles and political showdowns, and probably will do so for years to come.

To Madison, Hamilton, and Jay, the pamphlets and newspaper letters that the Lee faction churned out were an indication that the opposition was already working hard and that its leaders were some of the most prominent men in the nation.

Surely, Madison, Hamilton, and Jay assumed from these early efforts that the opposition to the Constitution would not only be vociferous but highly organized and very effective. To defeat them, they would have to put together a well-oiled and highly functioning political movement—and quickly.

It is unknown when and where Madison, Hamilton, and Jay held an initial meeting to form their Triumvirate and create a working group of men from different states to get the Constitution passed—or whose idea it was. They attended several parties in New York together in October and might have been at congressional sessions. There was no known formal written note between them acknowledging the formation of the Triumvirate, but any study of their activities leaves no doubt that they not only put one together, but planned one of the great lobbying campaigns in American history to get the Constitution ratified. It was a campaign in which the three men had to be in constant touch with each other and with their Federalist supporters in each state. There is ample evidence that they did so. As an example, Hamilton wrote Madison from New York in May 1788, that "We [he and Jay] shall leave nothing undone to cultivate a favorable disposition in the citizens at large" and then reminded him to write frequently and to continue their practice of hiring teams of riders and horses to carry letters back and forth between them as quickly as possible. He urgently told Madison, then four hundred miles away in Virginia, that "it is of vast importance that an exact communications should be kept up between us."

The trio, especially Madison and Hamilton, wrote hundreds of letters to their state allies over the winter and throughout the spring; Madison and Rufus King, of Massachusetts, alone exchanged more than sixty letters. The letters of local leaders outlined the close communications between leaders within states and state leaders with the trio of Madison, Hamilton, and Jay.[70]

What the three did not know, could not know, was that the fight to have the Constitution ratified would be a wild political donnybrook that would rival any that would follow in the history of the country, a drama full of villains and heroes in which the final act would result in either the creation or collapse of the United States.

# THE TRIUMVIRATE

M adison, Hamilton, and Jay realized that ratification would be easy in the small states but much harder in the large ones and were always mindful that, in the end, just a handful of votes would or would not carry the Constitution.[71] They believed small states, such as Connecticut, New Jersey, Delaware, and New Hampshire, would ratify because under the new government they had as much power in the Senate, two seats, as the large states. They were also smaller entities and needed the protection of a federal government. They gave up hope on the cantankerous leaders of the tiny state of Rhode Island, who were very happy with the old Confederation, even though they had been such trouble to that body. Rhode Island's congressmen seemed to vote no on everything others proposed, often bringing the operations of the Confederation to a standstill. They had been such staunch supporters of the Confederation, though, and were so parochial in their thinking, that few thought they would ratify. The Federalists simply wrote the state off and let its leaders do whatever they chose, hoping that they would join the new union after it was approved. Frontier states such as Georgia would approve swiftly because they needed federal forces to protect their citizens from Indian attacks and from any threats from the Spanish government, which still owned Florida, to the south.

They needed to win ratification in their home states, where passage seemed questionable from the start, and help others to win it in states where the vote might be close, such as Pennsylvania, Massachusetts, Maryland, and North and South Carolina. Some of the small states, eager to move under the federal umbrella, had scheduled their conventions early; easy passage there would build momentum for the close votes later on; of the first five conventions, four were in small states. Hamilton, Madison, and Jay also decided that if they did work together, they could serve as the hub of a network that could help shore up support in some states based on action in others (such as letting the delegates of one state know, in the middle of their deliberations, that delegates in another had just ratified, thus swaying their vote).

There could not have been three men so different from each other than Jay, Hamilton, and Madison. Hamilton was outgoing and egomaniacal, Madison was quiet and reserved, and Jay was a sophisticated man and one of the most experienced public figures in America.

## Alexander Hamilton: The Peacock

Alexander Hamilton rose to fame during the Revolution, when, just twenty years old, he became George Washington's most active aide, a predecessor to the American military's "chief of staff." No one is certain how they met. Washington had been told that Hamilton was brilliant, but that he was also a good soldier who had been one of his artillery leaders in the battles of Trenton and Princeton. He was a fine writer and an efficient, hardworking young man who possessed extraordinary administrative skills. He understood the soldiers and could offer considerable administrative help to Washington as the general ran the army. The pair became close friends during the war. Washington's admiration for Hamilton was well known. Washington wrote, "There are few men to be found of his age who have a more general knowledge than he possesses and none whose soul is more firmly engaged to the cause, or who exceeds him in probity and sterling virtue."

The commander completely trusted him. And the two men thought so much alike that Washington often permitted him to write his letters and circulars to the states and various governors and public officials. Hamilton ran a spy ring, worked with officers, interviewed deserters, and frequently met with local officials and merchants on the general's behalf. The two men were always together; many attributed much of the American success in the war to Hamilton's work as the chief of staff.[72]

He was an engaging companion at dinners and receptions. During the war, Washington often sat in the middle of the dinner table, placing Hamilton at the head, so that his aide could regale diners with his hundreds of stories, analyze European politics, or discuss classic literature.

Hamilton arrived at the Continental Army camp as a man with a checkered past. He was the illegitimate child of Rachel Faucett and James Hamilton, a Scottish merchant who lived on the Caribbean island of St. Kitts or, as John Adams sneered about him, "the bastard brat of a Scot's pedlar." James Hamilton left his wife and two sons, Alexander and James Jr., and the three moved to St. Croix, where she died when Alexander was still a young boy. The brilliant child could speak Hebrew fluently by the age of four and soon added other languages, such as French and Latin. As a child, he read entire books when classmates struggled with finishing pages. As a teenager, he worked as a clerk at a local import/export firm, Beekman and Cruger, in St. Croix and stunned all with his substantial abilities at mathematics and management.

He was an overly ambitious boy and felt hopelessly trapped on St. Croix. He yearned for fame and fortune just about anywhere else. He wrote a friend, Edward (Ned) Stevens, who lived in New York, that, "my ambition is prevalent that I [hold in contempt] the groveling and condition of a clerk or the like, to which my fortune, etc. condemns me and would willingly risk my life, though not my character, to exalt my station. I'm confident, Ned, that my youth excludes me from any hopes of immediate preferment, nor do I deserve it, but I mean to prepare the way for futurity. I'm no philosopher, you see, and may justly be said the man to build castles in the air. My folly makes me ashamed and beg you'll conceal it, yet Neddy, we have seen such schemes successful when the projector is constant." Then, at the end of the note, he added wistfully, "I wish there was a war."[73]

Hamilton became the manager of Beekman and Cruger when he was just sixteen. He impressed all, and a local minister, Rev. Hugh Knox, became his mentor. He helped Hamilton financially, as did Cruger and others, advancing the boy enough money to move to New York in 1772, at the age of sixteen. There, he resumed work in a large mercantile house whose owner understood his brilliance and introduced him to several public figures in town. They advanced him money to enroll at Francis Barber's prep school in Elizabethtown, New Jersey. As soon as Hamilton began classes at the prep school, his fortunes soared. William Livingston, of the wealthy Livingston family and a friend of Barber's, befriended Hamilton. An accomplished writer, he became the provincial governor of New Jersey and a close friend of George Washington's when the war began. Livingston allowed him to live in his mansion, Liberty Hall, near the school. There Hamilton met John Jay, who married Livingston's daughter Sarah.

Hamilton then attended King's College [Columbia University] where he became politicized, delivering an incendiary speech against the Crown in 1774. The success of the speech led him to write a series of scathing newspaper essays denouncing England and advocating independence. They all exhibited a grasp of political history and economic savvy, surprising all, especially from the pen of a mere teenager.

He soon joined a New York militia company formed by Jay, the New York Provincial Company of Artillery, and, with them, removed a battery of British cannon in lower New York. They were mobilized when the Revolution began and participated in several of the battles in New York City, all defeats, and then helped to cover Washington's hasty retreat across New Jersey in the fall and winter of 1776.

Hamilton and his company crossed the Delaware River with Washington on Christmas Day 1776, and defeated the Hessians at Trenton in a battle fought in freezing temperatures as four inches of snow fell. Hamilton's artillery aided in the victory. Ten days later, Hamilton and his artillery were instrumental in the American victory at Princeton.

The New York teenager, nineteen years old, could not be missed. Someone who saw him in action wrote that he was "a youth, a mere stripling, small, slender, almost delicate in frame." He had his "cocked hat pulled down over his eyes, apparently lost in thought, with his hand resting on a cannon, and every now and then patting it, as if it were favorite horse or a pet plaything."[74]

Hamilton left the army the year after the victory at Yorktown and began a career in Congress, representing New York. There, he worked tirelessly to assist the army in any way he could, to bolster the constantly collapsing finances of the Continental Congress and win more friends for America among the European diplomats who traveled to the United States. As in the army, Hamilton told anyone who would listen that the government of the Confederation was ineffective and a stronger, more nationalistic one was needed. "Experience must convince us that our present establishments are utopian before we shall be ready to part with them for better," he wrote Nathanael Greene, a general in the Revolution who had become his friend.[75]

He also warned everyone, as did Jay, that the British sympathizers had to be treated with respect once the war was over because the country could not move on if the majority of Americans continued to hate the minority that had remained loyal to the king. In 1784, in a legal pamphlet, Hamilton wrote prophetically of the new nation, "The world has its eyes upon America. The noble struggle we have made in the cause of liberty has occasioned a kind of revolution in human sentiment. The influence of our example has penetrated the gloomy regions of despotism and has pointed the way to inquiries which may shake it to its deepest foundation."[76]

Critics, and Hamilton had many, always felt he was too cocky. Hamilton acknowledged the accusation to be true, but saw no harm in it. He wrote in *The Federalist* No. 72 that the love of fame was "the ruling passion of the noblest minds." George Washington admitted his young friend was ambitious and that some saw him as "dangerous." Washington did not. "That he is ambitious I will readily grant, but it is of the laudable kind, which prompts a man to excel in whatever he takes in hand."[77]

Friends, and he had many, treasured him. Congressman Fisher Ames said that he was "the friend of his friends" and that "his power over their affections was entire and lasted through his life." A judge wrote that he was "blessed with a very amiable generous, tender, and charitable disposition. It was impossible not to love as well as respect and admire him."[78]

Hamilton became a lawyer when he left the army and either led or joined numerous organizations in New York City when the war ended. One of the most prominent was the New York Society for the Manumission of Slavery. He became the vice president of the society, at the urging of his friend John Jay, who was the president.

He advocated the gradual end of slavery, freeing slaves over the age of forty-five immediately and younger ones over a period of years. Ironically, two other members of the energetic group were Melancton Smith, who would become his chief rival at the New York convention to ratify the Constitution in 1788, and Aaron Burr, who would shoot him dead in a duel in 1804.

He had contentious relationships with the members of the society, as he often had with men across the country. His lightning-quick mind chafed at the ponderous thinking of others and his belief that he was always right did not permit him to understand opposing views. He clashed with other politicians instead of mollifying them. He could also never ignore a slur; he had to fire back with a verbal barrage that often put him in even more trouble.

Hamilton startled many delegates at the Constitutional Convention with his seemingly interminable six-hour speech that criticized the proposed American government and heaped praise upon both the British monarch and Parliament (he called it the best government on earth). In his rambling speech, he paid no attention to how people there would perceive it; he inflamed everyone by stating that the United States needed either an actual monarch or a president with the trappings and power of a monarch. Further, he insisted on a Senate whose members served for life, which rankled many as aristocratic elitism, and a large, twelve-man Supreme Court with similar lifetime appointments. If anything, the speech provided yet more ammunition for those who saw Hamilton as an overblown egomaniac whose government was for the wealthy aristocrats. It was just the kind of government everyone wanted to avoid, his enemies argued, and here he was, pirouetting all about the Convention chamber in this never-ending speech about his love for the country the Americans had just defeated and his plans for a government made up of individuals just like his insufferable self.

Always mindful that marriage, as well as friendships and connections, often led to success in life, Hamilton decided early to find a union with a woman that could make him comfortable. He wrote army friend John Laurens in 1779 that he was looking for a young and beautiful wife, "sensible (a little learning will do), well bred, chaste and tender…as to fortune, the larger stock of that the better…money is the essential ingredient to happiness in this world."

By sheer coincidence, he found the mate he was looking for, and more, in the war, when he met Eliza "Betsy" Schuyler, the lovely daughter of wealthy land owner and Continental Army general Philip Schuyler. He and Eliza became smitten with each other. They married and moved to New York City when the war ended and became members of the social scene at the same time that Hamilton began his career in politics and law.[79]

And it was on the Schuylers' schooner that Hamilton began to write the first essay of *The Federalist* in the waning days of October 1787.

## John Jay: Mr. Secretary

John Jay's roots went all the way back to the first Dutch families that settled New York and then prospered as merchants, shipping magnates, and farmers. His father, Peter, was a descendant of the French Huguenots. He was one of two intelligent and well-read brothers; his brother James was sent to England to study medicine at the University of Edinburgh. A third brother and two sisters suffered mental and physical disabilities. John Jay grew up in a comfortable home in Rye, New York, twenty miles north of New York City, and attended King's College at the age of fourteen.

As a student at King's College he met Robert Livingston, one of the sons of the wealthy and influential Livingston family. They became lifelong friends. Jay envied Livingston's personal skills, which he felt he lacked. Jay was shy, restrained, and felt he was a bit of a social failure. In an ironic line as a teenager, Jay, the man who would become the president of the Continental Congress, secretary of state, and the first chief justice of the U.S. Supreme Court, wrote to Livingston that "you [are] formed for a citizen of the world and I for a college or a village…"[80]

Upon graduation, Jay became a lawyer and struck all the attorneys and judges he met as someone who would eventually become one of the best. He had reached his full and commanding height of just over six feet. He had a handsome face accentuated by his sharp nose and clearly defined eyes, which were animated when he talked. He served as a law clerk to Benjamin Kissam in New York. One of the other clerks in that office wrote that Jay was "remarkable for strong reasoning powers, comprehensive views, indefatigable application, and uncommon firmness of mind."[81]

He worked with Kissam for four years and then struck out on his own, soon becoming a successful attorney and later forming a partnership with his college friend Livingston. Throughout these years, he cautioned political radicals in New York against taking violent measures against the Crown. He realized how unhappy the people were with the king and Parliament and soon found that he agreed with them.

The man who was so at ease at political rallies and in the courtroom was awkward around women. He was "more ignorant of women than in any other art whatsoever," wrote Livingston.[82] In college and as a young attorney, Jay met numerous attractive unattached young women, but never seemed to care much for any of them. The feeling among the young women of New York was mutual. Then, in 1768, he met and married the daughter of William Livingston. Sarah Livingston was a bright, well-educated, and adventurous young woman who seemed a perfect match for the successful young lawyer, who was now twenty-eight years old.

Jay was soon drawn into the revolutionary movement. In 1774, he was elected to the Continental Congress as a delegate from New York for the first of several terms. He began to write anti-Crown pamphlets, spurred on perhaps by the many pamphlets being produced by his young friend, Alexander Hamilton. In his stirring "Address of the Convention of the Representatives of the State of New York to their Constituents," written after the dramatic defeat of the American army in New York in the fall of 1776, Jay reminded all that the British could defeat an army but not a country. He wrote, "Millions, determined to be free, still remain to be subdued, millions who disdain to part with their liberties, their consciences, and the happiness of their posterity in futures ages..." He told Americans to support the army and Washington and stay resolute. If they did, in that desperate hour, he said, they would reap "all the blessings of freedom...you will be happy with God and liberty in heaven."[83]

Back in New York, he was elected to the New York Provincial Convention, a "Congress of New York" that monitored British activity and prepared for war if it should come. He was put in charge of a conspiracies committee, whose job was to hunt down loyalists to the crown who conspired against the American government. He was one of its hardest working members.

In 1777, just after the British chased Washington's army out of New York and occupied the city, Jay began a successful career as a spymaster. He came into contact with several American spies who gathered information in New York and, month by month, slowly expanded that network. It became one of the most successful spy networks in the Revolution. His spy ring reported to Hamilton and Washington, who ran a vast espionage operation that procured information on British troops, cannon, transports, and the plans of the high command throughout the war.

That same year he was asked to write the new constitution for the state of New York. Despite numerous additions from others, and a refinement of language, the constitution was mostly Jay's work. While the Constitutional Convention met, always with one eye on their deliberations and the other on the British armies that were roaming through the area, such as that of General John Burgoyne, Jay was asked to serve on a Committee of Safety that governed the state.

Jay had substantial support to run for governor under the new constitution, but urged everyone to support General Philip Schuyler instead. Schuyler lost the election to George Clinton, who would turn out to be one of the harshest critics of the U.S. Constitution in 1787 and lead the forces determined to quash it at the state's federal convention in 1788 as Jay and Hamilton fought for it.

Jay was elected the first chief justice of New York State instead. He was thirty-seven years old. He plunged into his new job with all the energy that he had tackled each of the jobs given him, or sought by him, since the eve of the Revolution. He enjoyed the chance to oversee the judicial courts of New York, at least those outside of British-held New York, but bridled under legislative interference. His horizons soon expanded when, just a year later, he was asked by the legislature to serve once again as one of New York's delegates to the Continental Congress.

By the winter of 1778, when he arrived in Philadelphia on horseback, Jay had become a very close personal friend of General Washington. The commander in chief and William Livingston, Jay's father-in-law, grew close during the war. Washington had attended many dinner parties at Liberty Hall, Livingston's mansion, during the winters of the war or at homes where Livingston and his family stayed as the governor of New Jersey, when he was forced to flee British army companies trying to capture him. Finally, Washington insisted that Livingston and his family live in the army's winter camp at Morristown, New Jersey, and later at nearby Branch Brook, so that they could be protected. Their friendship grew.

Jay and his wife were frequent visitors to the Livingston homes and hideaways and the army camp. He and Sarah were guests at many of the dinner parties that Livingston hosted for Washington and as well as those given by the general and his wife Martha. Not only did Governor Livingston insist that Jay and Sarah attend the parties, but so did his old friend Hamilton. Now Washington's top aide, Hamilton was delighted to see Jay again.

It was at those occasions that Jay, Hamilton, Washington, and others discussed not only the war, but what kind of democratic government the United States should have after the Revolution ended. They also discussed other key issues of the day, such as slavery. Jay owned several slaves himself, but was a staunch opponent of slavery and hoped to see it disappear. In 1777, when he wrote the New York State Constitution, he tried unsuccessfully to include a clause that called for the eventual abolishment of slavery in the state. One year later, he proposed granting freedom to any slaves in South Carolina who joined the army and supported Washington's later decision to enlist thousands of slaves in the army in exchange for their freedom. When the war ended, Jay freed one of his house slaves, writing that "the children of men are by nature equally free, and cannot without injustice be either reduced to or held in slavery."[84]

He continually urged Americans to end slavery, writing friend Egbert Benson from Spain in 1780 that "an excellent law might be made out of the Pennsylvania one for the gradual abolition of slavery. Till America comes into this measure her prayers to heaven for liberty will be impious.[85] Later, in 1792, Jay (who would, contradictorily, own slaves nearly all of his life, as did half the members of the New York antislavery group), again lashed out at the institution, writing in support of yet another antislavery bill, that "every man of every color has a natural right to freedom and I shall ever acknowledge myself to be an advocate for the manumission of slaves in such way as may be consistent with the justice due to them."

In 1785, along with Hamilton, Robert Livingston, and Melancton Smith, Jay worked to create the New York Society for the Manumission of Slavery. The group worked on legislative reform, sought religious backing for its goals, and, over the next few years, opened up schools for black students in New York and elsewhere. In 1799, New York, with Jay as governor, banned slavery.[86] Jay's close relationship to Washington made him an important man and when he arrived in Philadelphia for his next term as a congressman in 1778, he was immediately elected the president of the Congress when Henry Laurens suddenly resigned as its chief executive because he was unhappy with its effectiveness. The presidents of the Continental Congress were elected by the Congress, not the people, and only served one-year terms. They had no real executive power and had to work with the legislatures of the states to accomplish anything, but the position gave Jay considerable national status and yet more experience as an executive. He decided in his year as president that a powerless president was useless and began to agree with Hamilton and Washington that while an effective Congress was necessary to govern a democratic country, a strong national executive was also needed.

Jay had gained prestige as president of the Continental Congress and in his prior work and in 1779 Congress sent him to Spain as a minister to persuade the Spanish government to give America troops, ships, and money for the war. Soon afterwards, in 1783, Jay was named one of the peace commissioners assigned to haggle over the terms of the peace treaty that would follow the Revolution. As one of the negotiators, he earned high praise from all in his efforts to not merely end the war but to do so in such a way that the United States emerged not as a rump rebel offspring, but as a major world power.

Jay returned to the United States in 1784. He was forty-four years old and had already served as the president of the Continental

Congress, chief justice of New York, minister to Spain, and peace commissioner. The experienced New Yorker was asked to serve as U.S. secretary of foreign affairs (secretary of state). He had gained enormous respect in Britain and Europe for his work as a minister and peace commissioner and was perfectly suited for the job.

He became disenchanted with the government rather quickly, telling friends that "the construction of our federal government is fundamentally wrong" because one body of legislators passes bills, executes them, and decides whether or not they are legal. He wrote Washington that three separate branches of government were needed.[87]

He lived the part of foreign secretary, building an enormous, three-story stone mansion on lower Broadway, with stables and gardens run by a staff of servants. Over the years, he had reaped huge profits when he sold lands he had inherited from his father or purchased himself. In addition, he had money from his legal business and his salary as secretary of foreign affairs. He also had a substantial amount of inherited money of the wealthy Livingston family through his wife Sarah. As soon as the home was complete, the new secretary of foreign affairs and his wife became leaders of the New York social scene, hosting numerous parties in their mansion and attending those hosted by other influential and wealthy New Yorkers and members of Congress. The man who had once only seen himself as a figure in a small village was now a major figure on the world stage.[88] That's why, in the autumn of 1787, when it appeared that the new Constitution would be defeated, his longtime friend Hamilton asked him to help write *The Federalist* and to work with him and James Madison to get the Constitution ratified.

## James Madison of Virginia

Thomas Jefferson and George Washington often wrote that they yearned for retirement from the hectic pace of public life and the enjoyment they would find back home at their sprawling plantations at Mount Vernon and Monticello. Not James Madison. Perhaps no one in American history loved public life, thrived on it, as much as the Virginian.

Madison grew up on a large plantation, Montpelier, in central Virginia. There, he determined early on that he was too sickly to become a planter and turned to intellectual pursuits. His father sent him to the College of New Jersey (later Princeton University), where Madison plunged into his studies, reading every book he could find and overloading himself with course work. He managed to cram three years of study into two and then requested another year to take a personally designed "master's degree" in politics and government, reading yet more books and establishing himself as an expert not just on American history and government, but the politics of Europe going all the way back to ancient Greece and the Rome of the Caesars. His studies led him into a life in politics that stretched over nearly six decades and saw America rise from a collection of colonies to one of the great powers in the world.

He returned from college in the spring of 1772 to find himself living in a Virginia in political turmoil. Starting in 1765, the state had been torn apart by controversies over the Stamp Act and other British taxes. The royal governor of Virginia had disbanded the state legislature on several occasions and hundreds of men in the state had joined militia companies, ready for a war if it came. Different counties formed Committees of Public Safety to oversee the militias and provide political leadership to those opposed to the crown.

In 1774, just two years after his return, at age twenty-three, Madison was elected to the Orange County Committee on Public Safety. At age twenty-five, he was elected as the local delegate to the Virginia Convention, in Williamsburg, that declared Virginia's independence. One year after that, he was elected to the state assembly.

The slight scholar, more than perhaps anyone of his generation, was, as Edmund Randolph said, "a child of the Revolution."[89]

His movement to a position of leadership in the Revolution was rapid. The Virginia General Assembly sent him to the Continental Congress in Philadelphia in the winter of 1780, when he was twenty-nine years old; he was its youngest delegate. In Philadelphia, he continued to wear his traditional black clothing, which drew derision from some members, and perpetually carried armfuls of books wherever he went.

Madison had already met and befriended Thomas Jefferson when the latter was first governor of Virginia, elected in 1779. It was in Philadelphia, though, where his life changed. There, he began his lifelong relationship with George Washington. Because Washington was with the army, he did not meet Madison when the latter arrived at the Virginia state assembly for his first term in 1776. Like everyone, Madison saw in the heroic Washington the leader of the Revolution and the most admired man in America. The slight Madison, nearly a foot shorter than Washington, seemed just the opposite of the general and perhaps the last person the commander of the army would make a close companion and advisor.

Madison was not a polished public speaker. He exhibited none of the theatrical flourishes of the great orators, such as Patrick Henry. He was effective, though. Madison prepared for his speeches or committee meetings for hours, was well versed in the history of politics, and presented all of his arguments in a logical manner, full of facts and figures. A Massachusetts congressman wrote that he was "a man of sense, reading, address, and integrity" but "a little too much of a book politician and too timid in his politics."[90]

As its most active participant, he brought two other strengths to the Triumvirate. He was unemployed and a bachelor.

In addition to being a politician, Hamilton was a full-time lawyer, working hard at his law office on Wall Street to solicit new clients as well as additional assignments from old ones. For him, the crusade to ratify the Constitution was a part-time job, adding work to his busy schedule in courts throughout New York. Jay had been a lawyer all of his life, adding politics and diplomacy to his resume during and after the Revolution. As secretary of foreign affairs, his days were crammed with official meetings and travel and his nights filled with social and diplomatic parties. For him, too, time spent working for the goals of the Triumvirate was substantial, as well as an additional burden.

Both Hamilton and Jay were married. In addition to their full-time jobs, they were full-time husbands and the heads of households. Their free time away from their offices was taken up with marital and family responsibilities. Most of the Federalists who aided the three in their drive to gain passage for the Constitution held full-time jobs and had families, too.

Madison, thirty-one in the autumn of 1787, never held a job. He filled his days with reading and writing and working part-time as a congressmen during and after the war. He had not married. Being single gave Madison an enormous amount of time for the affairs of the Triumvirate. He did not have to host dinner parties with his wife, attend balls, tuck children into their beds at night, travel about the state to visit his wife's family, entertain mutual friends or devote nights and weekends to time with his spouse. That free time gave him the opportunity to work continually as he did to write the U.S. Constitution, lobby for its approval in Philadelphia and now, in the autumn of 1787, to get it ratified.

⁓

The trio of Madison, Hamilton, and Jay had to work quickly because the opposition to the Constitution was starting to organize and publish their complaints. The Anti-Federalists deplored the proposed new government in general, but each state had its specific grievances, too. Men in Massachusetts complained that there was nothing in the Constitution about religion and that the document had to have some sort of imprimatur from God. Merchants in Rhode Island were appalled that the Constitution called for a uniform system of paper money to be used by all of the states; Rhode Islanders wanted to have their own separate currency from that of the rest of the country. Residents of Maine, then a part of Massachusetts, argued that they were against anything the rest of the residents of Massachusetts favored.

Residents of Kentucky, then a part of Virginia, had begun talking about themselves as a separate state. They did not see why they should have anything to do with Virginia and the men who ran it. And they certainly did not need a Constitution to tell them how to run Kentucky. The people who populated the towns and counties distant from Philadelphia argued that their interests were more important than those of the merchants of Philadelphia, who received all the attention. Federal government opponents in Maryland feared that their state would be overwhelmed by a national government, just as they felt overwhelmed now because they were wedged between the goliath states of Virginia and Pennsylvania. Voters in Delaware felt the tiny size of their state even more acutely. The slave owners of South Carolina would not agree to any national government unless they had absolute guarantees that the government would protect slavery. Governor George Clinton and his faction in New York complained that New York was a premier seaport, with business ties to the entire world, not just the states, and could not be dictated to by fishermen in New England, slave owners in the South, and certainly not a federal government. Not only did the people there object to the Constitution, but they insisted that their terms be met because there could be no United States without New York.[91]

There were regional objections, too. The southern states with boundaries they claimed extended to the Mississippi River felt that the navigation of the Mississippi, important to them in the future, would be ignored by a federal government that cared more about the seafaring interests of the merchants in New York, Boston, and Philadelphia. All of the southern states feared a federal government that would curb slavery and favor industrial concerns over agricultural ones. Tied to all of this, opponents insisted, was anger that the Federalists were so determined to have their way that they not only ignored critics, but had started to denounce them in the public press in vitriolic terms, an obvious precursor of how the Federalists would treat any political opposition in the future.[92]

The opponents of the new government worried that it would not keep foreign powers out of the Midwest and the West, that it would be unable to keep the Mississippi open for traffic, that it would base its capital in some isolated area, and that its "necessary and proper clause" could mean that Congress could pass whatever laws it wanted to invest the federal government with more power, usurping many of the powers of the states to do so.

All of the Constitution's opponents had two overwhelming objections. In every state there was a large group of objectors who were convinced that the new government would not only be too powerful, but one designed to benefit the rich at the expense of both the poor and the ever-growing middle class, too. Wealthy aristocrats who cared little for the commoners would run the new government. Its wealthy lawmakers would pass legislation designed to make the rich richer and the poor poorer and force the people to accept that legislation with a powerful national army. Had not the American people just won a bloody revolution to separate themselves from that exact same uncaring, all-powerful, far-away government—Great Britain?[93]

There was widespread belief that the wealthy planters and well-to-do merchants would run the new government. Melancton Smith, of New York, continually insisted that "a representative body, composed principally of respected yeoman, is the best possible security to liberty." Massachusetts delegates were so committed to rule by the common man that they hesitated to embrace the new Constitution because they worried that it "[would] give birth to new hopes of an aristocratical faction which every community possesses."[94]

Amos Singletary, a farmer and congressman from Massachusetts, sneered of the rich that they were men who "talked so finely and glossed over matters so smoothly."[95]

This was not just a group of wealthy men meeting in a tavern across the street from the assembly hall for drinks, but, some Anti-Federalists believed, a far-flung cabal that included everyone of some station in life throughout the country. Congressman Samuel Osgood wrote that this secret conspiracy would "lord it over the rest of their fellow citizens, to trample the poorer part of the people under their feet, that they may be rendered their servants and slaves."[96] And other Anti-Federalists argued that the common people knew the rich aristocrats who wanted to control them. One pamphlet writer wrote that they all had that "dictatorial air, the magisterial voice, the imperious tone, the haughty countenance, the lofty look, the majestic men." Another said smugly that "you cannot be too cautious of men of advantage of every denomination."[97]

Not all of the Anti-Federalists shared this view of the wealthy, but they charged that the rich led lives that insulated them from the problems that beset ordinary people. How could they grapple with the problems of the common men and women?

The jealousy and hatred of the rich, scoffed at by many Federalists, was a very real problem and Madison knew it. In January of 1788, at the start of the raucous Massachusetts convention in Boston, Rufus King wrote him that it was impossible to bridge the divide between the rich and poor delegates. "A distrust of men of property or education have a more powerful effect upon the minds of our opponents than any specific objections against the Constitution," King wrote. "Any attempt to remove their fixed and violent jealousy seems hitherto to operate as a confirmation of that baneful passion…" And, he told him that the opposition to the Federalists because they were men of property and influence was "immovable." He informed the three that the Anti-Federalists felt that "some injury is plotted against them that the system is the production of the rich and ambitious…the consequences will be the establishment of two orders in the society, one comprehending the opulent and great, the other the poor and illiterate."[98]

The Federalists were exasperated by these charges and, in fact, were just as fearful that the new government would not be controlled by educated men like themselves but by uneducated men who would be carried into office in this crazed atmosphere in which a true democracy meant that anyone had the skills to serve in Congress. Throughout the 1780s, true democracies bloomed in the different states and seasoned lawyers found themselves losing elections to saddlemakers because the people insisted that a democracy had to be governed by people from all the ranks of society, not just the wellborn.

The unqualified men elected in the different state assemblies may have represented the people who voted for them, but many did not have the education to understand the bills they were voting on or the ability to explain themselves on the floor of their assemblies. Many had friends write their speeches because they could not. They had no knowledge of politics, government, parliamentary law, or the workings of the legislature. The result was assemblies that soon ground to a halt.

One newspaper editor called the election of these men "Whiggism run mad" and said that just because a man could patch a shoe did not mean that he could patch a state. Another fumed that the new legislators were, to the electorate, "men whose fathers they would have disdained to have sat with the dogs of their flocks…"[99]

They annoyed the Triumvirate. Jay complained that "effrontery and arrogance even in our virtuous and enlightened days are giving rank and importance to whom wisdom would have left in obscurity." Madison complained that the ill-trained men, "without reading, experience of principle," who were now in power, were often rejected in the next election by other untrained men. He said that in many state legislatures half the seats changed each year and, consequently, nothing was accomplished.[100]

Congressman Roger Alden, of New York, derisively put the Anti-Federalists into three categories, writing that they were "great men who would lose their consequence, little great men, conscious of their own talents who know they have not abilities to become really great men, and all those who are really enemies to the happiness of the country or have exposed themselves by their crimes, idleness, and wickedness to the just laws of society."[101]

New York Federalist Robert Livingston, angry at Melancton Smith and his New York yeoman, railed, "whom, in the name of common sense, will we have to represent us? Why, Smith must go out on the highways and pick up the rogue and the robber; he must go to the hedges and ditches and bring in the poor, the blind, and the lame."[102]

One elitist from Massachusetts, Henry Jackson, became so upset in trying to describe the lack of character in the Anti-Federalists that he gave up, writing a friend that "Harry, it is too much to think of!" Other Federalists said that they were elected by "false representations" and by "propagating impudent lies."[103]

James Otis put it even more bluntly. "When the pot boils, the scum will rise."[104]

These comments enraged the Anti-Federalists, particularly those middle-of-the-roaders for whom normal language might have persuaded a change in opinion. They did not like being ridiculed. "Oh, they [Federalists] cry out, shame upon you, low born gentry; to call such grand big men public defaulters, their characters are sacred, it is blasphemy to touch their names; if they owe the public millions, the people must sit down and bear it patiently without so much as a murmur," wrote one Anti-Federalist in the *New York Journal*.[105]

The fact was, though, that the Antis were right; most of the Federalists were financially comfortable and politically well connected. Federalists outranked Anti-Federalists among officeholders by two to one. Three times as many Federalists held a college degree as the Antis. Seven times as many ship owners, ship captains, and large manufacturers were Federalists as Antis. Five times as many merchants and twice as many lawyers and judges were Federalists. Yet, when the Federalists tried to explain their achievements, in defense of themselves, they often had a negative effect. Jay constantly raised the issue. He once said that the Constitution was "recommended by so many men of distinguished worth and abilities," yet the Antis answered that was exactly the problem.[106]

Another problem was that while Antis represented people who were mostly farmers or working-class shopkeepers, the Anti-Federalist delegates themselves were not. Many of the Antis were lawyers, merchants, and wealthy landholders. The Federalists knew that and yet constantly branded them all as ignorant farmers in comparison to the Federalists' highly educated, successful businessmen. In so doing, they made a large mistake.

What the Federalists had to do, and failed to do in the beginning, was convince the Anti-Federalists, and the entire country, that there was a natural aristocracy among men and women that went beyond wealth. There were many people who were not rich who were educated and eager to serve in a government in which they could use their skills to make life better for all, rich or poor. Success in doing so would be their crowning glory and failure would lead to the wreckage of the Constitution and end of their dreams for a republican government.

That was just part of the overall scheme, though, because the Anti-Federalists had leveled hundreds of questions at the Federalists. DeWitt Clinton, writing in his "Letters From a Countryman From Dutchess County," published in the *New York Journal*, wanted to know how a free people could continue to condone the slave trade, "that trade in blood and every vice of which the avarice, pride, insolence, and cruelty of man is capable." A Maine man wanted to know what happened to the president after the end of his four-year term and joked that until the next president was elected, "in the year 2000," the chief justice would serve as the president. What about the dozens of members of the Albany, New York, Anti-Federal Committee, that issued a manifesto questioning the Constitution's "great and extensive powers granted to the new government over the lives, liberties, and property of every citizen…"

Or Elbridge Gerry, who refused to sign the Constitution at the federal convention and asked for amendments, writing, "Should a free people adopt a form of government under the conviction that it wants amendment?" Or New York's Melancton Smith, who charged that the Constitution would bring about "aristocratic tyranny"? Or the many who reminded all that Madison and Washington had tried, unsuccessfully, to ram through a provision at the federal convention in Philadelphia, vetoed by a wide margin, to make all federal law supercede all state law? Or all of the men and women angry that under the new Constitution they would have to pay taxes to a federal government on top of the taxes they already paid to their state government? Or that federal taxes would grow and grow (one Anti-Federalist in Maryland insisted that any taxes were "the horror of a free people").[107]

When Madison moved back to New York at the end of September 1787, and assessed the fight that lay ahead for the Constitution's ratification, he knew that the wide divide between the rich and poor threatened passage of the constitution. So did the people's dread of a powerful central government, the second major argument against the new Constitution.

Most Americans were farmers, some middle class and some poor, and they all depended on other farmers, villagers, and residents of the large cities for revenue from the sale of their crops. They were interconnected to everyone. These men and women made up the majority of the Anti-Federalist movement. They all prospered on a local basis and they feared any kind of big government that would shape their lives.

Many of the Anti-Federalists who feared an all-powerful federal government reminded the Federalists, particularly Madison, that the people whom they quoted so liberally in defense of their policies were the same people who warned that governments just like the one they proposed would always turn tyrannical. Englishman James Burgh's *Political Disquisitions*, written in 1775, was one of the most quoted volumes in their arguments, as were those of Englishmen Thomas Gordon and John Trenchard, writing as Cato in *Cato's Letters, or Lessons on Liberty, Civil and Religious and Other Important Subjects*, published in 1748. Burgh argued that those who are given power want more and that power always expands and never diminishes. Trenchard and Gordon argued that men given power also abuse it.

Anti-Federalists strongly believed that no assembly should have too much power. After all, look at what the all-powerful British Parliament had done to the Americans in the 1760s and 1770s. Boston's Samuel Adams said that watchfulness "is necessary to guard against the infirmities of the best as well as the wickedness of the worst of men." Hugh Hughes, a former soldier and political figure in New York, said that "when bodies of men in authority get possession of, or become invested with [power]…whether it be by intrigue, mistake, or chance, they scarcely ever relinquish their claim."[108]

Richard Henry Lee, Madison's nemesis, expressed that worry best when he wrote that "'Tis really astonishing that the same people who have just emerged from a long and cruel war in defense of liberty should now agree to fix an elective despotism upon themselves and their posterity."[109]

The opponents of the Constitution insisted on a bill of rights. Almost all of the separate state constitutions had such a bill and most had eight or more rights protected. It had to be in the Constitution and not simply assumed by James Madison or promised by Alexander Hamilton and John Jay at one of their lavish receptions in their glistening New York City mansions.

The Anti-Federalists demanded freedom of the press, religious worship, speech, and the right to assemble in public. The people should be allowed to keep and bear arms, suffer no unreasonable searches of homes, obtain due process of law, grand jury charges for trials, speedy trials with juries, and representation by a lawyer with no high bails or cruel punishments if found guilty. The opponents, wary of a powerful national government, also insisted that any of the rights not specifically given to the national government must be turned over to the states so that the federal government and state governments shared power.

Many critics argued that the success of democratic government was not the strength of the majority, but of the minority. Brutus, the nom de plume (never clearly identified) of one of the most strident voices for individual rights, wrote that "informing a government on its true principles the foundation should be laid...by expressly reserving to the people such of their essential natural rights, as are not necessary to be parted with."[110]

And, Anti-Federalists said over and over again, while current public officials might be trusted, future leaders might be abusive of the people. Patrick Henry exclaimed that he could see future federal law enforcement leaders not only denying citizens their rights, but torturing them. Many argued, too, that in the future leaders might simply invent new laws under which to charge political opponents. Besides, as Richard Henry Lee told everyone, pro- and anti-Constitution, why not add a bill of rights? What was the big deal? He wrote that the bills of rights "won't do any harm, but might do much good."[111]

The Federalists genuinely believed that all the rights the people needed to protect themselves from the proposed national government were built into it. The Triumvirate never for a moment saw a need for a bill of rights; the trio steadfastly ignored all of their critics. They agreed with Benjamin Franklin, who wrote that "the first Congress will probably mend the faults of the Constitution and future Congresses the rest."[112]

All of the Antis saw their efforts as noble and despised the Federalists and the press for portraying them as the enemies of democracy. "The importance of the alternatives proposed, calculated to preserve public liberty by those checks on power which the experience of ages has rendered venerable, and to promote the happiness of the people, by a due attention to their ease and convenience, will justify the steps we have taken, to obtain them, to our constituents and the world," wrote a committee composed of William Paca, Samuel Chase, John F. Mercer, and Jeremiah Chase, four influential political leaders in Maryland.[113]

The problem with the Federalists, though, was not that they were elitists, or that they looked down upon the Anti-Federalists. They had dismissed efforts to put a bill of rights into the Constitution in Philadelphia and now stubbornly continued to do so. The more their enemies insisted on protection for the people, the more the Federalists, all of them, refused. Their intransigence made it impossible for the Triumvirate to see the opposition to a strong federal government and the unhappiness of so many people.

The Federalists, convinced they had created a wonderful government in Philadelphia, did not see themselves as stubborn at all, but the protectors of this new democracy. They were certain no one in the federal government, then or in the future, would ever abuse the people. Why didn't others see that? They did not look at the issue from the other side of the aisle and, unable to do that, did not gauge the depth of the opposition. They then became angry at the Anti-Federalists for their attacks.

What happened after that was classic feuding. Each time an Anti-Federalist criticized the Constitution, the Federalists then deepened their resistance to any changes in it. They came to see surrender on the Bill of Rights as a surrender of the entire Constitution, which it was not. The more critical the Anti-Federalists became, the more defensive the Federalist became. The two sides never understood each other and that turned the battle for ratification into a donnybrook that would tumble across the United States for nearly a year.

# THE RIGHT TO KEEP
# AND BEAR ARMS

The best example of why the public so strongly demanded a bill of rights was the determination of all Americans to continue to possess firearms, later recognized in the Second Amendment to the Constitution. It was as important to them as freedom of religion and freedom of the press, and, like those issues, they insisted that it had to be legally outlined in the Constitution. It could not be inferred or presumed. The heated campaign to keep guns was symbolic of the crusade to obtain a bill of rights. Freedoms had been ingrained in the American psyche and the people were not about to give them up. Guns were representative.

Thomas Jefferson had been a longtime devotee of firearms. He had a personal armory full of guns at Monticello, his mountaintop Virginia estate, and lectured visitors on their manufacture and use. He told friends that they should give guns to their sons when they reached the age of ten.[114] He wrote his own fifteen-year-old nephew that "a strong body makes the mind strong. As to the species of exercises, I advise the gun…Let your gun therefore be the companion of your walks."[115] He had been instrumental in supplying firearms to the Continental Army during the Revolution as governor of Virginia and in 1796 would write President Washington that "one loves to possess arms."[116] In the state constitution he drafted for Virginia, he wrote that "no free man shall be debarred the right to arms."[117]

At the Virginia Convention, George Mason pleaded with delegates for language that protected every Virginian's right to carry a gun. Patrick Henry told that state convention that "the great object is that every man be armed" and that "everyone who is able may have a gun." Samuel Adams in Massachusetts told delegates that several amendments were needed and that Congress could not infringe "on the just liberty of the press or the rights of conscience or to prevent the people of the United States who are peaceable citizens from keeping their own arms."

It was a long-standing law in Massachusetts not only that every man could be armed, but had to be to protect the colony from invasion; local communities paid for guns for men too poor to purchase them. Virginia also mandated ownership of firearms. New Hampshire insisted that it had to halt any attempt by the government to disarm the citizens. North Carolina did the same, reminding Congress that "the people have a right to keep and bear arms."[118]

There were several reasons why American political leaders advocated militias and firearms for citizens in 1787: (1) a fear that a future leader of the new American government might use a national army to oppress the people. An armed population, enrolled in state militias, could easily defeat any such army and preserve the nation's freedom; (2) a citizen army could be quickly mobilized to defend the country against a second invasion of the United States by England or another foreign power; (3) individuals needed guns for protection against criminals, Indians, and any wild game that threatened their farm animals; and (4) individuals needed firearms to hunt game to provide food for their families.

The authors of the Constitution had not included provisions to guarantee an armed citizenry because they assumed everyone understood that right as an accepted aspect of life in the United States in 1787. Madison, in responding to repeated calls for a firearms amendment, reminded critics that he had addressed that issue directly in *The Federalist* No. 46. He had written that any oppressive federal army "would be opposed a militia amounting to near half a million citizens with arms in their hands."[119]

Madison's contention that the right to bear arms would not be eliminated by the new federal government did not impress anyone. The clamor for a guarantee of gun possession within a general bill of rights persisted. One direct and visible way to assure state supremacy, they believed, was large and well-armed state militias. These militia supporters, led by Jefferson, insisted that strong state military units would serve as a forceful deterrent against any desire of a president or Congress to subjugate the people with a large national army. None were more blunt than Noah Webster, who argued in a pamphlet distributed to delegates to the Pennsylvania ratification convention that "the supreme power in America cannot enforce unjust laws by the sword because the whole body of the people are armed and constitute a force superior to any band of regular troops."[120]

Massachusetts' model bill of rights, under its state constitution's seventeenth amendment, stated that the people have the right to keep and bear arms "for the common defense."[121] Virginia's suggested collection of individual rights, too, connected the individual's possession of firearms to the militia. Article XVII of the bill of rights of that state asserted "that the people have a right to keep and bear arms; that a well regulated militia, composed of the body of the people trained to arms, is the proper, natural safe defense of a free state." Pennsylvania, too, was clear in its desire for weapons to be limited to those in the state militia. The arms amendment proposed by legislators there read: "That the people have a right to bear arms for the defense of themselves and the state..."[122] In two connected amendments, legislators in Delaware suggested "that a well regulated militia is the proper, natural, and safe defense of a free government" and that "standing armies of any kind could not be raised without the consent of the legislature."[123]

Today, this fanatical devotion to the state militia as a defense against the national government seems far-fetched, but at the time defenders of states' rights saw an armed militia as a necessity. These Anti-Federalist states' rights champions reminded their Federalist opponents who dismissed their fear of a despotic national government that the British Crown had seemed friendly for a long time, too. The entire concept of state militias may seem inappropriate now, but in 1788 the state military organizations were a legitimate yardstick of national defense. The thirteen British colonies in America had no national army when the war for independence began in the spring of 1775 and the colonies' only armed forces consisted of militia units from different counties and states, supplied and armed at first by their states and later by the new Continental Congress.

Most Americans believed that the state and county militias would always be able to defend the people against a runaway federal administration or foreign power. Others were not so sure.

In the beginning of the Revolution, George Washington had little use for the state and county militias. Soldiers from militia units, tired of the fighting, lack of food, and the brutally cold winter, deserted and went back to their hometowns long before their enlistment was supposed to end. "They often walk off for their homes a few days after they join the army," Washington complained. The number of deserters from the militia became so great in the winter of 1777 that an exasperated Washington wrote Continental Congress president John Hancock that "we shall be obliged to detach one half of the army to bring back the other."[124]

The loss of militia soldiers who left at the end of their short enlistment or deserters meant that Continental Army officers had to continually train the new recruits who replaced them. This required time for drills and money for new uniforms. The departure of troops also meant the loss of thousands of firearms. The army supplied almost all of its newly recruited militia soldiers with muskets upon arrival. The men who departed picked up their muskets and brought them home. No one stopped them. "No human prudence could secure but a small part of those [muskets]...from being embezzled and carried off when their time of service expired," Washington exploded to Congress. Men who fought for an agreed upon year or, later, three years, and those who stayed in the army for the duration of the war, also brought their weapons home.[125]

In the early years of the war, Washington had become so disgusted with the militia that he once referred to them as "a motley crew, here today, gone tomorrow."[126]

During the Revolution, the militia became far better disciplined. In June 1780, the British army attacked Springfield, New Jersey, twice in an effort to crush Washington's army. Fearful of such an invasion, Washington asked New Jersey's governor, William Livingston, to call up the entire state militia and tell them to get ready to march at a moment's notice. A timely and efficient coordination of a single county militia, much less the entire state troops, would have been unthinkable early in the war, but by 1780 the militias had improved so much that all of the New Jersey men were ready for action within just three days and won both battles convincingly.[127]

The militia had impressed the British. General Wilhelm Knyphausen, a Hessian general fighting for the English, said that the American militia was surprisingly strong. But even more impressed was George Washington. He proudly told Robert Howe that they fought "with admirable spirit."[128]

The success of these militias, as Springfield had proven, was the ability of men already armed to be quickly mobilized for a battle. After all, as one writer expressed in a letter to the Philadelphia *Freeman's Journal*, the United States did not have any army at all when the revolution began and relied on state militias. "Is not a well regulated militia sufficient for every military purpose of internal defense?" he asked. "And which of you, my fellow citizens, is afraid of any invasion from foreign powers that our brave militia would not be able to immediately repel?"[129]

All of the reasons men wanted guns seemed valid at the time. Men did need arms to hunt and provide food for the table. Guns were required to kill and ward off wild animals that threatened farmer livestock. There was a constant fear of Indian raids during the Revolution. Indians in Pennsylvania had carried out raids on farmers with land in rural areas, killing several. Those raids, and others in New York, resulted in a small war against the Indians by the Continental Army that resulted in the deaths of many and the destruction of Indian villages. There were no police departments in the United States until 1842 and residents of villages, and especially cities such as New York and Boston, believed that without such protection they needed guns to defend themselves, their wives, and children against physical assaults and robberies.

Even Hamilton wanted guns, writing in *The Federalist* No. 29 that of any oppressive force, "that army can never be formidable to the liberties of the people while there is a large body of citizens, little if at all inferior to them in discipline and the use of arms, who stand ready to defend their rights and those of their fellow citizens."[130]

Virginia's Richard Henry Lee echoed his remarks, stating that all of the citizens of a state, or the nation, under arms are "too strong a body of men to be openly offended…They will take care of themselves. Men who shall govern shall not dare pay disrespect to their opinions."[131]

The writers and philosophers whom the colonists trusted all felt the same way. One of the most prominent was Thomas Paine. He wrote that, "the supposed quietude of a good man allures the ruffian; while, on the other hand, arms, like laws, discourage and keep the invader and plunderer in awe and preserve order in the world as well as property."[132]

Some political philosophers of the era, such as Joel Barlow, argued that to disarm men who had carried weapons all of their lives was to morally and emotionally emasculate them. Disarmament, he wrote, "palsies the hand and brutalizes the mind" and wrecks the human moral compass.[133]

Others felt that guns were a part of the overall makeup of the American frontiersman, a symbol of the individual pushing ever forward into the woods and mountains of North America, expanding American territory and bringing the greatness of the American people into whatever meadow or valley he found, using his gun to clear the way. That image of the gritty and heroic frontiersman was given mythic stature in the novels of James Fenimore Cooper in the 1820s and 1830s, such as *The Last of the Mohicans*, and, a hundred years later, in American Western movies.

There was also the strong belief that the man who kept and maintained arms and was ready to use them to defend his country, or his family, even if never called upon to do so, was a good citizen. In keeping weapons and letting everyone know that he was prepared to use them, to give his life in battle for home and country, he exhibited staunch character. In the postrevolutionary era, Americans did not believe that their new nation would flourish just because of its democratic institutions or economic success; they believed it would thrive because of the virtue and character of its people. In 1787, firearms were a very visible sign of that virtue and character.[134]

The near unanimity of opinion among the people and the leaders of the different states that an amendment was necessary to protect the people's right to bear arms was representative of the way the Americans felt about all of the rights they insisted on in a bill of rights of some kind in the Constitution.

Madison, Jay, and others could not dissuade the people from this belief and they could not convince them that these rights were inherent in the Constitution. Madison, especially, was oblivious to the strong arguments in favor of a bill of rights. He insisted, as did Hamilton and Jay, that the Constitution, as written, offered ample protection to the people from a national government, even a very strong national government. The three branches of government protected the people from an overly powerful president, Congress, and Supreme Court. Besides, all three argued again and again, if there was, in fact, a real need for a bill of rights, legislation to provide such a bill could be introduced and approved when the new government was formed.

They did not, even for a moment, understand the people's belief that once in power, a strong national government would ignore cries for a bill of rights and, being a strong national entity, forever block the passage of legislation to provide such a bill. The members of the Triumvirate were deaf to the cries for a bill of rights and their lack of understanding made the passage of the Constitution very difficult.

## The Fury of the Anti-Federalists

The Anti-Federalists were angry at Hamilton, Madison, and Jay, especially at Madison, because they saw them as aloof, condescending, and intransigent, and this further strengthened the resolve of the opponents to reject the new government.

They were right. Hamilton and Madison, in particular, looked down at the Anti-Federalists and had nothing but personal disdain for them. "Out of the vast number that composed [the Anti-Federalists], there was scarce a man of respectability, and not a single one capable of leading the formidable band," Madison wrote Pendleton of the Massachusetts Anti-Federalists.[135]

Madison, an even-tempered man, remained perplexed that the Anti-Federalists did not see that the three branches of the federal government would protect the people from tyrants. He, Hamilton, and Jay had continually stressed the power of the people in *The Federalist*. In No. 22, Hamilton had written that "the fabric of American empire ought to rest on the solid basis of the consent of the people…original fountain of legitimate authority." In No. 42, Madison had agreed, writing that "the express authority of the people alone could give due validity to the Constitution."[136]

It seems ironic that three men who were genuine elitists—wealthy, educated men who owned valuable property and mingled with the most important people in America at parties—had created a democratic government that seemed to be designed to protect the rights of the middle and lower classes as well as their own elite class. The trio openly sponsored a national government of, by, and for the people that helped all, not just their own class. Perhaps this dedication to a great democratic government, met with such opposition, made them resent those who opposed them, creating much of the problems they encountered in the ratification fight.

Madison felt that those in opposition had no real goals except the destruction of the Constitution and the proposed new government; they offered no plans at all.

Madison fumed at cries that the federal government was being created for the rich, people just like himself, Hamilton, and Jay, and that the well-to-do would blithely ignore the poor in order to benefit themselves. The Federalists told people repeatedly that the guarantees for the rights of the people were assured and did not have to be spelled out. Pennsylvania judge Thomas McKean, as exasperated as Madison, Hamilton, and Jay, said that "the whole plan of government is nothing more than a bill of rights—a declaration of the people in what manner they choose to be governed."

One of the most powerful and effective arguments that Hamilton and Jay adopted from the start in their campaigns was that the Anti-Federalists were against a single national union, which they were not, and that the rejection of the Constitution would not only lead to civil war, but perhaps result in the British again taking over the United States, a spurious argument at best.

The pair embraced it because they understood that while the people might argue over exactly what form the new government should take and specifically what powers were given to the national government and the states, and what protection the people had of their personal rights, everybody wanted to preserve the nation they had fought for in the Revolution. Again and again, their alarm and warnings would frighten their fellow citizens that their country might plunge into war and be divided into three or four separate nations. In doing so, they hurt the Anti-Federalists' efforts—unfairly so.

Hamilton used this threat first right after the Constitutional Convention ended in Philadelphia. He argued that the Anti-Federalists intended to create a nation of strong states because they currently not only ran those states, but became wealthy by using their power to help their businesses there. If the states became powerful, Hamilton argued, "in the course of a few years, it is probable that the contests about the boundaries of power between the particular governments and the general government and momentum of the larger states in such contests will produce a dissolution of the Union."[137]

Jay hammered away at the same theme, predicting continual wars between different confederations carved out of the thirteen states if one united country could not be formed under the Constitution.

Prophetically, he predicted a war between the North and South over slavery. And Jay, like Hamilton, twisted history a bit. The United States in 1788 was a polyglot nation of many different immigrant groups from Europe and South America, Indian tribes, and also a black and white country. All of these people had different backgrounds, religions, and political interests, but Jay rather whimsically and neatly wrote, "Providence has been pleased to give this one connected country to one united people, a people descended from the same ancestors, speaking the same language, professing the same religion, attached to the same principles of government…the country and people seem to have been made for each other…"[138]

Many Federalists adopted Washington's view that the new government was a pretty good plan that could be amended and improved later. They pushed for adoption despite the faults of the Constitution, reminding their opponents that no system was perfect. One of the most successful Federalist lobbyists was James O. Wilson, a congressman from Pennsylvania, who argued that over the years common sense, and not political philosophy, would determine public policy and the faults of the Constitution would be overcome by the people. He told crowds. "I will confess, indeed, that I am not a blind admirer of this plan of government, and that there are some parts of it which, if my wish had prevailed, would certainly have been altered." But he added quickly that it was probably the best blueprint that could be put together, could always be changed with amendments and would, in the end, produce "the best form of government which has ever been offered to the world."

Wilson, like Jefferson and Washington, believed that the wisdom of the people would always overcome the failings of some political leaders. He drew an analogy between democratic government and a pyramid, reminding listeners that the large and solid base, the people, would always determine who rose to the top and that those selected would succeed because they had the support of all the people at the bottom.[139]

Madison spent the entire autumn and winter angrily and unfairly denouncing the opposition, writing that they were "ignorant or jealous men who had been taught or had fancied that the Convention at Philadelphia had entered into a conspiracy against the liberties of the people at large, in order to erect an aristocracy for the rich and well born."[140]

Such claims hurt his cause.

Nor would the three men listen to their friends. Madison's closest friend Jefferson read the Constitution and wrote him back immediately that it was a wonderful document but absolutely had to have a bill of rights and the argument that the rights were implied was weak.

"I will tell you what I do not like. First, the omission of a bill of rights, providing clearly…for freedom of religion, freedom of the press, protection against standing armies, restrictions of monopolies, the eternal and unremitting force of the habeas corpus laws and trials by jury." In another letter, he declared nothing could be "implied" in the new government and that "a bill of rights is what the people are entitled to against every government on earth, general or particular and what no just government should refuse or rest on inferences."[141]

The stubborn Madison, Hamilton, and Jay ignored all arguments about the bill of rights, even from Jefferson, a friend whose intelligence and political savvy they admired. In the federal convention, Madison snipped abruptly that "the [state] legislature may be safely trusted."[142]

Madison simply did not acknowledge the pleas of his opponents and that inability to look at the issue through their eyes crippled him. He could not compromise with them because he could not understand them. The more that the opponents insisted on a bill of rights, the more stubborn Madison became in his opposition to the idea. There were rights for the people in the Constitution, he argued often, and if anyone wanted more rights, they would come in legislation after the Constitution was passed and the new government in office. Why worry about it now?

The Anti-Federalists gained strength, too, because many of the leading Federalists had become easy targets for critics. Southerners in particular despised the elitist John Adams of Massachusetts, who had belittled them ever since he first arrived at the Continental Congress back in 1775 and wrote Joseph Hawley that "gentlemen in other colonies have large plantations of slaves and the common people among them are very ignorant and very poor. These gentlemen are [more]... habituated to higher notions of themselves..." He soon began giving speeches and writing letters supporting a strong national government with a powerful president. Opponents seized on that, asking why Americans had jettisoned one monarch, King George III, only to replace him with an American monarch? Critics gleefully denounced Adams's belief in a strong national executive as his "King Project."[143]

One of the great threats that loomed over the states, the Anti-Federalists insisted, was the Constitution's provision that the federal government could tax the states and the people in order to obtain revenue to meet its financial obligations. The Congress did just that in the waning years of the Revolution, when it was bankrupt, and it caused a furor among the states. "Taxation is the necessary instrument of tyranny. There is no tyranny without it," said John Brown of Rhode Island, a former Congressman and shipping magnate.[144]

What worried Madison the most was that across the country, political figures using pseudonyms began to denounce the new government in large printed broadsides, thick pamphlets, and lengthy letters to the nation's newspapers. These denunciations were vitriolic and instilled fears of despotism in the people. The early critics were soon joined by more, all eager to assail Madison's work and to insist that the new government would emasculate both the states and the people. Lee supposedly corralled all of his essays into a series called *Letters from a Federal Farmer* (actually, Melancton Smith was the author of *Letters*).[145] James Winthrop in Massachusetts, of the influential Winthrop family that arrived with the Pilgrims, wrote as "Agrippa," issuing a long chain of critical newspapers letters. In Virginia, George Mason wrote a pamphlet called *Objections to the Proposed Federal Constitution*. Luther Martin, of Maryland, penned scathing letters against the Constitution called *The Genuine Information* that he had published in Baltimore newspapers. The secretive "Brutus," reportedly Robert Yates, a delegate to the Philadelphia convention from New York, wrote that the new federal government leaders would "exercise this power to annihilate all the state governments and reduce this country to one single government."[146]

Thomas Wait, of Massachusetts, agreed with him. He cried, "The vast continent of America cannot be long subjected to a Democracy if consolidated into one government. You might as well attempt to rule hell by prayer."[147]

As was the custom, essays that appeared in one newspaper were then reprinted in a dozen more. These early attacks against the Constitution appeared as a torrent of criticism to Madison and he felt overwhelmed by the negative press. "The newspapers here begin to teem with vehement and violent calumniations of the proposed gov't," he wrote frantically to Washington soon after his arrival in New York. Three days later, having read yet more newspapers, he wrote Edmund Randolph that "the newspapers in the northern and middle states begin to teem with controversial publications…judging from the newspapers, one would suppose that the adversaries were the most numerous and the most earnest."[148]

He worried, too, that those writing the essays were among the best writers in the nation. He must have cringed when he read the flowery arguments of New York governor George Clinton, writing as "Cato," in varied New York newspapers.[149]

Madison feared, as did the other Federalists, such as Nathan Dane, that the negative and flowery press would sink the entire project. "You know many people always believe all they see in the newspapers without the least examination," Dane complained.[150]

Even Madison's own father had reservations about the Constitution because he thought the powers given to the new president were too great and that the chief executive, who could serve for life, like a monarch, would quickly turn into a tyrant worse than King George III. In a letter that must have depressed Madison, his father declared that while Virginians at first seemed to be in favor of the Constitution, now they were not and that "hearing the many objections made to it altered their opinions and have influenced others," adding with finality that the opposition in the Virginia press had turned many against it, too. In another letter, he gave him the gloomy news that all of the state's Baptists were now against the Constitution.[151]

In October, with autumn in New York and the opposition in full bloom, Madison began to realize that ratification of the Constitution was going to be a hard sell. He wrote Jefferson of the many articles and clauses in the Constitution that "the whole of them together formed a task more difficult than can be well conceived" and that its passage in Philadelphia was nothing "less than a miracle."[152]

If Madison feared opposition, his friend John Jay was certain of it. Jay was one of the most politically connected men in the country and a man who was adept at understanding politics at all of its multifaceted levels, from the views of those in highest councils of the government to those of the working class New Yorkers. He knew right away that there would be an uphill battle to gain approval for the Constitution. Jay approved of the document, although he thought even more power should have been given to the national government. He wrote Jefferson, though, that "the majority will be in favor of it, but there will probably be a strong opposition in some of the states," especially in his New York.[153]

Hamilton, too, had great apprehensions. He wrote Washington from New York in early October that he was worried. He told him with great enthusiasm that "the new constitution is as popular in this city as it is possible for anything to be—and the prospect thus far is favorable to it throughout the state." Then, in the very next lines, he told Washington that Governor Clinton and others ardently opposed to it had not spoken out in the press or publicly yet. "There is no saying what turn things may take when the full flood of official influence is let loose against it," he warned.[154]

Washington sent back an ominous note. He told Hamilton that in the northern part of Virginia, where he resided, the Constitution was wildly popular, but he added bluntly, "I expect, notwithstanding, violent opposition will be given to it by some characters of weight and influence in the state."

The general told Hamilton that it was unfortunate that men of "talents and character" should disagree strongly on something that he believed was necessary for the public good. "Unfortunately, this ever has been, and more than probably, ever will be the case, in the affairs of man."[155]

At that same time, Washington wrote Madison that George Mason was going to make trouble in Virginia. The former head of the army shrewdly noted that while his friends Hamilton, Madison, and Jay were trying to convince the people that the Constitution was a good thing with rational arguments and intellectual concepts, Mason and his allies were trying to achieve just the opposite with raw passion. "To alarm the people seems to be the groundwork of his plan," Washington said of his longtime neighbor Mason. He also warned Madison that the fight for ratification in Virginia would be tough, that

Patrick Henry's opposition to it would be a "bar" to its passage and urged Madison to go to the state convention and lead the fight.[156]

After Hamilton had time to size up the feelings of New Yorkers on the Constitution, and a few days after the first installment of *The Federalist* was published, he wrote a depressing letter to Washington. In it, he told him that feelings were so evenly balanced in the country that he could not tell if ratification would be approved and that "the artillery of the opposition" would have great effect. He told Washington that while the Constitution had "warm friends," it also had "warm enemies." Henry Knox wrote Washington that "the city [New York], and the enlightened and independent men of the country are generally for it," but that it was unpopular upstate.[157]

The even divisions in several key states presented a larger problem to the Federalists and especially to Madison, Hamilton, and Jay, whom all assumed would be key figures, along with Washington, in the running of the new government. Their goal was not simply to get the Constitution ratified, though by doing so they would alienate half of the people in the country. The goal was to win ratification while at the same time convince the opponents to support the new government and give it a chance to succeed.[158]

A key to their plans was George Washington's public support of ratification in correspondence to leaders of both sides and highly publicized letters in dozens of important newspapers. That was not forthcoming because the retired general, the hero of the Revolution, the Great Man, did not want to get mixed up in the politics of ratification. He feared, too, that his entry into the fight would be a signal to many that he wanted to be the first president of the United States. So the most influential man in the country remained on the sidelines— publicly. He even wondered if the firestorm over the Constitution might be a good idea, even though it rankled the trio.

Washington told one friend, "Upon the whole, I doubt whether the opposition to the Constitution will not ultimately be productive of more good than evil; it has called forth, in its defense, abilities which would not perhaps have been otherwise asserted, that have thrown a new light upon the science of government: they have given the rights of man a full and fair discussion, and explained them in so clear and forcible a manner as cannot fail to make a lasting impression."[159]

The general also told anyone who discussed the Constitution with him that the opposition to the document was strong. "The opponents are indefatigable," he warned.[160]

They were so determined that they even attacked Washington, accusing him, and Franklin, of permitting the Federalists to use them as pawns in their game to have the Constitution approved. In the Philadelphia *Independent Gazetteer*, "Centinel" wrote that the much-admired duo was being used by the Federalists in their "schemes of power and aggrandisement."[161]

No one was safe from criticism; ratification would be a long, hard fight.

# THE FEDERALIST

Alexander Hamilton created *The Federalist* to get pro-Federalist delegates elected to New York's ratification convention and to convince them, and wavering Anti-Federalists, to approve the Constitution.[162] *The Federalist* was at first a series of eighty-five newspaper essays and later a book written by the Triumvirate.

The Constitution was Madison's project. No one worked harder to design it and to have it approved in Philadelphia than Madison, and no one understood all of its principles and nuances more than the Virginian. He had realized, firsthand, the need for a strong federal government as he watched the Continental Army practically crumble and the Revolution nearly collapse because the weak federal government under the Articles of Confederation could not help it. As a state and federal legislator, he knew that some sort of national government was necessary. He had studied the governmental structure of every monarchy, republic, democracy, and confederation since ancient Greece—obtaining many of his books, including the thirty-seven-volume *Encyclopedie Methodique*, through purchases and mailings from Jefferson in France—and was sure that the proposed Constitution was better than all of them.[163]

George Washington had been urging Madison to become involved in a newspaper campaign to win ratification, reminding him, as he told everyone, that the power of the press was far greater than most political leaders imagined. "Much will depend upon literary abilities, and the recommendation of it by good pens should be openly, I mean, publicly afforded in the Gazettes," he wrote in early October.[164]

Jay had already accumulated enormous experience in government. He was also a persuasive writer, like Hamilton, whose previous pamphlets had met with great success. Jay was completely behind the Constitution.

The three were ideally suited to *The Federalist* project.

At first, Hamilton, Jay, and Madison wanted to add more writers to reduce the work load, which they saw as considerable. They approached Gouverneur Morris and William Duer, but after conversations with each they decided against it, even though Duer's writing was seen as "intelligent and sprightly" and so was that of Morris, whom Hamilton at first "warmly pressed" to join them. The three came to the conclusion that five writers might be too many for a string of essays that had to get into public print immediately. The Triumvirate saw themselves in a race against time and felt it imperative to produce the essays as speedily as possible and worried that with five writers there would be delays, especially since Duer and Morris were contemplative and could not write as quickly as the trio.[165]

There was only a sketchy plan for the number, structure, and content of the essays, and the timing of their publication. Hamilton decided to write the first few, followed by Jay and then Madison, who started writing his share with the famous No. 10. Jay fell ill with rheumatism, though, and dropped out of the project after writing a total of five. Hamilton and Madison then assumed his work load, with Hamilton eventually writing fifty-one essays and Madison twenty-nine.

None of the three thought for a moment that they were writing for posterity, that the essays would eventually be published as a book or that their work would serve as the foundation for the study of democracy in nations around the world for centuries. Their lone goal was a succession of newspaper essays to influence New York delegates to approve the Constitution and, at the same time, perhaps convince the readers to influence those delegates that they knew.

They understood, too, beginning at the end of October, with the conventions looming just weeks ahead in some states, that they had to write quickly. There would be no writers' conferences, no editors to go over their work, and, in fact, very little coordination between the three. The essays were produced so fast that in one stretch of just six weeks, Madison wrote twenty-two. Madison later said that speed needed for writing the essays was so great that "[there] was seldom time for even a perusal of the pieces by any but the writer before they were wanted at the press, and sometimes hardly by the writer himself."[166]

To their amazement, Federalists throughout the country, especially in New York, lobbied their newspaper friends to publish the essays, getting them printed in numerous newspapers. One, James Kent, a New York lawyer, even convinced the editor of the Poughkeepsie *Country Journal*, where the New York ratification convention would be held, to print a number of the Federalist essays as supplemental sections to his newspaper.[167]

Remarkably, the writing styles of Hamilton, Jay, and Madison were surprisingly similar. There was intense speculation over who "Publius" (the common Latin phrase—"to proclaim," or "to bring before the public"—was the pseudonym the trio adopted) really was as soon as newspapers began to print the essays, but most assumed it was one man because the writing in each seemed identical. This style not only enabled the trio to write effectively, but to hide their identity and prevent those who read the essays from having their judgment tainted by their personal view of the authors.

Other than themselves, apparently the only other people who knew the identity of the three authors were George Washington and a few close friends in Virginia. They were alerted within several weeks after *The Federalist* essays began to run in an effort to recruit them as supporters and leaders in the ratification fight. Madison wrote Virginia governor Edmund Randolph in December that he was one author and that another was a member of the convention (Hamilton). Those men kept the secret.[168]

The secret identities of the authors created a national guessing game, even among their friends. Shortly after the work of "Publius" began to bombard the reading public, Federalist James Kent wrote a friend he was certain of one of the contributors. He wrote, "The author must be Hamilton, who I think in genius and political research is not inferior to Gibbon, Hume, or Montesquieu." Newspapers played the game, too, with the Philadelphia *Freedman* coming dangerously close in January 1788 in an article in which they guessed that Madison and Hamilton were the writers.[169]

George Washington admired everything about *The Federalist*. He wrote Chevalier de la Luzerne, a French diplomat he knew from the war, that "the merits of this Constitution have been discussed in a great variety of newspaper and other publications. A periodical essay in the New York gazettes, under title of *The Federalist*, has advocated it with great ability."[170]

The multitasking abilities of Hamilton were never so apparent as in his work on *The Federalist*. He not only wrote dozens of the essays, but managed to scurry about New York to convince editors of different newspapers to publish them, or reprint already published numbers, in an effort to reach as many readers as possible. Through his connections, *The Federalist* essays were printed in four of the city's five newspapers. The essays often ran in two newspapers at the same time, prompting one Anti-Federalist reader to complain about the "nauseous" Publius that he was forced to pay to read twice on the same day.[171]

The three may have faced a storm of opposition, but they had substantial support, too, and had since the Convention ended. Men from all over America chafed at the early criticism that had appeared in the press and applauded the activities of Publius. They saw the bold defense of the proposed federal government as necessary for the creation of a workable democracy; they also approved the call for governmental restraints on the people expressed in Nos. 1, 4, 5, 6, 7, and 10 as needed. Many urged Publius to fight on and to pay no attention to the scathing denunciations of the Constitution and the Triumvirate.[172]

One of their early backers was David Humphreys, a wartime aide to Washington and a friend of Hamilton. Humphreys wrote Hamilton right after the Convention that if the Constitution was defeated, "our political ship will be left afloat on a sea of chance, without a rudder as well as with a pilot" and urged him to carry on the fight against its opponents, especially Governor Clinton of New York. "I am happy to see that you have the honest boldness to attack in a public paper, the Antifederal Dogmas of a great personage in your state. Go on and prosper…Were there no little jealousies, bickerings, and unworthy sinister views to divert them from their object, they might by perseverance establish a government calculated to promote the happiness of mankind and to make the Revolution a blessing instead of a curse."[173]

Archibald Stuart, a Virginia lawyer, was one of the men to whom the trio had been sending copies of *The Federalist* for distribution throughout the states. Stuart assured them that *The Federalist* was a great success. He wrote, "'Publius' is in general estimation, his greatness acknowledged universally."[174]

Many Federalists opted not to explain why they wanted a Constitution, and just told friends to read *The Federalist*. James Kent told one friend it would answer all of his questions. He wrote, "I recommend Publius to you as the best thing I have seen hitherto in print on the federal side, I hope with my knowledge of your candor and firmness I may say it will silence some of the difficulties which may have been presented to your eye..."[175]

The reaction of Roger Alden, a congressman from New York, probably unknown to the trio, was the most telling. They did not need to convince the ardent Federalists and knew they could not change the minds of the staunch Anti-Federalists. Their goal was to sway the minds of the large number of delegates, and the people in the middle, those who saw the good and bad points of the arguments from both sides and were struggling to make a decision. To do that, the three men decided from the start, they had to write persuasive essays that neither pleaded for help or insisted upon agreement, just essays that presented their case fairly and asked for understanding. Alden's reaction showed that they succeeded. He complained about all the columns from both sides, telling a friend that they were so numerous that "the public ear has become deaf to [their] cries." But then he added, "'Publius' takes up the matter upon the best grounds, and is a very fair, candid, and sensible advocate upon the federal side. There is nothing personal or scurrilous in his writings—he only means to convince by plain reasoning, by arguments drawn from facts and experience."[176]

The members of the Triumvirate were so secretive about their identity that they even mused about who wrote the essays to each other. Hamilton, as an example, told Madison in an April letter that he was sending him several copies of *The Federalist* that he had just "read." One can almost see him writing, eyebrows raised, who Publius was. "If our suspicions of the author be right, he must be too engaged to make a rapid progress in what remains," he wrote. Those who suspected

Madison and Hamilton often asked George Washington, the duo's most trusted friend. He always replied with his own query, such as in a February letter to Henry Knox, when he innocently inquired of Knox, "Pray, if it is not a secret, who is the author 'Publius'?"[177]

*The Federalist* had several goals: explain the proposed, new, national government, criticize the Articles of Confederation, analyze and showcase the virtues of the new Constitution, and examine the good and bad things about democratic government—at length.

The trio eviscerated the Articles of Confederation, like most Federalists, but they did so in a way that everyone, regardless of their station in life, could understand. Their condemnation of the Articles set up the introduction of the Constitution and national government. Madison spent most of Nos. 10 and 51 hailing the large, pluralistic society America had become, and would be in the future. He said that factions would balance off each other, leaving as a result good government. "Let ambition counteract ambition," he wrote in No. 51. Hamilton hailed executive power in No. 70.

The trio often did not paint a pretty picture of their Federalist dream and admitted, again and again, that such a democratic government would anger many people and cause disturbances. Hamilton wrote in No. 6, "Are not popular assemblies frequently subject to the impulses of rage, resentment, jealousy, avarice, and other irregular and violent propensities?"[178]

In essays No. 11 through No. 13, Hamilton argued that a successful democratic government would, in turn, mean a successful economy for the United States, with federal and state officials working together to be certain that U.S. businesses prospered. These businesses would then pay higher taxes that would pay the expense of both federal and state governments.[179]

The trio argued that a large national government was needed to fight any war and that it was folly for Anti-Federalists to maintain the view that the Atlantic and Pacific oceans separated America from any foreign conflicts. Americans lived in an ever-shrinking world and had to be prepared for war at any time. They argued, too, finally, and with great strength, that although the proposed Constitution was not perfect, no constitution was. Hamilton wrote, "If mankind were to resolve to agree in no institution of government until every part of it had been adjusted to the most exact standard of perfection, society would soon become a general scene of anarchy and the world a desert."[180] Madison added later that if people did not want to live in a monarchy, and disdained democracy, then they had to "look for a Utopia exhibiting a perfect homogeneousness of interests, opinion, and feelings nowhere yet found in civilized communities..."[181]

In essay after essay, the three men supported the overall promise of the Constitution to deliver good government through a carefully devised system of checks and balances. This system, they cried out, would prevent any and all of the ills the Antis wailed about. The more checks the better, they argued, and a national government with so many checks—with three branches designed to safeguard the people from the other two—could not fail. The large House of Representatives and Senate would not promote factions, but eliminate their power and result in good government.[182]

The men pushed this agenda, but at the same time, in some essays, each reminded their readers, from all over the United States, that the Constitution and the new government was not simply a collection of checks and balances and laws. It was something grander than that—it was a new system, under which men and women could govern themselves in ways to ensure the freedom of all, a new epoch on earth.

Madison offered the first reference to "the American dream." He warned readers in No. 14 not to listen to the critics, but to dream along with him. "Hearken not to the unnatural voice which tells you that the people of America, knit together as they are by so many cords of affection, can no longer live together as members of the same family; can no longer continue the mutual guardians of their mutual happiness; can no longer be fellow citizens of one great respectable and flourishing empire."[183]

Those who read the papers were struck by both the manner and length of the writing style of the essays. Whoever wrote them was one of the best writers in America, and each essay was just as good as the last. When Jefferson learned that it was Madison, Hamilton, and Jay, he was overjoyed. He had told Madison that his notes on the federal convention in Philadelphia were superb, "the ablest work of this kind ever executed...a labor and exactness beyond comprehension" and was very pleased that he had written *The Federalist.* "It does the highest honor (to you)," Jefferson wrote to Madison of *The Federalist,* "as being, in my opinion, the best commentary on the principles of government which ever was written." He told him that it had "rectified me in several points."[184]

*The Federalist* appeared just about everywhere as essays and then in book form, published after pleas from Madison, Hamilton, and Jay, or their friends, such as George Washington, who persuaded his son-in-law David Stuart to convince Richmond, Virginia, publisher Augustine Davis to print the essays (Davis later served as the editor of the book version of the papers). Washington told Stuart, "If there is a printer in Richmond who is really well disposed to support the new Constitution, he would do well to give them a place in his paper."[185]

The Anti-Federalists dreaded the publication of each *Federalist* essay, and their reprinting in dozens of newspapers across the country. The beautiful writing, deft arguments, and persuasive demeanor of the essays overwhelmed their cause.

The essays of the trio certainly had loud critics, who charged they were simply too ponderous for the average reader, a complaint that is repeated today by general readers and by college students who are assigned them as part of their class work.

Anti-Federalist DeWitt Clinton, who later became governor of New York, scoffed, "[A]s to Mr. Publius, I have read a great many of his papers and I really cannot find out what he would be at; he seems to me as if he was going to write a history; so I have concluded to wait and buy one of his books when they come out."[186]

Clinton argued that the long and ambitious essays made no point. "The only thing that I can understand from [Publius] is that it is better to be united than to be divided and…to get all the world to join with us so as to make one large government."[187]

The Antis said the elegant writing in *The Federalist* might intrigue the very small percentage of intellectuals who appreciate that, but was "not well calculated for the common people." Other critics wrote that the papers were too long and too complex. French diplomat Monsieur Otto complained that the essays were "of value whatever to well informed people and…too learned and too long for the ignorant."[188]

Yet another charged that Publius was "a New York writer who, mistaking sound for argument, has with Herculean labor accumulated myriads of unmeaning sentences…he might have spared his readers the fatigue of wading through his long winded disquisitions." Yet another wrote that *The Federalist* was so dense that Publius should try to use "conic sections by which he will be enabled, with greater facility, to discover the mazy windings of his favorite system."[189]

The defenders of *The Federalist* were just as proud of their essays as their detractors were angry. Thomas Jefferson wrote from France that they were "the best commentary on the principles of government which was ever written," and James Kent said that he could not think "of any work on the principles of free government that is to be compared, in instruction, and intrinsic value, to…*The Federalist*, not even if we resort to Aristotle, Cicero, Machiavelli, Montesquieu, Milton, Locke, or Burke."[190]

Few book-length versions of *The Federalist Papers* were bought; only a few hundred were sold in stores at one dollar each. About five hundred copies of the book were distributed, free, to political figures in New York and shipped to delegates at state conventions throughout the country. Other political pamphlets, such as *The Federal Farmer* and *The Columbian Patriot*, sold several thousand copies each. Augustine Davis, the publisher of *The Federalist*, complained bitterly that the Triumvirate produced eighty-five essays, instead of twenty-six, as anticipated, and yet paid him for the publication of twenty-six. He argued that he should have been paid twice as much for printing the book in a lengthy letter of complaint to the Federal Committee, a group appointed after the new government took office in 1789, and was eventually paid the amount he asked for. Copies of the first run of *The Federalist* were sold through 1799, when they ran out.[191]

The three men made certain that *The Federalist* essays were printed in as many newspapers as possible, especially in New York City, because their goal in writing the long string of eighty-five essays was to influence delegates to the New York convention. Altogether, counting eighteenth-century book editions, there were nearly four hundred publications of one or more essays.[192]

Newspapers started to publish the essays in late October, but they were not all published at once. They appeared as quickly as the trio could write them, and that meant that newspapers carried them throughout the entire winter and summer of 1788.

The number of essays, their reprinting, and their collection in book form did not achieve their immediate goal of convincing all of the delegates, especially those in New York, to vote for Federalist delegates to the Constitutional conventions, but they did serve as a set of reference essays for anyone who wanted to examine the entire Federalist argument at length. They helped all of those who read them understand not just the proposed new government, but the government that was installed in 1789. They helped the trio of Madison, Hamilton, and Jay understand their own arguments, too, as they began to battle for the Constitution.[193] Finally, over the years, they explained democracy to anyone throughout the world who read them.

Over two hundred years later, historian Charles Beard wrote of the enduring strength of *The Federalist* essays, that they showcased "the best pledge that mankind, tormented by wars for countless generations, may at last establish tranquility throughout the earth…springs to the front as an indispensable treatise for all people, at home and abroad, who believe that in a federal union of nations lies the one assurance of perpetual peace."[194]

The newspaper editors were glad to have the essays because, within a month or two after the end of the convention in Philadelphia, most of them decided to back the Constitution and swung their complete support behind it.

# NEWSPAPER SUPPORT ACROSS THE COUNTRY

Throughout the heated battle to ratify the Constitution, the support of the nation's newspapers for the new government surprised Madison, Jay, and Hamilton. The outpouring of essays opposed to it in a few newspapers in October of 1787 alarmed the trio. That initial surge collapsed quickly. In the ensuing months, nearly 90 percent of the papers came out strongly in support of the Constitution. It is uncertain whether the editors of those papers did so on their own or because the brilliant writing and powerful arguments of *The Federalist* influenced them, but they did.

The newspapers did not defend the Constitution merely because of its political theory and concepts, but for different reasons in each of the thirteen states.

Many were certain that the government proposed in the Constitution would keep the United States from collapsing into chaotic revolutions like those that seemed on the horizon in France and other European nations. The editor of the *Middlesex Gazette* wrote that, "while the revolutions of governments in other countries

have given rise to the most horrid scenes of carnage and bloodshed...
[only the United States] could boast of a Constitution formed by her
chosen sages."[195]

Many saw unity among the people as a great accomplishment.
"Nothing but union and a vigorous continental government can save
us from destruction," wrote the editor of the *Connecticut Courant*.[196]

Many editors believed that a new government devised by the best
minds in the country could work. An essayist in the *Massachusetts
Centinel* wrote, "America can scarcely hope ever to see so respectable a body of her citizens convened on a similar occasion—so great
in unanimity we cannot expect again." A writer in the *Independent
Chronicle* agreed because the people had "calmly and deliberately,
in time of peace, unawed by arms, and uninfluenced by party faction, appointed their wisest and best men to form a Constitution of
government...most productive of the prosperity, felicity, safety, and
welfare of the whole."[197]

Many newspapers urged their readers, and the delegates to the
ratifying conventions in each state, not to think so much about what
might happen in the future under the proposed Constitution, but
what might happen without it. One editor pleaded that "the consequence of the people's rejecting the federal Constitution will be anarchy in the extreme."[198]

Many New England newspapers urged people to stand with the
new government because it was necessary to aid the region's shipping
business that went into decline with the end of the Revolution.[199]
Some went to the Bible. "A house divided against itself cannot stand,"
wrote the editor of one paper, reminding readers that the separate,
feuding states could not survive without a federal government.[200]

Editors sent one another editions of their newspapers and reprinted
stories from them. They all knew what each was writing and saw
overwhelming support for the Constitution everywhere. "The public

prints from every quarter of the United States are filled with accounts of the unanimity…on the proposed government," wrote the editor of the *New Hampshire Gazette.*[201]

Most supported the Constitution because, collectively, while they may have worried about prospects for success of the bold new democratic government, they were concerned that for four years the Confederation had failed to govern. One New England editor expressed the feelings of most when he wrote of the Confederation leaders that "they may DECLARE everything but can DO nothing." Many editors reprinted an essay critical of the Confederation government written to Virginia's House of Burgesses before the Constitutional Convention sat there, warning that the Confederation would prove in the end "…a tragedy to ourselves."[202]

They all felt, too, that everything that people sought in government, whether it was personal liberties, economic safeguards, or protection from foreign invaders, only a strong federal government could guarantee. There was the possibility that England could launch another invasion of America, that the radical new leaders in France could produce some ancient land deeds from America and Canada and stage an invasion to reclaim them, that the Spanish could move into the United States from their position in Florida, that a foreign power could shut down the Mississippi or blockade the Atlantic seaboard. They were convinced, and often said so, that if the Confederation did not work, something else must be tried.[203]

Further, those editors believed that the Revolution had created an opportunity for a revolutionary new form of government that would change the world forever. An essayist writing in the *Providence Gazette* framed that argument well, writing that "the American war is over, but this is far from being the case with the American Revolution. On the contrary, nothing but the first act of the great drama is closed. It remains yet to establish and perfect our new forms of government and to prepare the principles, morals, and manners of our citizens." Another declared, "May the national blessing resulting from this political revolution continue, and continually expand, from generation to generation till the last shock of time buries the empires of the world in one undistinguished ruin."[204]

The Anti-Federalists claimed later that editors of most newspapers refused to print their essays and that the massive number of overwhelmingly favorable essays in some states made it impossible for any public debate to be held and resulted in lopsided conventions. Beginning with the passage of the Constitution in Philadelphia in September 1787, through Connecticut's ratification convention in the spring of 1788, only six articles critical of the new government were printed in all of Connecticut's papers. Fourteen essays by Federalists Roger Sherman and Oliver Ellsworth were published in the ten Connecticut papers and then mailed to newspapers in other states for publication there. Other Federalists also published in the ten papers. Only one paper published more than one Anti-Federalist's article. The *Connecticut Courant* underscored its feelings by publishing a copy of the Constitution under a headline that used the largest type ever published in the state to that time.

Anti-Federalists also charged that the newspapers that favored their cause were sabotaged. They argued that the man in charge of the nation's mail, Postmaster General Ebenezer Hazard, curtailed the free mailing of many newspapers, especially theirs, in order, he said, to save the government money (in one of his first official acts as president, Washington fired Hazard for his actions). They also charged that mysterious people had gone from state to state convincing thousands of people to cancel their advertising and subscriptions to Anti-Federalist newspapers, forcing them to reduce publication and to go out of business.[205]

The Anti-Federalists' most bitter complaint, though, was that the editors of pro-government newspapers, like the leaders of the pro-government forces in the state conventions, belittled them. They said they were made to appear to be fools in the eyes of the convention delegates and the people of their states, publicly charging that they were ignorant and dishonest. A writer in the *Massachusetts Gazette* was typical. He declared, "If the anti-federal cause…is as base and contemptible as the scribblers who advocate it, the federalists have very little to fear, for certainly a more despicable junta than the herd of anti-federal writers were never leagued together."

This press treatment incensed the Anti-Federalists; as Richard Henry Lee put it, "I fear it is more in vicious manners, than mistakes in form, that we must seek for the causes of the present discontent."[206]

Were they right? One study of newspaper coverage in Connecticut showed the power of the pro-Constitution press. The highest number of delegates voting for the Constitution at the state convention was from counties that had the most newspapers; the lowest number of pro-Constitution votes came from the counties with the least number of newspapers.[207]

In the press, both sides attacked the other as being traitors, liars, and scoundrels. The nastiness of the columns from both sides became so virulent that at one point Benjamin Franklin begged his fellow newspaper editors to place a moratorium on all diatribes connected to the storm over the Constitution. (Franklin, though, did not take his own advice and continued to publish pro-Constitution rants.)[208]

The newspapers could print whatever they wanted and had demonstrated that freedom in the raucous debates over the Constitution. Madison's friend Jefferson had reiterated the stand of those in favor of press liberties in a famous letter in which he wrote that "were it left to me to decide whether we should have a government without newspapers or newspapers without a government, I should not hesitate a moment to prefer the latter."[209]

The Triumvirate did not understand the great passion of the people to have press freedom guaranteed in an amendment since the newspapers enjoyed that freedom already. It was another of the mistakes they made that threatened to doom the Constitution and the new government.

# A WINTER OF WORRY

M adison, Hamilton, and Jay never called themselves the Triumvirate, and neither did the loosely organized group of several
dozen congressmen, governors, judges, and other political figures who
worked with the trio in different states to get the Constitution ratified.
They did not form a political party or a civic organization, publish
their own newspaper, or rent out rooms as a headquarters. The only
name they ever used was "Publius." Yet, working together from early
October 1787 through the end of the winter of 1788, Jay, Hamilton,
and Madison managed to use their homes in New York City to successfully launch a national campaign involving several hundred men
that could rival any powerful, well-financed political movement over
the next two hundred years of American history.[210]

The movement involved lobbying for the Constitution with
congressmen in New York City before they returned to their states
for the conventions, writing essays for home state newspapers, and
recruiting like-minded Federalists to run for seats as delegates to the
ratification conventions, working hard to make certain that these men

were elected in their home districts or, if that seemed impossible, to get them elected from a neighboring district, or just about any district where their selection would be "safe." They convinced some states to insist that a man elected as a Constitution supporter remain that way when he went to the convention; those candidates who said they might change their mind were removed and replaced by a Federalist. They convinced other states, though, to let someone who was elected as an Anti but changed his mind in the convention to remain and vote Federalist.[211] The Triumvirate, in New York, had to relay all the information it received from one state leader of the crusade to the leaders of the others so they knew what was going on from state to state. They continually scanned newspapers for stories about state conventions and mailed them to their floor leaders in the other state conventions. The trio, especially Madison, provided an ongoing analysis of the support of the Constitution, or the lack of it, in each state, county by county, city by city.

The Triumvirate needed a simple, yet complex, strategy to win over the middle-of-the-road delegates who would, in the end, determine ratification. They decided not to argue against them with their national versus state philosophy, but to show them that the weak national and strong state government under the Confederation simply did not work. They might not change the minds of staunch Anti-Federalists, but they could win over the moderates.

These moderates were fed up, Madison wrote, "of the vicissitudes, injustice, and follies which have so much characterized public measures and are impatient for some change which promises stability and repose." It was the same argument that had succeeded in the federal convention—any government would be better than the one they had.[212]

Benjamin Rush, a Pennsylvania congressman and former chief surgeon of the Continental Army, explained it well when he said,

"Although we understood perfectly the principles of liberty, most of us were ignorant of the forms and combinations of power in republics."[213]

❧

Madison, Jay, and Hamilton knew, too, people who were completely against any strong national government and could never be swayed. Virginian Henry Lee put it best, writing that the Antis were "opposed to any system, was it even sent from heaven, which tends to confirm [federal government]..."[214]

Madison surprised many that winter with his clever understanding of issues, politics, and people. In a lengthy letter written to Thomas Jefferson in Paris in late October, Madison sized up the chances for passage, state by state. "The legislature of New Hampshire was sitting when [the Constitution] reached that state and was well pleased with it," he told Jefferson. "Boston is warm and almost unanimous in embracing it. The impression in the country [the rest of the Massachusetts] is not yet known...The legislature of [Massachusetts] is now sitting, through which the sense of the people at large will soon be promulgated with tolerable certainly. The paper money faction in Rhode Island is hostile. Its passage through Connecticut is likely to be very smooth and easy. There seems [now] to be less agitation in [New York] than anywhere. The discussion of the subject seems confined to the newspapers. The principal characters are known to be friendly... New Jersey takes the affirmative side, of course. Meetings of the people are declaring their approbation and instructing their representatives. Penn[sylvania] will be divided."

He added, "The city of Philad[elphia], the Republican party, the Quakers, and most of the Germans espouse the Constitution. Some of the Constitutional leaders, backed by the western country [counties], will oppose. An unlucky ferment on the subject in their assembly just before its late adjournment has irritated both sides, particularly the opposition, and by doubling their exertions of that party may render the event doubtful. The voice of Maryland, I understand from pretty good authority, is, as far as it has been declared, strongly in favor…Mr. Chase is an enemy but the town of Baltimore, which he now represents, is warmly attached to it and will shackle him as far as it can. Mr. Paca will probably be, as usual, in the politics of Chase." (Madison was happy that Maryland approved the Constitution but unhappy that the state added a suggested bill of rights, yet another state to do so.)[215]

Madison told Jefferson he was most worried about the vote in their native Virginia and former governor Patrick Henry. He wrote, "The part which Mr. Henry will take is unknown here. Much will depend on it." He counted North and South Carolina in but warned that politics could change that.[216]

Even before he agreed to write *The Federalist* with Hamilton and Jay, Madison began a strenuous letter-writing campaign to solicit support for the Constitution around the country. Madison and Rufus King, of Massachusetts, the Federalist leader there, alone exchanged dozens of letters in that winter of 1787–1788, and Madison was just as prolific in his correspondence with others. He wrote dozens of letters to any political ally he could think of, including those in the far reaches of Georgia and North Carolina. He wanted to keep those whose votes they needed up-to-date on the progress of the Constitution in others states and in so doing wrote breathless analyses of the state-by-state vote, like an announcer at a racetrack describing a stretch run by two horses, each neck and neck as they approached the finish line.[217]

His numerous, often worried letters to leaders in other states elicited equally worried letters from them. He immediately relayed his concern to others around the country. Madison rewrote the letters from others, or important sections of them, at the end of his own letters. He also enclosed stories from any newspapers he purchased and newspaper clippings that were sent to him from others. His letters included his own analysis of the vote, the assessment of other people, information that appeared to be accurate, and a general view of politics in each state's cities and counties. He broke up many larger states into cities and "country," meaning the rural parts of the state, and tried to impress on the delegates he was writing that they had to worry about the country delegates and could not dismiss them as uninformed farmers (this would become crucial in his own Virginia later).

Throughout these months, communication between Madison, Hamilton, and Jay was close. As an example, Madison sent Hamilton a letter about the Massachusetts fight containing information and assessment of it, including a newspaper clipping to look at and told him to "read the above immediately and send it back by the bearer who will wait for it." Men in different states not only sent Hamilton, Jay, and Madison newspapers, but copies of delegates' letters, speeches, broadsides, minutes of group meetings, and even extracts from the diaries of state commissioners. The couriers traveled during rain and snowstorms. They set up a comprehensive network of way stations and riders that crisscrossed the different states so that a courier knew what route to follow and at what towns he could obtain meals and change horses or transfer his mail to another rider.[218]

Sometimes messages would be sent several ways in order to insure that they arrived quickly. As an example, news of Virginia's vote was sent up to reach New Hampshire by stage, courier rider, and by boat, all at the same time.[219]

They reminded all that the ratification of the Constitution was topic number one all across the country. As Madison wrote Jefferson that February, "the public [is]...attentive to little else."[220]

Collectively, these letters began to turn the ratification race into a real national melodrama, with people in different states eagerly awaiting news from the trio or the press on what had just happened, and what would happen next as events unfolded rapidly and political figures became key players in the ever-turning plot of the story.[221]

Letters of support such as David Stuart's to Washington, predicting victory in Maryland and "exceedingly well disposed to the adoption of it..." were forwarded to Madison.[222] Marylander Thomas Johnson wrote, "There is no American of observation, reflection, and candor but will acknowledge men unhappily need more government than [they] imagined..."[223]

Others, though, such as Tench Coxe of Pennsylvania, told Madison the people were split. "The people of the party in the city are chiefly federal, 'tho not so I fear in the counties," he wrote.[224]

Madison received numerous angry letters from the opponents of the proposed new government, too. Joseph Jones, a longtime friend from Virginia, wrote him at the end of October that Jones and his friends there thought the new Constitution gave too much power to the president, Senate, and Supreme Court and that the country absolutely needed a bill of rights. He told Madison bluntly that the number of supporters in Virginia for the new government was dwindling, and fast.[225]

Madison, distraught from Jones's letter, opened one just two days later from another Virginian, Dr. James McClurg, who had served with him at the federal convention in Philadelphia and was against the Constitution. He told him, too, that the new government invested too much power in the president and the Senate and said he expressed the feelings of many that the president and Senate would often work as a "dangerous Junta" against the people. He went through numerous other objections, including the huge state debts from the war that were still unpaid. He told Madison, whose hopes were sinking with each line that he read, that the Constitution was seen as "obnoxious" to the people of all the states and that "I am so fearful of its loss."[226]

Federalists throughout the country were worried. Rufus King of Massachusetts wrote, "What will be its fate, I confess I am unable to discern."[227] He added, "By the last calculation we made on our side, we were doubtful whether we exceeded them or they us in numbers."[228]

The members of the Triumvirate were glum as the first large state, Pennsylvania, met to argue ratification.

# PENNSYLVANIA: THE FIRST TOUGH SKIRMISH

It was Pennsylvania that first called for a ratification convention. It was Pennsylvania that first held elections of delegates to that convention. It was Pennsylvania where the Declaration of Independence had been signed and the Constitution had been written. It was Pennsylvania that was home to one of the country's most beloved figures, Benjamin Franklin. And it was in Pennsylvania, in December of 1787, where the first major fight over ratification took place between two sides that represented the supporters and opponents of the new government across the nation.

Pennsylvania, with 434,373 people, was one of the largest states in the country, one of the most prosperous, and home to the country's largest city, Philadelphia, with its 28,522 people, and some of its Revolutionary heroes. The state was also the shining example, its residents believed, of true democratic government. Under its 1776 state constitution, there was a single, large state assembly with enormous power and strict term limits for its members that even required rotation in office. To be approved, a bill had to pass not once, but twice, in successive sessions of the state assembly, by two different sets of officeholders. The state executive had little power. Every seven years a committee, elected by the public, rewrote the state constitution to adjust to the changing times. The residents of Pennsylvania believed so strongly in true representative government that they sent shoemakers and farmers as well as lawyers and physicians to the legislature.

The state, like Massachusetts, Virginia, and New York, was also made up of two sections, urban and rural, often pitting cities versus rural counties. Like everywhere else, in Pennsylvania the residents in rural counties, mostly farmers, did not like the residents of the cities whom they saw as overdressed, over-educated rich people with over-inflated egos who looked down their noses at the common folk.

The idea of representative national government over effective state government would be severely tested in Pennsylvania for those reasons and because the people of Pennsylvania fervently believed that all of the people, from small villages as well as cities, in large assemblies, had a better chance to achieve good government than a few elected representatives who purportedly represented the masses—the heart and soul of the Constitution and the new government.

The Pennsylvania ratification process got off to a catastrophic start because of headstrong Federalists. The Federalists tried to get the state legislature to pass a motion to vote on ratification on October 28, making them the first state to do so and, they were certain, the first state to approve the Constitution. The Anti-Federalists feared that an immediate vote meant defeat for them and stayed away from the session in which the vote would occur, preventing the necessary quorum. Irate gangs of Federalists went through Philadelphia looking for the missing legislators. One group found two of them and physically dragged them through the city to the legislative hall and pushed them down in their seats to make the needed quorum (the vote was delayed anyway). The strong-arm tactics of the Federalists received wide publicity. These tactics were deplored throughout Pennsylvania and in the other states and underscored the Antis contention that the thuggish Federalists would do anything to get their way.

The Federalists had one of their best leaders in Pennsylvania, former congressman James O. Wilson. He was a veteran state legislator, signer of the Declaration of Independence, and delegate to the Constitutional Convention. Wilson was a good writer and his *Considerations on the Nature and Extent of the Legislative Authority of the British Parliament* had been considered one of the most effective pamphlets in winning support for the Revolution in his state. He, like few Federalists, was an effective backroom politician as well as a political theorist. He understood that the pro-Constitution forces did not have to explain their vision of the new national government so much as persuade the opposition that it was not that much different from their own.

Wilson did that effectively in a speech in the yard of the state house on the day that delegates were elected to the ratification convention. Representing himself as a man of both Pennsylvania and the United States, he ardently defended states' rights at the same time that he called for a national government. He reminded everyone, Federalist and Anti-Federalist, that the national government only had the powers given it in the Constitution and the states retained all other powers, which were numerous. The bill of rights? The states retained all of those rights for the people within their own laws; there was no need for them to be enumerated in the Constitution. An elitist Senate? The state legislatures elected the senators and would make certain that the rich were not sent to the national capital if the people objected. A tyrannical president? State electors selected the president and the states, therefore, would make certain tyrants were not put in power. In the end, Wilson promised, the new government offered a system of checks and balances that would work and as a separate entity from the states would make them equal partners by sharing power with them.

The Federalists mounted several strong arguments to counter the prevailing feeling that a true people's democracy was better than representative national government, an idea that was embraced in Pennsylvania. Wilson insisted, like Madison, that the strength of any democracy is the overriding wisdom of the people. He linked that to religion and told Pennsylvanians that their collective conscience was "the voice of God within us." Then he told them that "all sound reasoning must rest ultimately on the principles of common sense."

Wilson insisted that the true people's democracy and the Federalist cause were one and the same. Common sense and grassroots representatives would produce a federal Congress with members who reflected the sentiments of the people and, at the same time, governed fairly. This enabled "common" people to be just as effective in acting in the best interests of the people as the people of influence the Federalists seemed to cherish. It would also produce a Congress of people from different occupations who would, as Madison claimed, create a sensible balance of opinion within the large body. From all of those diverse Congressmen from many states and backgrounds would come sound government.[229]

Wilson spoke frequently at the convention and his rhetoric improved with every passing day. He soon began to reframe his argument to remind the Antis and Federalists alike that the "We the people..." preamble to the Constitution said it all—the new government would represent everyone fairly and the states would lose nothing. The more he spoke, the more the opposition seemed to melt. Delegate Francis Hopkinson wrote of Wilson, "The powers of Demosthenes and Cicero seem to be united in this able orator."[230]

The Antis published an effective broadside in which they listed their fears that the national government would overwhelm them and complained that in the Senate tiny Delaware had as much power as mighty Pennsylvania. They quoted Montesquieu that it was impossible for a small number of men in any representative government to truly represent the feelings of millions of Americans and asserted that those men would become mad with their power. They asked the people to wonder why, if the Constitution was such a good thing, it had to be written in secret? Why, if its authors were such good men, did they drag delegates into the legislative hall and shove them into their seats to make a quorum?

Throughout the state, Anti-Federalist groups produced other broadsides, wrote newspaper columns, conducted petition drives, staged large indoor and outdoor rallies, and even started a riot in Carlisle as they burned in effigy Federalist leaders Wilson and Thomas McKean, former president of the Continental Congress, in front of a large and loud throng of Pennsylvanians.

Following parades, demonstrations, shouting matches, scathing newspaper columns, and rancorous debates, the Federalists won the vote, 46–23, but in winning the battle might have lost the war. The Federalists looked bad in their oppressive behavior and the Antis looked good in pleading that the masses of the people, and not the elite few, should run the country. The vote was a political victory but a public-relations disaster for the Triumvirate.

Federalists there celebrated the victory with glee anyway. Philadelphia political leader Samuel Powel wrote that "all ranks of people here rejoice in the event...repeated shouts and huzzas..."[231]

Federalist leaders knew that the battle had been won with great difficulty, though. Could they learn from their mistakes in Pennsylvania at the next scheduled convention of a contentious state, Massachusetts, where influential state leaders and revolutionary heroes such as John Hancock and Samuel Adams had announced their opposition to the new government?

*Chapter Nine*

# SNOWSTORMS AND POLITICAL STORMS: THE FIGHT IN MASSACHUSETTS

The ratification convention in Boston, population 18,320, was marred by snowstorms, rainsqualls, and howling winds that created high snow drifts throughout the city. On January 23, 1788, the city was buried under eight inches of snow and the weather had turned "severe cold...the coldest day of the year," according to one delegate. The storms delayed the arrival of travelers from the remote sections of the state and Maine (part of Massachusetts then). One man who rode from Bath, Maine, wrote in his diary, "We mounted our horses at Bath in order to join the delegates at Boston; the large fall of snow that fell the day before made our traveling heavy..."[232]

The 355 delegates, the largest number at any state convention, turned the gathering into a madhouse. Some were Anti, some Federalist, some uncommitted. They were elected by most towns in the state and served as a broad cross section of the population, even though twelve towns sent no representatives. They were, as minister and historian Jeremy Belknap wrote, "good, bad, and indifferent." They jammed the snow and ice palace that was Boston.[233]

Despite the snowstorms, Bostonians filled the hallways and the ground floor below the auditorium of the state house, seeming to hang on every word of the debates and eager to be a part of history. All of them were transfixed by the great drama of the day. One wrote, "With the fate of Massachusetts, anxiety sat on every brow."[234] Nearly one thousand spectators, some from other states, packed the galleries each day; they had to arrive more than an hour before the proceedings began and then had to wait in a long line to obtain a seat. They were a noisy crowd, too, and local newspapers had to admonish the spectators to keep quiet during the debates.[235]

The hall and the city were filled with lobbyists. Since the Federalists heard that a number of Baptist preachers had been elected as Anti-Federalist candidates, they managed to have Rev. Samuel Stillman, a Boston Baptist clergyman, sent to the convention. He held daily meetings in an attempt to woo the Antis over to the Federalist side. Some of them scoffed that Reverend Stillman was not a true preacher at all, but a former shoemaker who was there just to be "a vociferous brawler."[236] The Antis countered by bringing in Rev. James Manning, former congressman and the president of Brown University, another well-regarded Baptist preacher. He attended the convention each day for two weeks and tried to convince the Baptist delegates to vote against ratification.[237]

The Federalists brought out important political figures, such as former governor James Bowdoin, to wine and dine delegates who seemed to not have made up their minds.[238]

Massachusetts deeply worried Hamilton, Madison, and Jay. At first, it was believed that the Federalists had a majority. After all, Massachusetts had produced one of the very best state constitutions in the country in 1780, a document that called for a state assembly, a state Senate, an elected governor who could veto legislation, and a court system. It was remarkably like the proposed new federal government.[239]

But in the opening days of the debates, the feelings of the delegates seemed evenly divided. The three most powerful men in the state, Revolution heroes John Hancock, Elbridge Gerry, and Samuel Adams, were against it. (John Adams was in England at the time.) That really worried the Federalists. Hancock, the state's governor, just elected to yet another of his several terms, wielded enormous power over delegates. Gerry, former congressman and a nondelegate who attended most sessions anyway, had refused to sign the Constitution in Philadelphia and Sam Adams, as one unhappy Federalist put it, was "an arch Devil."

In late January, Madison wrote Washington that "the intelligence from Massachusetts begins to be very ominous to the Constitution. The anti-federal party is reinforced by the insurgents, and by the province of Maine, which apprehends greater obstacles to her scheme of a separate government from the new system." He warned the Federalist leaders that if Massachusetts voted down the Constitution, it would set an ominous precedent and dire consequences for passage in the remaining states.[240]

Henry Knox, a Bostonian and Revolutionary War general, was gloomy about prospects there. He wrote Washington that about one-third of the delegates were "insurgents" and were for "an annihilation of debts public and private" and would not approve the new Constitution.[241]

Different delegates, pro- and anti-Constitution, offered opposite estimates of the vote, confusing all. A week later at Mount Vernon, Washington heard from Madison, who worried, "what will be its [the Constitution's] fate, I am unable to discern. No question ever [faced] the people of this state in a more extraordinary manner..."[242]

The Anti-Federalists in Boston were pleased with their numbers and their work to hold them together at the convention. "It appears pretty evident that there is a decided majority against the new

Constitution," wrote one. Melancton Smith, the lawyer who led the Anti-Federalist forces in New York, thought that if the Antis did not have a majority, they had at least enough votes to force a close fight and perhaps win at the end of it. Staats Morris, in New York, the half-brother of Gouverneur Morris, wrote that "from the large number of vile insurgents who compose a part of that body of people, it is feared it will not go down…"[243]

The delegates and those in the galleries listened to the best speeches their colleagues could give. "The [Federalist] speeches would do honor to any assembly on earth. Mr. Parsons was…stupendous…" wrote one man in the crowd. "Judge Dana thunders like Demosthenes," wrote another. "[He talks] with such energy that it seemed as if his feeble frame could scarcely have supported him. He expressed the feelings of an honest mind which had taken an early and decided part in the cause of the country and wished to see its labor and sufferings crowned with success, but would all be lost if this Constitution should be lost. He was greatly admired."[244]

One man there excoriated the Antis, calling them "hardened anti-federal infidels" and claimed that "nothing but insuperable ignorance can withstand such a torrent of good sense embellished with all the charms of the most engaging and winning manners" of the Federalist speakers.[245]

Each side criticized the other. One haughty Federalist, seeking a historical reference for his venom, wrote that the Antis "are as trouble-some as Homer's babbling speakers." One sarcastic Anti, referring to the high-profile men at the federal convention in Philadelphia, asked, "Can it be supposed that a Constitution so pregnant with danger could come from the hands of those who framed it?" One asked that since state representatives had to be closer to the people than federal congressmen it was obvious that the states, and not Congress, should run the country.[246]

Other Antis suggested, no matter where they lived, that their state did not need to be part of the United States, that they could simply merge with neighboring states and form a small country.[247]

The state's newspapers offered extensive coverage of the debates, with many filling their pages with nothing but convention stories. Between February 2 and 13, nine state newspapers printed Hancock's Federalist speeches in their entirety and dozens of delegates sent copies of the papers to colleagues in other states as soon as they finished reading them. King sent a copy to Madison who read it and immediately sent it via courier to the homes of Hamilton, Jay, and Washington. The newspapers offered saturation coverage, the editor of the *Worcester Magazine* wrote, so that readers could "discover [the Constitution's] imperfections as well as its perfections and thereby form a better judgment…"[248]

There were stories of personal courage, too. The son of Massachusetts delegate Benjamin Lincoln, a Revolutionary War general, died in the middle of the convention, but Lincoln remained there, unwilling to take time for mourning if it meant that the Constitution might not pass.

Hamilton, Jay, and Madison, in New York, did not understand why there were so many problems with the Constitution in Boston. Everyone acknowledged the failure of the Confederation. James Bowdoin put it best when he said, "Our lands have sunk in their value, our trade has languished, our credit has been daily reducing and our resources are almost annihilated. Can we expect in such a state, that the people will long continue their allegiance to systems of government…so many calamities?"[249]

After all, this proposed government was designed very much like the state government, with a separation of powers that made it impossible for one of the three branches to crush the others. They paid no attention to the fact that the Massachusetts constitution also had a bill of rights. They ignored local arguments that a federal bill of rights was needed, along with protections to prevent the new national government from overwhelming the states.[250]

Madison, in New York, blind to local arguments, could not figure out how the tide of the convention was going; neither could most Federalists in Boston. On some days delegates lamented that the Antis were mounting a powerful campaign and that prospects looked "gloomy" and on other days bragged that "the opposition decreases every day and the party themselves confess that they have not a majority of more than 15 whereas a few days since they boasted of a majority of a hundred."[251]

Madison kept up steady correspondence with different delegates in Boston to convey the ideas of the Triumvirate; he exchanged dozens of letters with Massachusetts Federalist leader Rufus King alone. Madison was also frustrated by the attitude of some of the Federalists who were his correspondents from Boston, such as King, who always dwelled on any negative rumor or piece of bad news. "His anxiety... may give greater activity to his fears than to his hopes," Madison groaned to Washington.[252]

During the last days of January, delegates noted a shift in momentum toward the Federalists. Benjamin Lincoln wrote Washington not to get his hopes up too high for success, but that "I have now higher expectations that it will pass."[253]

Madison was just one of thousands all over the country who could not determine the feelings of the men in Boston from letters. Melancton Smith, who would be an Anti-Federalist leader at New York's convention, had people telling him that the Antis might win by as much as 201–119, while others insisted that the Federalists were ahead. He wrote, "It is impossible in this variety of reports to form an opinion that may be relied upon." [254]

Rumors flew and many believed that the Anti-Federalists were going to force a complete adjournment of the Massachusetts convention so that it would be held last, after New York and Virginia, when the Anti-Federalists could kill the Constitution. The vote was supposed to be so close that one New York newspaper gleefully reported that the Antis had actually voted down the Constitution, even while the convention was still in progress.[255]

Delegates changed their minds daily, and with flowery oratory. One judge told the assembly he had come to Boston undecided, but now stood with the Federalists because the question was "whether the people of America should be an industrious, flourishing, happy and respectable people or a divided, disunited, miserable and ruined country."[256]

It was here that, for the first time, the Federalists bent a bit on the bill of rights. The Triumvirate decided that the Federalists in Massachusetts, and in the remaining states, would agree to add amendments to protect the rights of the people to the Constitution after it was approved. This, they felt, would solve the problem. The Antis would know that their desperately desired bill of rights would become law—someday.

Or would it?[257]

The biggest change came from Elbridge Gerry and Samuel Adams, who now seemed to favor the new government. Adams had told Bostonian friends that he was "full against it [the Constitution]." At a meeting of delegates on the eve of the convention, he said so in even stronger terms, but his criticism softened considerably after a large group of Boston tradesmen passed a resolution that supported the Constitution and denounced any tradesman who was against it. Adams, who ran a family brewery, was one of the most respected tradesmen in town and felt that he could not weather such opposition from his friends.

In a newspaper essay, Elbridge Gerry had complained about the Constitution when it was first passed. "Beware! Beware! You are forging chains for yourselves and your children..." he had written in a newspaper essay. Now, after some thought, he decided that the new government might have its faults, but was better than the anemic present one. The swing of Adams and Gerry to the Federalist side seemed to turn the tide after February 2. Newspaper articles and personal letters directly showed a shift in opinion toward ratification. At the same time, the lobbying of the Federalists increased, and as the moment for the vote drew close it seemed possible that the Constitution would be ratified.[258]

King wrote Knox at that time that "the opposition are less positive of their strength."[259] And, too, several more essays in *The Federalist* had been published in Boston just prior to the Convention, strengthening the Federalists' cause.

All that was left was for Governor Hancock to make up his mind.

The popular Hancock's decision would sway a sizable number of delegates and probably determine the outcome. On January 31, Hancock arrived. He was so sick with gout that his servants had to carry him, wrapped in blankets, from his carriage into the assembly hall and help him to his chair. He then broke the logjam when he sided with the Federalists as long as they backed a bill of rights amendment to be added later.[260]

On February 6, with the galleries packed and a large crowd gathered outside the assembly hall on a bitterly cold day, the delegates were addressed by Governor Hancock, who spoke in favor of ratification. There were rumors, never proved, that the Federalists promised to reward Hancock for this switch with Federalist support in his next campaign for governor, or a run for the first vice presidency. Other rumors claimed he changed his mind only to gain more fame.[261] He assured the Antis that their suggested bill of rights would be approved once the new government was installed. He had assurances from the Federalists and he trusted them. He pleaded with the losers, whomever they might be, to abide by the vote, no matter how it went, in order to create a united country. Hancock reminded them, too, that on that cold winter day in Boston they might be about to change the history of the world. He told the delegates, and the people packed into the hall, with hundreds standing and hundreds more outside in the cold, that "no nation on earth" ever made such a decision on government. He exclaimed that "we must all rise or fall together."[262]

Sam Adams then rose and supported Hancock's call for ratification, a move that gathered still more votes. The Constitution passed, barely, with 187 in favor and 168 opposed. Immediately following the vote, the leaders of the Anti-Federalists acknowledged defeat but, as so many had hoped, followed Hancock's lead. They pledged allegiance to the Constitution or, as one put it, to "devote their lives and fortunes to support the government."[263]

What Madison, Hamilton, and Jay did not consider in their analysis of the Massachusetts vote, and all of the votes, was the complexity of the decision for the middle-of-the-roaders. Many believed the proposed government would help them in some areas and hurt them in others. Abraham Clark, a delegate to the Constitutional Convention from New Jersey, was a perfect example. He wanted a strong federal government to help his state economically—as a small state it was financially tied to the success of the larger states nearby. But he feared that the same strong federal government would overwhelm them politically. Where was the balance? Many delegates to the state conventions simply sided with the Federalists believing that the new government would be a good one under which different states' problems would have to be ironed out.[264]

When the Massachusetts' vote was announced, jubilation erupted throughout Boston. Hundreds of people poured into the streets to celebrate, muskets and cannons were fired, and flags were hoisted on ships in the harbor and hung from windows of homes. The firing of

guns was so long and so loud that residents complained that the vibra-
tions from the explosions caused furniture to shake and glassware to
break. When the news reached towns throughout the state, cannons
boomed in thirteen-gun salutes, one for each American state, muskets
were fired in joy, dinners were held, and the men who ratified the
Constitution were toasted into the wee hours of the morning. Two
days later, a huge parade was held in Boston that was only exceeded
in size several years later when President Washington visited the city.
A Federal Ball two days after that, with bands and dancing, attracted
hundreds of Bostonians, who danced until 4:00 a.m.[265]

Despite the close vote, the people of Massachusetts were satisfied,
even the malcontents. Henry Van Schaack, one of the members of
Shays's Rebellion, may have put it best when he wrote, "I shall now
rejoice that I am an American…the adoption of this Constitution will
give us lustre and dignity throughout the world…"[266]

The success in the Bay State also reflected the strong off-stage, distant leadership of the Triumvirate, particularly Madison, as they wrote
flurries of letters back and forth to Federalist leaders in Boston. Their
work had been so unrelenting that on the day the Constitution passed,
Rufus King wrote Madison of his help, "God bless you!"[267]

There, as in all of the states, Madison, Jay, and Hamilton, although
not physically present, worked closely with local Federalist leaders to
gain passage.

The news rapidly reached Connecticut, New York, and other
states. In New Haven, Connecticut, all of the church bells in the city
were rung throughout the day and cannons repeatedly fired thirteen-
gun salutes. Dozens of people attended a special dinner served at the
City Coffee House, toasting the leaders of the Federalists, such as
Hancock and King.

Throughout the country, Federalists were relieved over the passage
and kept many taverns open until the early hours of the morning as

they celebrated. There was no joy in Mrs. Ellsworth's boarding house in New York where James Madison lived, or in the nearby homes of Jay and Hamilton, though. The vote was far too close and the losers had been leaderless. The opposition, Madison wrote Jefferson, "was made up partly of deputies from the province of Maine who apprehended difficulties from the new government to their scheme of separation, partly of men who had espoused the disaffection of Shays's [Rebellion], and partly of ignorant and jealous men who had been taught or had fancied that the Convention at Philadelphia had entered into a conspiracy against the liberties of the people at large in order to erect an aristocracy for the rich and well born...they had no plan whatever." He then added in a note to Washington that "the minority is also very disagreeably large."[268]

Pennsylvania had been close and Massachusetts was even closer. What would happen in Virginia and New York, the crucial states, when those delegates learned that the margin of Federalist victory in Massachusetts, perhaps the most patriotic state in the country, had been razor thin?

Then, incredibly, just a week later, the delegates to the New Hampshire convention, split from the start, found themselves embroiled in daily arguments and unable to accomplish anything. On February 22, frustrated and tired after lengthy debates at the two-story-high meetinghouse in Concord, they decided to suspend their proceedings and renew their efforts in June, at the same time the Virginia and New York conventions met. Perhaps four months would give the delegates time to rethink the arguments of both sides, get new instructions from their towns, and make a sound decision. What really hurt the Federalists was that just before they broke up, the delegates took a preliminary vote and the Federalists came out ahead, 57–46, but the ballot did not count. News of the vote was sent to Hamilton via the Triumvirate's system of couriers.[269]

The New Hampshire collapse caught Madison, Jay, and Hamilton off guard. They knew the vote would be close, but they thought they could win there. A victory, on top of the Massachusetts triumph, albeit slender, would have given them momentum coming into Virginia and New York. Now not only was New Hampshire uncertain, but would remain so for months. It was just the kind of news that Madison, Hamilton, and Jay did not need.

Throughout the autumn and winter, Madison had been corresponding frequently with Washington. The general told him, as did others, that prospects for passage in their native Virginia were dim and that the opposition was organizing, an easy task because they all lived near each other in the state capital. "The opposition should have gained strength at Richmond," Washington wrote. "The great adversaries to the Constitution are all assembled at that place, acting conjointly, with the promulgated sentiments of Colonel Richard Henry Lee as auxiliary."[270]

Madison had been telling Washington from the start that although Richard Henry Lee was a well-known opponent, his following was small. Washington responded in several letters that he was wrong and that the loquacious Lee had stirred up many Virginians against the proposed new government and continued to do so while Madison sat in New York.[271]

A morose letter from Cyrus Griffin, of Pennsylvania, must have really demoralized Madison. Griffin wrote, "The adjournment of N. Hampshire, the small majority of Massachusetts, a certainty of rejection in Rhode Island, the formidable opposition in the state of N. York, the convulsions and committee meetings in Pennsylvania, and above all the antipathy of Virginia to the system, operating together, I am apprehensive will prevent the noble fabric from being erected."[272]

Washington and the others underestimated the diminutive political theorist from Virginia. He did know everything about the political history of ancient Greece and Rome, but he also knew who the heroes and villains of those ancient governments were. He fully understood that throughout history, and during 1787–1788 as well, leaders had to understand the ulterior motives and agendas of their foes. As an example, after extolling John Hancock's public announcement to support the Constitution, Madison warned all that they should not be fooled by Hancock, that "his character is not entirely free from a portion of caprice..." and that he was "weak, ambitious, a courtier of popularity given to low intrigue and lately reunited by a factious friendship with S. Adams."[273]

He understood from history, too, as some Federalists did not, that there could be no United States with just nine states in the union. How could the United States succeed without all thirteen states? How could it succeed without its three largest and most important states, Virginia, Massachusetts, and New York? How could the established nation succeed in either domestic or foreign affairs as a government in which just two-thirds of its states supported it? No, the members of the Triumvirate agreed, in order for the United States to become a nation all thirteen states had to ratify the Constitution. The Federalists had to win their battle in every single state. The decision had to be decisive and unanimous.

James Madison left New York on March 4, 1788, to return to his home in Virginia to run for election as a delegate to the Virginia convention, as many had begged him to do to ensure a well-led battle for ratification at that state's convention. On that day he was more demoralized than ever. New Hampshire's convention had adjourned and scheduled its final vote for June, right in the middle of the New York and Virginia conventions. He was certain New Hampshire did so on purpose, so that regardless of what New York or Virginia did, New

Hampshire could vote the Constitution down and ruin everything. "This event...is no small check to the progress of the business. The opposition here [New York], which is unquestionably hostile to everything beyond the federal principle, will take new spirits," Madison wrote Edmund Randolph the day before he left, adding that the close votes in Pennsylvania and Massachusetts would strengthen the resolve of Anti-Federalists in the remaining states to defeat the Constitution.

He had reason to be worried. Members of the New Hampshire delegation admitted that the arguments of the Anti-Federalists had been powerful and that perhaps when New Hampshire reconvened, the Constitution would be defeated. One delegate there, writing that the nationwide efforts of the Anti-Federalists were "indefatigable," whimsically hoped for terrible tidings to befall their leaders. "Had it been pleasing to the preserver of man, in the super abundance of his tender mercies, to have removed [Patrick Henry] and [George Mason] to the regions of darkness, I am induced to think the new system of government would have been adopted," he wrote. He added that Henry and Mason's strengths made the prospects for passage in New Hampshire, Virginia, and other states "alarming."[274]

Madison received no reassurances from his Federalist allies, either, who were as upset about the New Hampshire debacle as he was and feared the worst in Virginia, too. Pennsylvanian Cyrus Griffin reflected the depression of many Federalists. He saw no hope, writing that the New Hampshire collapse meant that everything now depended on Virginia, and passage there seemed doubtful. "I fear the consequences," he wrote in a letter to fellow Federalist Thomas Fitzsimmons.

But the melancholy Griffin was sure that if anyone could win in Virginia, it was Madison. Perhaps he could save them all at the last minute, like the hero of a romantic novel. "I am doubtful that all of his virtues and abilities will avail to nothing," Griffin concluded to Fitzsimmons.[275]

The depressed Madison departed from New York the next morning. He was not headed directly home to his family plantation in Montpelier, as all expected, though. Madison was on his way for a secret rendezvous with the unofficial, fourth, silent member of the Triumvirate, the man who had clandestinely helped the trio from the end of the Philadelphia convention onward and whose influence in the ratification fight, although unknown, was enormous and would grow in the next few months.

James Madison was headed for Mount Vernon.

# Chapter Ten

# THE FOURTH, SILENT MEMBER OF THE TRIUMVIRATE: GEORGE WASHINGTON

The Constitutional Convention had succeeded, all agreed, because George Washington had served as its president. The former commander in chief of the Continental Army, the national hero, was the most admired man in the United States. The newspapers adored him. A writer at the *Pennsylvania Gazette* expressed the idolatry of Washington felt by all Americans when he wrote, "We behold him at the head of a chosen band of patriots and heroes, arresting the progress of American anarchy, and taking the lead in laying a deep foundation for preserving great liberty by a good government, which he had acquired for his country by his sword. Illustrious and highly favored instrument of the blessings of heaven to America—live—live forever!"[276]

His leadership at the Convention gave the body legitimacy, not only in the United States, but throughout the world. Had he not been in attendance, the Convention would have been seen at home and abroad as a rump parliament full of political whiners who were never satisfied with anything.

Washington attended it, and agreed to serve as president, because he, more than anyone else, was certain the brand-new United States would collapse if a new form of federal government was not instituted. As commander of the army, he had seen the federal government totter during the war and afterwards. When he arrived in Philadelphia for the Convention, he did not know what form the new Constitution would take, but realized that a new and different government was needed to replace the old one.

He wrote his son-in-law, David Stuart, that, "happy indeed would it be if the convention should be able to recommend such a firm and permanent government for this union, as all who live under it may be secure in their lives, liberty, and property...the primary cause of all our disorders lies in the different state governments and in the tenacity of that power which pervades the whole of their systems. [Now] this great country is weak, inefficient, and disgraceful. It has already done so, almost to the final dissolution of it—weak at home and disregarded abroad is our present condition and contemptible enough it is."[277]

Washington had changed his daily routines at Mount Vernon to spend more time working on the campaign to have the Constitution passed. He did most of his letter writing in his spacious study, located just below his bedroom in a wing of the home that overlooked the Potomac River to its north. The study was jammed with books, telescopes, a large globe of the world, a washbasin, and stacks of letters. Here he kept up his voluminous correspondence with men and women all over America and in Europe, rising at dawn each day to tackle his daily mail. He met with visitors to discuss the Constitution fight in his main dining room, where dinner was served at about 3:00 p.m. Men from across the nation dined with him and talked for hours about the political drama unfolding across America.

Amid all of this busy time, Washington continued to maintain his role as gentleman planter. He rose early, ate breakfast, and before

7:00 a.m. was riding away from his stables to oversee the production of crops on his large plantation. He worked with slaves throughout the day, returning home for dinner. The general also managed the fish business he had developed, utilizing a ship moored in the Potomac for fishing expeditions in the Chesapeake Bay area. He supervised all of the household help, with his wife Martha; tended to the Mount Vernon paperwork; gambled with his friends; went fox hunting early in the mornings when he could; took trips to Annapolis and Williamsburg with his wife; served as an elder at a nearby Protestant church; and when he could, greeted the hundreds of Americans who came to Mount Vernon to see him, the hero of the Revolution. Now, in addition to all of those activities, he had plunged into the campaign with his three friends to have the Constitution passed by each state.

He approved of the Constitution, but told all that he would have no public role in the crusade to have the Constitution adopted because he was a man above politics. His intervention alone might sway public opinion on the new government, he said, and the people would make decisions based on their respect for him and not the proposed government itself. He wrote, "[It] is not for me to decide, nor shall I say anything for or against it—if it be good I suppose it will work its way good…"[278]

Most importantly, he feared that many would see his support as an early campaign to be elected the country's first president. He did not want to convey that impression and, he repeatedly told everyone, he certainly did not want to be the president. All he wanted to do was to continue to enjoy his retirement from public life at his beloved plantation at Mount Vernon on the shores of the Potomac River.

He did not understand why there was opposition to the Constitution, either. He wrote former army aide David Humphreys, "The Constitution that is submitted is not free from imperfections, but there are as few radical defects in it as could well be expected considering the heterogenious [sic] mass of which the convention was composed and the diversity of interests that are to be attended to. As the Constitutional door is opened for future amendments and alterations, I think it would be wise in the people to accept what is offered to them..."[279]

He scoffed at the Anti-Federalists' notion that the new government would be too powerful and trample on the freedoms of the states and the people. He wrote the Marquis de Lafayette, "These powers...are so distributed among the legislative, executive, and judicial branches into which the general government is arranged, that it can never be in danger of degenerating into a monarchy or an oligarchy, an aristocracy or any other despotic or oppressive form, so long as there shall remain any virtue in the body of the people."[280]

He thought, too, that the proposed federal government would not only survive, but succeed beyond anyone's imagination. "I cannot help flattering myself that the new Congress...will not be inferior to any assembly in the world," he wrote.[281]

He believed that the people would always do the right thing. "The power under the Constitution will always be in the people," he declared after the Constitutional Convention ended, insisting that any elected official who abused his office, the people would deem a "tyrant" and recall from office. And he always looked beyond 1787 to the American future, writing that "the people can, as they will, have the advantage of experience on their side, decide with as much propriety on the alterations and amendments which are necessary [as] ourselves. I do not think we are more inspired, have more wisdom, or possess more virtue, than those who will come after us."[282]

But he was worried that it would not be ratified.

Washington's fears that the new republic he and his troops had fought so hard to create would disintegrate—and again become a target for foreign conquest—had first surfaced while he was still commander of the army, in 1783, the final year of the rebellion. In a general circular to the people that year, he wrote, "This may be the ill-fated moment for relaxing the powers of the Union, annihilating the cement of the Confederation and exposing us to become the sport of European politics. Without an entire community to the spirit of the Union, we cannot exist as an independent power." He lamented to a friend that summer that the United States had already become a nation "directed by thirteen heads" and worried that the country would soon "sink into…anarchy and confusion" and "moulder into dust."[283]

His fears for the new country grew rapidly throughout the 1780s. As he sat at Mount Vernon, determined never to return to the army or hold public office, he watched as the states, counties, and cities feuded with each other and all battled with a Congress that had little power to tax and seemed to have no power to govern. He was appalled. Washington wrote Virginia governor Benjamin Harrison about the battles between the states that the former colonies had "run riot until we have brought our reputation to the brink of ruin." A year later he complained to John Jay that the country faced "a crisis" and that he saw no hope to prevent it, telling Jay that Congress "appears to me the very climax of popular absurdity and madness."[284]

From the very beginning of the Constitution fight, George Washington carefully projected an image to all of the gentleman farmer. He was now the happily retired national hero. In letter after letter, he reminded all that he had not only retired from the army and public life, but, in fact, knew very little about what was going on in the world. He meekly told all, as he wrote Henry Knox, that he did not leave Mount Vernon, "never going from home and seeing nobody except those who call upon me."[285]

As always, Washington was aghast at any suggestion that he knew anything or expected people to tell others what he told them. He was similarly "appalled" at the wide press distribution of his famous letter to Charles Carter, suggesting that the country would simply collapse unless the Constitution was passed. "I had not the most distant idea of its ever appearing before the public," he wrote of the letter, although he surely knew Carter would make it public.[286] This naïve, perplexed attitude worked, just as his I-am-no-politician persona worked so well during the Revolution, when his superb political skills helped him to keep the army together and win the war. He maintained this for years after the war ended, telling army aide James McHenry during the Constitutional conventions, "I meddle as little as possible with politics…I am less likely than almost any person to have been informed of the [conventions]…"[287]

In reality, Washington was the fourth, silent member of the Triumvirate. "A greater drama is now acting on this theater than has heretofore been brought on the American stage, or any other in the world," he wrote of the ratification parade in the different states and yearned to be an important part of it.[288]

Washington, more than anyone else, had a vision of the American government that was part federal, part state, and designed for the benefit of the all the residents of the country. "The power under the Constitution will always be with the people," he insisted.[289]

The general conducted an extensive private campaign to have the Constitution ratified. He spent innumerable hours writing letters. He kept in close touch with Hamilton, Madison, and Jay, showing adroit political assessments of the fight for ratification in each state. He wrote letters to leaders in each state supporting the Constitution on behalf of the Triumvirate and added that support in replies to just about anyone who wrote him. The commander in chief, who knew how persuasive newspapers could be, asked all of his correspondents to mail him any newspapers they purchased so that he could keep up with the opinions of the press in every single state, not just Virginia.[290]

He knew that he had to be very careful about how his words were measured and that he had to remain "behind the curtain," as he loved to say. Despite the public idolatry of him, Washington always understood that there was a fine line between the perception of strong leadership and tyranny. "A dictatorial style, although it may carry conviction, is always accompanied with disgust," he wrote his nephew.[291]

In perhaps the most important development, Washington invited Madison to spend several days with him at Mount Vernon when he returned from New York to Virginia in the middle of March 1788. Washington took time off from his plantation to discuss the Constitution and the battle for its ratification with Madison. Most importantly, he offered his young friend needed advice on how to win over the opponents of the new government at the upcoming Virginia convention through hardscrabble politics, not more soaring addresses.[292]

Washington developed a successful strategy as a silent partner. He stressed four things: (1) no one who supported the Constitution should worry about its passage because everyone in the country understood that a new government was needed; (2) it would pass in the states where the vote appeared to be close, especially in Virginia and New York, because delegates there could not possibly vote it down when every other state had already approved it; (3) the Constitution would be amended again and again as necessary over the coming years—the opponents who called for a bill of rights now, especially in Virginia and New York, should realize that they would get every protection to the liberties of the people that they wanted eventually; and most importantly (4) those who opposed the Constitution were not enemies but well-intentioned friends of democracy.

Washington told the Triumvirate again and again that this was a political war. Simply winning in a state was not enough; the Constitution had to win by a sizable margin. He told Madison the victory by a bare majority in Massachusetts was preferable to rejection, but "is also to be deprecated." He explained to Madison that a close vote in one big state would give the enemy ammunition and a chance to "blow the trumpet of discord more loudly."[293]

And it was rapidly becoming a personal war in which men's pride and egos often meant as much as political victory or defeat. The opposition, he told his three friends, had to be beaten but not bloodied. Anti-Federalists in other states could not be permitted to seek revenge on the Federalists there for any poor treatment their friends received elsewhere. A simple thing like gentlemanly conduct might turn the tide in other states where the vote would be close and many of the Anti-Federalists who would end up in Congress would be needed to make the new government work. They had to be kept as friends. "Friends to the new system may bear down the opposition," he told Massachusetts's Benjamin Lincoln. Washington applauded the Federalists who agreed and maintained cordial relations with the Antis. "The conciliating behavior of the minority will strike a damp on the hopes which opponents in other states might otherwise have formed from the smallness of the majority and must be greatly influential in obtaining a favourable determination in those states which have not yet decided upon it." The general wrote and expressed the same feelings in a letter to Henry Knox.[294]

That campaign of persuasion for the new government began right away, the very week that Washington returned home to Mount Vernon following the creation of the Constitution in Philadelphia. Washington and Madison knew that their main opponent in Virginia was Patrick Henry, and he was the first prominent Virginian that Washington tried to win over. He told Henry candidly that "I wish the Constitution which is offered had been made more perfect," but that it was the best that could be hoped for at the time. He assured the former governor that in the near future the amendments Henry and others desired would be added. Henry and his friends had to end their quibbling in order to save the country. Washington wrote that "the political concerns of this country are, in a manner, suspended by a thread" and that most people favored it. He warned Henry that "if nothing had been agreed on by that body, anarchy would soon have ensued, the seeds being rich sown in every soil..."[295]

In those first weeks after the convention ended, Washington did everything possible to win over the opponents in Virginia, again, in a private way. When he heard that George Mason, the ringleader of the Anti-Federalists with Henry, had been injured in a carriage accident, he sent him a condolence note, writing, "I am sorry to hear you met with an accident on your return. I hope you experience no ill effect from it."[296]

Washington and Madison had been in touch since the day Madison arrived in New York and Washington returned to Mount Vernon. The general was certain that Madison would lead the fight for ratification and assumed that Hamilton would at least command the battle in New York. It is not known how he viewed Jay that early, except that he seemed pleased when Jay issued a statement assuring all that an early letter with his name denouncing the Constitution was a forgery.

The very first letters that Madison wrote when he arrived in New York City were to his father and General Washington. He advised Washington of the divisions over the Constitution and his reluctance to push for a bill of rights. It was the first of a flurry of letters between the two men and the start of Washington's role as the silent partner of the Triumvirate. By the middle of October, Washington was sending Madison his own advice, and that of others, copies of newspaper columns for and against the Constitution, and pamphlets on both sides. Anything he received in the mail, he forwarded to Madison, and Madison did the same. Both men kept their correspondence a secret.

Washington was helpful to Jay, Madison, and Hamilton in sizing up how the key political figures in the state would vote on the Constitution, especially in Virginia. In his letters to Madison, he broke down the vote region by region, county by county, and man by man, constantly warning Madison to watch out for Patrick Henry. He offered this wisdom in letters, never in public, staying in the shadows of the battle.

Madison had worried about Massachusetts before the federal convention even convened. He was certain that the ever-shifting political alliances there would produce delegates to the ratification convention that would wreck any new government. Two months prior to the opening of the federal convention in Philadelphia, referring to the "insurgent spirit" of states' rights advocates there, he lamented that John Hancock had replaced James Bowdoin as governor and others of Hancock's states' rights persuasion had won other elections and would carry their "wicked measures." He wrung his hands over Hancock, of whom he wrote "his merits are not a little tainted by a dishonorable obsequiousness to popular follies."[297]

In those early letters to Madison, Washington began to analyze people and suggest strategies. He was able to do so because dozens of writers of pamphlets and newspaper editors sent him printed copies of their work in order to influence his opinion and, because he was so famous, to bathe in the glory of his attention.[298]

The general always thanked the leaders of any Federalist effort to approve the Constitution. As an example, he wrote Jonathan Trumbull, of the politically powerful Connecticut family, "I congratulate with you on the adoption of the new Constitution in your state by so decided a majority and so many respectable characters."[299]

He sized up the opposition in Virginia quickly, targeting Mason and Richard Henry Lee as the heads of the movement against it, with Lee the one influencing Mason. Patrick Henry would aid them.

Washington let Madison know he had little regard for the views of any who opposed the Constitution. Richard Henry Lee "rendered himself obnoxious" about the Constitution when it was passed in Philadelphia. He wrote that "his conduct is not less reprobated in this country [Virginia]."

But, he added, Madison had to watch out for Lee and Mason because they were both loud and effective. He said of Mason that "the highest coloring would be given to his objections" and that "to alarm the people seems the groundwork of his plan."[300]

The general harped on the noisy antics of Mason, Lee, and Henry and continually reminded friends that these tactics garnered attention and often worked. He told Henry Knox of the opposition's objections in Virginia, that "it is highly probable that these reasons will be clothed in [the] most terrific array for the purpose of alarming; some things are already addressed to the fears of the people and will no doubt have their effect."[301]

In the middle of October 1787, just after his return to Mount Vernon, he warned all of the supporters of the Constitution not to underestimate the opposition because its members "had sinister and self important motives" and that "they were driven by personal agendas." He reminded them that the Antis were "indefatigable in fabricating and circulation papers, reports etc. to its prejudice; whilst the friends [of the Constitution] generally content themselves with the goodness of the cause and the necessity for its adoption, supposing it wants no other support."[302]

Washington worked hard to always be a step ahead of the competition. He was aware that George Mason was returning to Virginia at the end of October and planned to hand out his published *Objections*. Washington made certain that the Virginia newspapers printed copies of James Wilson's pro-Constitution speech the week before Mason returned home to blunt the effect of his criticism.[303]

He stepped up his letter-writing campaign on New Year's Day 1788, appropriately enough, hoping the new year would bring a new government. In a letter to William Gordon, he offered what would become his standard reassurance to all that the new government would be approved, hopeful that his continual guarantees would, in fact, make it so. "There is the great prospect of its being adopted by the people. It has its opponents, as any system formed by the wisdom of man would undoubtedly have, but they bear but a small proportion of its friends and differ among themselves with respect to their objections. Pennsylvania, Delaware, and Jersey have already decided in its favor, the former by a majority of two to one and the two latter unanimously. The dispositions in the other states, so far as I have been able to learn, are equally favorable…and it is expected that their conventions will give it a similar decision."[304]

He carefully counted up the states who ratified early and used their numbers as ammunition to promote the passage of it everywhere, blithely ignoring the close votes in states such as Massachusetts and Pennsylvania. He wrote Samuel Powel that "it is with pleasure I find that the states of Pennsylvania, New Jersey, and Delaware have adopted the proposed constitution for a federal government; the two latter unanimously and the former by a majority of two to one. Of the unanimity of Maryland there can be little question."[305]

He offered the trio analyses of the public leaders and the problems of each state, explaining that they were all different and that the Triumvirate would be mistaken to see all the Anti-Federalists as a united group and the problems of all the states similar. He pointed out in one letter that while some states worried about an oppressive federal government, some a tyrannical president, and others clamored for a bill of rights. Georgia had distinctly different problems, such as Indian raids to the west and Spanish-owned Florida to the south. "If a weak state with the Indians on its back and the Spaniards on its flank does not see the necessity of a general government there must I think be wickedness or insanity in the way," Washington told one friend in mid-March.[306]

Washington's office in Mount Vernon was so cluttered with his letters and men from all over the colonies who had traveled to see him about politics that his aide, David Humphreys, said that the room was "the focus of political intelligence for the New World." Washington's secretary, Tobias Lear, wrote that "the Constitution and its circumstances have been almost the sole topics of conversation" at Mount Vernon in those winter months.[307]

Yet, throughout all of these weeks, Washington's involvement with the Triumvirate was never made public.

By December 1787, Washington's mail had turned negative. A Virginia assemblyman wrote him that he had taken a straw poll of all the members of the legislature and found the supporters in the minority. "The Constitution has lost ground so considerably that it is doubted whether is has any longer a majority in favor," he wrote.[308]

On the eve of the critical conventions in Virginia and New York, Washington spent much time, in personal meetings at Mount Vernon and in letters sent across the United States, reassuring the Federalists that the success the Constitution had enjoyed in other states would bring about its success in the final two. Nothing and no one had derailed it so far, and nothing would, he constantly told them in fatherly tones.

"I have not at any moment despaired of this state's [Virginia's] acceptance of the new constitution and entertain more confidence since the ratification of it in Maryland by so large and decided a majority. The fury of the opposition, I believe, is spent. The grand push was made at the elections. Failing of success there, the hopes of the leaders begin to flag and many of them (or I am mistaken) wish the business was to commence de nova, in which a different line of march would be taken up by some of them," he wrote Gouverneur Morris in early May.

On that same day, he sent a reassuring letter to the very troubled Madison, reminding him that the Anti-Federalists had used up all of their arguments in the Maryland fight and lost. "Mr. Chase, it is said, made a display of all his eloquence. Mr. Mercer discharged his whole artillery of inflammable matter—and Mr. Martin did something—I know not what—but presume with vehemence—yet no converts were made—no, not one. So the business, after a very short season, ended and will if I mistake not, render yours less tiresome."[309]

He emphasized again and again that the leaders of foreign countries with whom the United States did business all favored the Constitution, attempting to persuade opponents that domestic animosities should not wreck foreign policy and world trade. Washington assured French general Comte de Rochambeau, with whom he won the battle of Yorktown, that with its passage "we shall regain thus [the] confidence and credit among the European powers which a want of energy in the present confederation has deprived us of…this event must be extremely pleasing to every friend of humanity and peculiarly to you…[for your part] in establishing her liberty and independence." He reiterated those feelings to the Marquis de Chastellux, a French diplomat.[310]

Perhaps at Madison's behest, Washington began to lobby the leaders of the Anti- Federalists in early January, laying the groundwork for the success of the Virginia Convention, six long months away. He told all of them that although the Constitution was not perfect, it could be amended later, but they had to approve it now.

To amend the Constitution now would be folly, he told Edmund Randolph, adding that "[I] do firmly believe that, in the aggregate, it is the best Constitution than can be obtained at this epoch." He warned him bluntly that the only alternative to ratification was "dissolution of the Union."[311]

Washington never sent copies of any of his letters to newspapers, where they might have had much positive effect, for fear of having his secretive mission with the Triumvirate made public. It was a careful strategy and it worked.

Throughout the winter, Washington dined with hundreds of visitors to Mount Vernon and at each dinner lobbied all of them to persuade their convention delegates to back the Constitution, disdainfully referring to the Anti-Federalists and all politicians he did not like as either "[men] who have no great objection to the introduction of anarchy and confusion" or, more bluntly, "babblers."[312] He invited dozens of influential politicians from the New York and Philadelphia area to visit him at Mount Vernon, usually political friends, and remain for several days for a series of dinners at which he asked them to support the Constitution. His most important dinners were held for his influential friends and neighbors in Virginia to get them to persuade the delegates to the Virginia Convention from their area to back the new government.

The Great Man, as always, took pains to look and act like an ordinary Virginian, despite his heroic status, in order to get what he wanted. "[He was] dressed in a plain drab coat, red jacket, buff breeches and white hose," remembered Olney Winsor, an Alexandria merchant who was invited to one such lobbying dinner in March. Winsor, who was pleased that Mrs. Washington was dressed plainly, too, said that the general, in very deliberate fashion, urged them to back the Constitution. "The General expressed himself on the subject with real concern for the united happiness of the states and at the same time with such clearness on those parts of the Constitution which have been objected to…I was so much pleased with him, as a private man, as I have heretofore been in his military character," Winsor wrote his wife, adding that the campaign afoot that Washington was going to become the tyrant of America under the new Constitution was "black infernal ingratitude" on the part of the whisperers."[313]

It was at these dinners, too, that he peppered guests with questions about their feelings on the Constitution and their assessment of how people in their towns felt about it. This enabled him to gauge the temper of the public and to keep Madison, Hamilton, and Jay up-to-date on public opinion. The feedback he received at these numerous dinners convinced him that Madison and the others were up against more formidable foes than they had anticipated.[314]

The general warned his three friends, too, that while they were busy writing more speeches, the Anti-Federalists were successfully organizing "town hall" type of meetings to solidify opposition to the new government. In one clever maneuver, he told Madison, they convinced a famous debating society in Richmond to sponsor talks on the Constitution so that the Anti-Federalists had a respected public forum to denounce it. The opposition then managed to get every single member of the Assembly to attend the debating society meetings. "The enemies to the Constitution leave no stone unturned to increase the opposition to it," he told him.[315]

He was annoyed, too, that the Federalists in the state were taking victory for granted. In January, though, Archibald Stuart assured Madison that the first batch of *The Federalist*, which had just been published in Richmond, had been very effective and that victory now seemed certain. He wrote Madison, "The anti-constitutional fever which raged here some time ago begins to abate and I am not without hopes that many patients will be restored to their senses."[316]

The general's efforts to win approval were relentless. On Christmas Day, when just about every other man relaxed with his family and enjoyed the holiday, Washington retired to his study at Mount Vernon and wrote a letter of support for the Constitution to a man in England, who had heard much about the Anti-Federalists, assuring him that the Constitution would easily pass.[317]

When the news arrived that Massachusetts had ratified, dozens of Federalists in Richmond walked to the Union Tavern in the middle of the city, hoisted a flag to the top of the roof, and began a celebration that lasted until nearly midnight and emptied the tavern of its beer and wine bottles. One man there chortled about the Virginia Convention that "there seems to be little or no opposition."[318]

Washington fretted over their lack of worry and, as the spring began, stepped up his own efforts to help the Federalists gain victory in his home state.

Washington loved *The Federalist*, and not just because three of his closest friends produced it. He saw it as a complete guide to democracy. It was "an antidote to these [opposition] opinions, and in order to investigate the ground of objections to the Constitution which is submitted the people, the Federalist...is written. They [the essays] are written by able men and before they are finished will, if I am mistaken not, place matters in a true point of light," he wrote at the end of November 1787.

Washington did not wait for anyone to distribute copies of *The Federalist* in Richmond, where the state convention would be held. He did so himself, enlisting friends to talk Richmond newspaper printers into publishing all of the essays.[319]

Washington knew that the Constitution was in trouble in both New York and in Virginia. He wrote Jefferson on New Year's Day of his worry and nine days later wrote Henry Knox that New York was "most problematical."[320]

The general intervened wherever he thought activity was taking place that might derail the Constitution. His interest was often welcome, but sometimes it was not. He had learned there was an effort underway to postpone the Maryland convention, as New Hampshire had done, so that the delegates would have a better idea of how the other states voted. The general fired off a letter on April 20 to Thomas Johnson, the state's governor during the American Revolution and one of the men Washington had always been able to rely upon throughout the Revolution to find food and supplies for his soldiers. Johnson was now a delegate to the Maryland ratifying convention. "An adjournment (if attempted) of your convention to a late period than the decision of the question in this state [Virginia], will be tantamount to the rejection of the constitution," he told Johnson. The Marylander, intent on having his state determine its own fate, was happy to hear from the general, but very annoyed at Washington's interference in his own political affairs.[321]

The way in which Washington was used most ably was the constant reminder by the Federalists, in every state, that the general would surely be the first president. Leading Federalists continually wrote Washington to ask him to consent to election as the first chief executive, even though he remained silent on the subject. In letters to Federalists and Anti-Federalists, and in essays printed in newspapers up and down the Atlantic Coast, the Triumvirate and their allies asserted that the commander in chief, the most respected man in the country, perhaps the world, would be the president. Therefore, the argument went, there is nothing to worry about. Washington has said he likes the Constitution and favors amendments later on. We all trust him and know that he will do the right thing. No one should worry about nuances of power or federal versus state battles as long as he is in charge.

In an unsigned letter published in the *Connecticut Courant* in February 1788, the author wrote that "General Washington will unquestionably be the President and Governor Hancock Vice President. With these great men at the head of government, all Europe will again acknowledge the importance of America."[322]

Could Washington be elected?

Washington was so beloved throughout the country that when toasts were given at a Fayette County, Kentucky, gathering that spring he was toasted third, only behind "the United States of America" and "the western world."[323]

# Chapter Eleven

# VIRGINIA

Everything was coming down to Virginia, as Jay, Hamilton, and Madison had suspected it would. One by one, all of the other states large and small, by margins wide and thin, had ratified the Constitution. Now a ninth and deciding state, according to the rules, was needed to make the new government official, and it could be Virginia (the Federalists were determined to convince all of the states to ratify, though). The delegates in New Hampshire had adjourned their convention in the winter and reopened it in June, but they were hopelessly bogged down in debates and would take weeks, perhaps months, to vote. Virginia would be the deciding state.

Virginia was the largest state in population, geography, commerce, and importance. It had provided many of the most influential leaders of the Revolution and the Continental Congress: George Washington, Thomas Jefferson, James Madison, James Monroe, Richard Henry Lee, George Mason, Henry Lee, Edmund Randolph, and others. It seemed fitting that Virginia could be the final state needed to ratify the Constitution. It also seemed fitting that Virginians represented both sides of the Constitutional question better than any other state and opponents there could sink it. Which would it be?

Madison, Hamilton, and Jay had worried about Virginia for months. When Madison finally arrived home at Montpelier at the end of the horrid winter of 1788, a winter whose temperatures had been below freezing for long periods of time and that had dropped several feet of snow on the ground, he knew that his political plate was full. To win ratification he had to: (1) get as many pro-Federalist delegates elected as possible, including himself; (2) blunt the force of Richard Henry Lee, George Mason, and Patrick Henry; (3) somehow turn recalcitrant Anti-Federalist Governor Edmund Randolph into an ally; (4) let everyone know that George Washington would be the first president of the new country; (5) get all of the pro-Federal forces to work together; (6) win the fourteen delegates from the western region, Kentucky, whom he did not know, to the cause; and (7) make certain everyone had a copy of *The Federalist*.

The Virginia state election returns for delegates to the Constitutional Convention showed a slight majority for those in favor of the Constitution, Madison thought. He told Jefferson, "A large majority of the most intelligent and independent are equally so to the plan under consideration."[324]

Among the men elected were the most important public figures in the state and nation. There were many others who had no great national reputation, but were eminently qualified for the convention, such as John Jones. The Brunswick County planter had been a justice of the peace and served in the House of Burgesses for two years, the state senate for eleven years, and would go on to be the speaker of the Senate in 1789 and, later, serve in the state House of Delegates.[325]

There were many unknown men who saw selection as a great honor. William Fleming, of Botetourt County, said that his neighbors "chose those of the candidates they can best confide in. Who will offer [to run] I know not; should the voters choose me for one, I will serve them, as I look on it to be my duty and the last service I can render my country."[326]

Others who did not serve did all they could to help those who did. Archibald Stuart, on hearing that those running in his county said they might or might not vote for the Constitution if elected, rode seventy-five miles, an all-day journey through snow squalls, to the polling place at Fincastle and demanded that voting be suspended so that he could give a speech outlining the importance of the Constitution and the new government. He convinced the townspeople to force those elected to vote for the Constitution.

There were touching scenes, too, such as an argument between a Federalist delegate and a second man who harangued him on a village green, full of solid arguments, about why the Constitution should not be approved. At the end of the argument, in which the Federalist nobly defended himself, someone said that the complainer should run against the Federalist for the delegate's seat. No, the complainer answered, he would not because the Federalist had made such a strong argument against him.[327]

At local conventions, some delegates won election by aligning themselves with others they knew could be elected. Popular men who apparently knew little about the great arguments concerning the Constitution were elected. One man "remarkable for little but his vices was elected by a great majority," according to a neighbor.

There was some chicanery in Fairfax County, where George Washington declined the urging of all to be a delegate and instead convinced people to vote for his son-in-law, David Stuart.

George Mason, increasingly unpopular, was asked to run in another Virginia county, where he was elected, rather than his native Fairfax. James Hughes in Fairfax wrote, "Should Col. Mason offer himself he would hardly get twenty votes in the whole county for he has made himself odious."

There was vote fraud when some delegates argued that unknown "settlers" not on the tax rolls had been permitted to vote in clusters in some counties; votes were disputed in others.

The counties responded as Madison had assumed they would, giving each side about the same number of delegates, with the Federalists obtaining a very slender edge.

James Mercer sneered at all the rich people elected. "High toned gentry can never be sound Republicans. They but deceive themselves if they think so, like the Lady in the Fable, that they will catch mice if ever one comes in their way."

Some men who lived in one county where they were certain they would lose ran in another county and won. Some surprised everybody. Federalists Martin Pickett (225 votes) and Humphrey Brooke (210 votes) were elected in Fauquier County, thought to be Anti-Federalist. Some men thought to be popular lost. Some men did nothing except give a speech on election day, at the polling place, while others engaged in heated newspaper letter-writing with each other prior to the elections. Some anonymous writers campaigned against candidates, particularly Governor Randolph, an Anti-Federalist who won anyway.

Madison, who hated campaigning for anything, delivered a single speech, that lasted nearly two hours on a day with snow blowing in the air, and was elected handily, with 202 votes, leading James Gordon, with 187, Thomas Barbour, 56, and Charles Porter, 34.

Arguments raged for weeks in Powhatan County about delegate selection. One candidate in Prince William County campaigned with his snuffbox, constantly pointing to it and telling his audiences that all the other states in size and importance were that of the snuffbox compared to Virginia. Some candidates blustered for hours about their love, or hatred, of the Constitution. One man sniped at William Graham, a Revolutionary War veteran from Rockbridge County, that "he has sounded the bell of sedition and raised an uncommon commotion."

Everybody had something to say. One voter in Fredericksburg urged a friend to tell his brother to sell his land because when the Constitution went into effect, the entire county would slide into bankruptcy.[328]

Ratification would not be easy; there were many obstacles. There was the stubborn Mason. He "is growing every day more bitter and outrageous in his efforts to carry his point and will probably in the end be thrown by the violence of his passions into the politics of Mr. Henry," Madison wrote Jefferson.

Madison feared, too, that the delegates would demand a second convention for a bill of rights that he thought would wreck the entire Constitutional procedure. He wrote, "The very attempt at a second convention strikes at the confidence in the first and the existence of a second by opposing influence to influence would…destroy an effectual confidence in either."[329]

The Federalists breathed a sigh of relief when Madison was elected. His skills were needed—vitally. One man wrote, "[Madison] is the only man in this state who can effectually combat the influence of Mason and Henry…if left out, not only this state but the whole continent will sustain a considerable loss."[330]

Virginia's ratification was questionable because it was such a huge state. Its combined black and white population numbered just over 800,000, of which more than 300,000 were slaves. In size, it additionally comprised what is now West Virginia and Kentucky and stretched all the way to the Mississippi River. The state was three quarters as large as all of New England, almost twice the size of Pennsylvania, and nearly three times the size of New York. It represented 75 percent of the population of all the southern states. The commerce of the state in 1788 was perhaps the strongest of any state in the Union. Its total commercial trade value was just over $20 million and the people paid only a 2 percent state income tax. The state's planters and small subsistence farmers not only produced the world's largest amount of tobacco, but also flour, corn, hemp, lumber, animal skins, iron, and wheat. A milder climate permitted ships to reach all of its sea and river ports safely year round. If any state could go break away from the Confederation and become independent, it was massive Virginia.[331]

That's why its adoption of the Constitution was so critical. "It would be truly mortifying if anything should occur to prevent or retard the concurrence of a state which has generally taken the lead on great occasions," Madison wrote Edmund Pendleton, a Virginia Supreme Court judge, back in October 1787.[332]

Madison worried about everything. He fretted about Richard Henry Lee. It was Lee who was one of the first to insist on a bill of rights and Lee who had written letters to many influential Virginians outlining the need for rights involving press, assembly, religion, legal fairness, and unreasonable search and seizure. Madison's view that Lee was an enemy prevented him from listening to Lee's other ideas, such as an eleven-man presidential council made up of experts in different areas of governmental services. (Washington remembered that suggestion and used the idea to form his Cabinet.)

He paid no attention to Lee's plea that the states take their time in ratifying the Constitution because a civil war would not follow, as the Triumvirate and their Federalists insisted in letters and speeches. "To say a bad government must be established for fear of anarchy is really saying we should kill ourselves for fear of dying!" Lee said.[333]

The Federalists—it is not certain who ordered them to do so— attacked Lee from the start. In December 1787, Oliver Ellsworth, a Federalist from Connecticut, wrote in the sixth of his series of "Landholder" pro-Federalist newspaper essays that Lee was the author of the powerful anti-Constitution *Federal Farmer* articles that had been running in New York newspapers (the author was Melancton Smith, not Lee). Ellsworth then reminded readers that Lee had been connected to a conspiracy, the Conway Cabal, to depose Washington as commander of the army in 1778 and replace him with the hero of Saratoga, Horatio Gates. Now, Ellsworth wrote, Lee was getting back at Washington and his Federalist friends with these *Federal Farmer* columns.

The attacks increased and within weeks Federalists throughout the country were connecting Lee to the Anti-Federalist essay series and to the seemingly long dead Conway Cabal. It became known that Lee's son was in favor of the Constitution, and many newspapers simply invented stories about the progeny that Lee seemed to be working so hard against. Other newspapers questioned his postwar relationship with George Washington, wondering whether the general really thought as highly of Lee as Lee said he did of the general.[334]

Why did Madison detest Lee, whose goals of rights for the people seemed noble enough? It was the same reason he and his friends were angry at every one of the Anti-Federalists—the opposition's belief that the Triumvirate and all of the Federalists were power-hungry. Lee wrote that history had shown that "the most express declarations and reservations are necessary to protect the just rights and liberty of mankind from the silent, powerful, and ever active conspiracy of those who govern."[335]

Madison dismissed him and reminded everyone that the Philadelphia Constitutional Convention had already voted down Lee's bill of rights proposals unanimously; he chafed that Lee persisted in his quest.[336]

Lee was just as angry as Madison and told the Federalists that the Anti-Federalists supported the proposed new government and believed that it was a good one—but could be better with a bill of rights. They were not out to wreck the government but to improve it. These rights,

Lee insisted to Washington, were "the opinions [that] our people have for ages been fixed on" and that "I am led to fear the danger that will ensue to civil liberty from the adoption of the new system in its present form."[337]

It annoyed Lee and other Anti-Federalists that Madison, Jay, Hamilton, and their Federalist friends did not understand them and made no effort to do so. He wrote in early October, "If all men were wise and good there would be no necessity for government or law—but the folly and vice of human nature renders government and laws necessary."[338]

Lee did survive the wrath of the Federalists longer than his friend George Mason. Mason had been a neighbor and friend of George Washington's for thirty years, a long-standing and productive and highly admired member of the Virginia House of Burgesses, a signer of the Declaration of Independence, and one of the most forceful and helpful members of the Constitutional Convention. Why was he so against the Constitution?

Mason had two worlds to protect, the greater United States and the local Virginia where he and his friends lived. He had serious problems with the Constitution because it seemed to him that the national government would become as corrupt as some state governments. His primary interests were in Virginia and with the planters of the northern counties. He wanted navigation acts passed to protect the ships that transported the tobacco grown by himself and his friends. He also strenuously opposed the suggestion by John Jay that Spain should hold the navigational rights to the Mississippi, not America. He wanted a strong House of Representatives that worked for the people and a weak president and Senate that worked for the elite so that the problems of the states could be taken care of by the states. He had also opposed the slave trade most of his life and was certain that it would end soon. What would happen to him and his rich planter friends when it did? How could the national government help them then?

He saw his views as those of many southerners and waited for the Constitutional Convention to address them. They did not and then, eager to go home, they quickly dismissed his efforts for at least a bill of rights to protect individuals. That made him very angry. He returned home "in an exceedingly ill humor," Madison wrote.[339]

Prior to leaving Philadelphia, Mason and Lee agreed to put together a very small group of men to delay passage of the Constitution without any bill of rights. Mason went to work writing his "Objections," paced by his own anger at having been so sharply dismissed in Congress. The objections he raised covered all of the ground of those in the other states, but they were sharper and better organized than most because he was such a good writer. They were not long, either, and that permitted many newspapers to publish them.

He argued against the office of the vice president, demanded less power for the Senate and president, more for the House, and a two-thirds voting margin on any commercial bills. He was solidly against the "necessary and proper" clause that enabled Congress to pass new laws to deal with new problems as they arose. Mason saw that as an open door to political treachery. "This government will set out a moderate aristocracy; it is at present impossible to foresee whether it will, in its operation, produce a monarchy, or a corrupt, tyrannical aristocracy; it will probably vibrate some years between the two and then terminate in the one or the other," he gloomily predicted.[340]

Mason permitted the anonymous publication of "Objections" in several northern newspapers, but strangely declined to have it printed in the Virginia press, despite the urging of many Antis there that the publication would help their cause.

When the federal convention ended in Philadelphia, Mason headed home toward Virginia intent on forcing the Constitutional delegates there to adopt a bill of rights or else lose the Constitution. He encountered nothing but trouble on his way.

First, Tobias Lear, Washington's secretary, wrote against the "Objections" and told everyone that Mason was the author of the "Objections." Once that was made public, Federalists in Virginia and around the country immediately lambasted Mason for his remarks. The criticism would continue for all of the long nine months until the Virginia convention.

Second, Washington himself turned on his old friend, letting everyone know that he was unhappy with his actions. Washington then arranged for Virginia newspapers to print the Federalists' opposition to Mason's "Objections," naming Mason as their author.

Third, writing in Connecticut, Oliver Ellsworth blasted Mason in his newspaper columns, writing, "Mr. Mason would prefer the subjects of every foreign power to the subject of the United States who live in New England."

Fourth, Mason received a chilly welcome by the residents of Alexandria, the closest large community to his plantation, Gunston Hall. He apparently had a town crier read his Anti-Federalist report on the convention. The crowd listened quietly; no one cheered. That was not the worst of it, though. Federalist newspapers concocted a wild story that town leaders had ordered Mason out of Alexandria within the hour after he arrived and that the Anti-Federalist chief and longtime state legislator had to flee. Retractions were printed later, but the story stuck in the minds of Virginians.[341]

Mason's critics were loud. Numerous newspapers denounced him. Writers attacked his mental faculties. "Imbecility," screeched one editor about Mason's views. He had become such an easy target for all that Madison feared the mildly antagonistic Mason might swing over into the radical Henry's camp, giving him a bevy of votes from Mason's supporters at the state convention.[342]

Mason had his supporters throughout Virginia. Hugh Williamson wrote John Blount in New York that "all eyes here are looking with hope or fear toward Virg[inia]. We all admire the beautiful trope of Col. Mason in the court house in the county where he was elected" and added derogatorily of the Federalists scattered throughout the United States that "from the eastern states there were knaves and fools...they were a parcel of coxcombs and from the middle states office hunters not a few..." Nineteenth-century historian George Ticknor Curtis said of Mason that he was "one of the most profound and able of all the American statesmen opposed to the Constitution while...inferior in general powers and resources to not more than two or three of those who framed or advocated it."[343]

Many Virginians also thought a bill of rights was necessary. They loved George Washington and wanted him to be the first president, but feared the presidency in general. They did not like the powerful Senate and, as the largest state, wanted more rights than the smaller states. Many Virginians owed money to the British from before the American Revolution and did not want to pay it; they saw the new federal judiciary as a legal system designed to make them do so.

In the end, there were probably just as many Federalist delegates as Anti-Federalists. The newspapers thought that the Federalists had a ten-vote lead out of the 168 total, based on the backgrounds of the elected delegates, although no one was sure how the fourteen men from the western region, Kentucky, would vote.

Madison should have been happy with the returns. He and his friends had engineered most of them, running heroic former soldiers, popular judges, wealthy planters, and well-known merchants as candidates. Some, unable to claim victory in their own county ran in other counties and triumphed there.

"The majority will be but small, and may possibly be yet defeated," Madison concluded. Congressman William Grayson, an Anti, had a different view. He knew the vote would be close, but wrote, "The district of Kentucky is with us and if we can get over the four counties which lie on the Ohio between the Pennsylvania line and Big Sandy Creek, the day is our own."[344]

The Federalists won in counties north of the James River, the Antis took most of the seats south of the river. The Federalists did better than expected along the Atlantic Coast and the mountains; the Antis just about swept the western region.

Madison had hurried home, urged by all to become a delegate and take charge of the Federalist efforts. Archibald Stuart had warned him that "opposition to your Constitution had been heard of from different parts of your state…pray, let nothing prevent you from coming to your convention."[345]

One thing Washington must have surely done in his days with Madison was to help his chronically depressed friend see the brighter side of the pro-Constitution votes in the states. He must have reminded Madison that the Federalists were winning, not losing, and that the insistence on a bill of rights, or even an attached suggested bill for later implementation, did not matter. An example of Washington's half-full and not half-empty cup was the vote in Massachusetts. He dismissed the fight over the bill of rights and told friends that it was a victory and would help the drive in Virginia.[346]

The Antis had a distant ally, Thomas Jefferson, a former governor and one of the most influential men in the state, then serving as ambassador to France. Jefferson had been upset about the lack of a bill of rights since the day Madison mailed a copy of the Constitution to him in the fall of 1787. He told Richmond political leader Edward Carrington that he had hoped the states that had ratified it would have approved the Constitution conditionally, provided a bill of rights was added. Now, in Virginia, he hoped for passage but said a bill of rights proviso was essential, "so much in the interest of all to have."[347] Carrington, an ally of Madison, saw Jefferson's letter as a time bomb and did not distribute it. Others did.

Madison had tried to persuade Governor Edmund Randolph to join him in supporting the Constitution since the federal convention ended in September 1787, and throughout the winter had tried to ingratiate himself with the governor.[348] He had written Randolph fawning letters, telling him that he seemed troubled about supporting the Constitution and that he should remember that whatever weaknesses he saw in the Constitution were certainly not those that the general Anti-Federalists perceived and that, in fact, he was not really an Anti-Federalist. Back in January, he wrote the governor after he read his pamphlet defending his opposition to the Constitution that "I read it with pleasure, because the spirit of it does as much honor to your candor as the general reasoning does to your abilities. Nor can I believe in this quarter that the opponents of the Constitution will find encouragement in it."[349]

The Triumvirate had been worried about the vote in Virginia for months. Before Christmas, Madison sized up the state in a perceptive letter to Jefferson in Paris. He saw the ratification vote being determined by three different parties in the state and then assessed the feelings of the leaders of each in a cogent analysis. "The first [is] for adopting without attempting amendments. This includes Gen'l W [Washington] and other deputies who signed the Constitution, Mr. Pendleton, Mr. Marshall, I believe, Mr. Nicholas, Mr. Corbin, Mr. Zach Johnson, Col. Innes, Mr. B. Randolph as I understand, Mr. Harey, Mr. Gabriel Jones, Doctor Jones etc.

"At the head of the second party which urges amendments are the Governor and Mr. Mason. These do not object at the substance of the government, but contend for a few additional guards in favor of the rights of the people."

The third class, led by Patrick Henry, was the strongest group against the new government. Madison wrote, "This class concurs at present with the patrons of amendments but will probably contend for such a strike at the essence of the system and must lead to an adherence to the principle of the existing confederation which most thinking men are convinced is a visionary one, or to a partition of the Union into several confederacies. Mr. [Benjamin] Harrison and the late Gov. is with Mr. Henry. So are a number of others. The general and the admiralty courts with most of the bar oppose the Constitution but on what particular grounds I am unable to say. General Nelson, Mr. Jon Page, Col. Bland, etc. are also opponents, but on what principle and to what extent I am equally at a loss to say."

The real problem, he told everyone, was Patrick Henry. "Mr. Henry is the great adversary who will render the event precarious. He is, I find with his usual addresses, working up every possible interest into a spirit of opposition," Madison wrote, adding that his great fear was that a few powerful politicians would wreck the chances for passage of a Constitution that Madison felt the ordinary citizens of the state favored.[350]

Washington had worried about Henry, too. He wrote, "[Henry] has only to say let this be law, and it is law."[351]

He had urged Henry to support the Constitution because as a longtime governor, distinguished orator, and charismatic leader, Henry had enormous influence in the state. But Henry wrote back that he could not. "I cannot bring my mind to accord with the proposed Constitution. The concern I feel on this account is really greater than I am able to express. Perhaps mature reflections may furnish me reasons to change my present sentiments into a conformity with the opinions of those personages for whom I have the highest reverence."[352]

He did not change Henry's mind, and in June, Henry was still dead set against the new government. His continued opposition incensed Washington. The general wrote Charles Carter, former House of Burgesses legislator and scion of the powerful Carter family, that if any one state refused to approve the Constitution, it would cause "anarchy" throughout the nation. He reminded him, and all, that amendments could be made later.[353]

The general's dismay was great. He warned ominously, "Should the states reject this excellent Constitution, the probability is that an opportunity will never again [arrive] in peace—the next will be drawn in blood."[354]

Patrick Henry was not trying to be the spoiler, though. He was sincere in his feelings that the government seemed overpowering and that the people would be trampled without a bill of rights to protect them. He represented the southern counties of Virginia, and most people there were against the Constitution, and told him so. "It is a matter of great consolation," Henry told John Lamb, a Revolutionary War veteran and customs collector from New York City, "to find that the sentiments of a vast majority of Virginians are in unison with those of our northern friends. I am satisfied that four fifths of our inhabitants are opposed to the new scheme of government. Indeed, in the part of this country lying south of the James River, I am confident nine tenths are opposed to it..."[355]

Others told Madison not to worry about Henry. He could not be turned into a supporter and he was so against it that many delegates to the Convention might not pay any attention to him. Henry Lee wrote Madison that "One [set of men] are opposed to any system, was it even sent from heaven, which tends to confirm the union of the states—Henry is the leader of this band..."[356]

Madison would need the skills of a smoky backroom deal-maker, and not those of a lecturer in a crowded auditorium, to get the Constitution ratified. Congressman Edward Livingston complained that Madison never acted until forced to do so and did not care for wheeling and dealing.

Others, though, saw a new Madison emerging. A Connecticut congressman wrote, "He has no fire, no enthusiasm, no animation but he has infinite prudence and industry. With candor, he calculates upon everything with the greatest nicety and precision. He has unquestionably the most personal influence of any man in the House of Representatives. I never knew a man that better understood [how] to husband a character and make the most of his talents. And he has the most artificial, studied character on earth."[357]

There were signs that Madison was becoming more involved. His strenuous work for the Triumvirate in New York, keeping in touch with a dozen or more key Federalists in the different state conventions, had built a strong coalition. He had engaged dozens of congressmen, judges, and other public officials in conversations about the Constitution there. He plunged into the work of writing the essays for *The Federalist*, churning out tens of thousands of clear and concise words about the need for a new government, discarding his former stodgy style of writing that was meant for the intellectuals and not the masses. During his very first year in the new Congress, in 1790, others would fondly refer to him as "the Big Knife" for his ability to cut political deals.

The late 1780s saw an enormous change in Madison's public personality. He was morphing from an intellectual into a political street fighter, but he was doing it in a way that kept his old political allies and gave him the chance to add new ones.

By the time the Virginia convention was held, though, Madison was firmly against any bill of rights. He had been against it from the federal convention in Philadelphia and now, after months of arguing, he had become completely defensive of his position, stronger against the bill of rights as more and more people clamored for it.

Madison's early stubbornness on the issue had grown larger each time the Constitution was opposed in a state. By the time the ratification parade reached Virginia, blocking a bill of rights had become very personal for him, the other members of the Triumvirate, and

George Washington. Their intransigence on the issue prevented any compromise to have a bill of rights, or even some rights, inserted into the Constitution.

The "Big Knife" had his work cut out for him at the ratification convention in Virginia, and, although he did not know it, he was about to embark upon a breathless race to the finish for his precious Constitution.

Triumvirate member JOHN JAY was one of the most politically experienced men in the country by the time he joined Madison and Hamilton in the ratification fight. He had been a member and president of the Continental Congress, a New York state justice, head of numerous Revolutionary committees, and the secretary of foreign affairs in the Confederation government.

Courtesy of National Independence Historical Park

SARAH JAY. The wife of John Jay traveled throughout the world with him, becoming one of America's first "diplomat wives." She became quite ill in the 1790s. He left public life in 1800 to care for her; she died two years later, at age 45. Jay lived twenty-nine more years but never remarried.

Courtesy of the New York Historical Society

GEORGE CLINTON. The very popular longtime governor of New York was opposed to the Constitution from the beginning and voted against it.

Courtesy of National Independence Historical Park

DEWITT CLINTON. Later governor of New York, spoke out early and often against the Constitution in New York.

Courtesy of National Independence Historical Park

The fiery ALEXANDER HAMILTON, Washington's top military aide during the American Revolution, wrote many of the essays in *The Federalist* with Madison and Jay and led the fight for ratification in his home state of New York.

Courtesy of National Independence Historical Park

RUFUS KING. Was the ringleader of the Federalists in Massachusetts who worked closely with Madison, Jay, and Hamilton.

Courtesy of National Independence Historical Park

FISHER AMES. Was a longtime Massachusetts congressman who was closely connected to the Triumvirate.

Courtesy of National Independence Historical Park

JOHN HANCOCK. The governor of Massachusetts, sat on the fence over his feelings on the Constitution until the very last moment, when he gave a stirring speech in support of it.

Courtesy of National Independence Historical Park

JOHN ADAMS. Would have been the leading advocate for the new Federal Constitution at the Massachusetts convention, but he was away in Europe at the time.

Courtesy of National Independence Historical Park

SAMUEL ADAMS. A Revolutionary War patriot and beer brewer, was originally opposed to the Constitution but was swayed by the overwhelming support for it by his fellow tradesmen in Boston.

Courtesy of National Independence Historical Park

GEORGE MASON. Was one of the chief opponents of the Constitution from the federal convention in Philadelphia right until the very day Virginia voted on it. The Federalists painted him as one of the villains of the ratification process.

Courtesy of National Independence Historical Park

RICHARD HENRY LEE, with Mason and others, was an early opponent of the Constitution and, like Mason, was portrayed as a scheming villain by the Federalists.

Courtesy of National Independence Historical Park

JAMES MADISON. The nation's youngest congressman, wrote most of *The Federalist* essays and spearheaded the drive to have his home state, Virginia, ratify the Constitution.

Courtesy of National Independence Historical Park

The vivacious DOLLEY MADISON married the usually sour, disgruntled James Madison, changing his personality and enlivening the White House when he was elected president later, in 1808.

Courtesy of National Independence Historical Park

Virginia's JAMES MONROE was at first against the Constitution, but like many others changed his mind after listening to Madison's lengthy arguments in favor of it.

Courtesy of National Independence Historical Park

GEORGE WYTHE. Was the chair of the committee that ran the daily operations of the Virginia convention and on the day the vote was taken made an eloquent speech supporting the Constitution.

Courtesy of National Independence Historical Park

GEORGE WASHINGTON. Was the fourth, silent member of the Triumvirate who did all that he could from his Mount Vernon plantation to get the Constitution passed in the different conventions.

Courtesy of National Independence Historical Park

HENRY KNOX. Was one of the influential people with whom the Triumvirate, and George Washington, corresponded during the Constitution ratification process. He later was named the first secretary of war.

Courtesy of National Independence Historical Park

The bombastic PATRICK HENRY, perhaps the nation's best public speaker, led the intense battle against the Constitution in Virginia.

Courtesy of National Independence Historical Park

The sickly EDMUND PENDLETON was the chairman of the Virginia convention; when Madison fell ill, he ably replaced him in the debates with Patrick Henry over the Constitution.

Courtesy of National Independence Historical Park

THOMAS JEFFERSON liked the idea of a federal government, but was very critical of the new Constitution, even urging states to vote it down so that it could be rewritten and amended before becoming law.

Courtesy of National Independence Historical Park

ABRAHAM CLARK, a delegate from New Jersey, expressed the feelings of many when he said that although he had complaints about the new Constitution, overall it was the foundation for good government.

Courtesy of National Independence Historical Park

The support for the Constitution by the esteemed BENJAMIN FRANKLIN was at first minimal, but at the end of the Federal Convention, to the surprise of many, he came out strongly in support of it.

Courtesy of National Independence Historical Park

Pennsylvanian JAMES O. WILSON gave several public speeches in which he expressed his support for the Constitution in elegant yet simple language that many said helped to carry it in that state.

Courtesy of National Independence Historical Park

This map of the United States, drawn shortly after the Revolution ended in 1783, shows the vast sizes of the new states.

Courtesy of the Colonial Williamsburg Foundation

George Washington's home at Mount Vernon, on the banks of the Potomac River in Virginia, served as a clearing house of information on the national debates on the Constitution. Washington kept his involvement in the push for ratification a secret.

Courtesy of the Mount Vernon Ladies Association

In the summer of 1788, Richmond was still a quiet little town of some 5,000 residents on the banks of the James River, as shown in this early 1808 painting of it.

Courtesy of the Virginia Historical Society

New York City was exploding in population at the time the Constitution was debated, its size doubling in ten years. This portrait of the Tontine coffeehouse and the streets surrounding it is an example of the crowded neighborhoods where Madison, Jay, and Hamilton lived and worked.

Courtesy of the New York Historical Society

Independence Hall, Philadelphia, where the Constitution was debated and signed.

Delegates debating the Constitution at Independence Hall.

The story of the ratification of the Constitution ended with George Washington's inauguration as the first president of the United States at Federal Hall, in New York City, in April of 1789.

Courtesy of the New York Historical Society

Washington attends Congress, Wall Street, 1789.

President Washington arrives at Congressional Hall in New York to deliver a speech to Congress during the first year of the new government.

Courtesy of the New York Historical Society

# Chapter Twelve

# VIRGINIA'S WILD CONVENTION BEGINS

The Virginia ratification convention in Richmond had all the elements of an exotic eighteenth-century adventure novel. It had the single hottest issue of the time—the new government. It had an ever-approaching deadline and a ticking clock. It had the eyes of the nation upon it. And it had, yearning for the fight, some of the great men of the century on the convention floor, their sleeves rolled up.

Richmond was a city of five thousand people that was growing so rapidly that the local government leaders did not have time to keep up with its explosion. In just the decade since it had been named the state capital, the town had doubled in population. Its shipping business boomed, its wharves filled with large, tri-masted ocean-going ships just in from the Caribbean or South America or bound for Europe. Landlords constructed flimsy boardinghouses as fast as they could, but that never seemed to be enough for the ever-growing horde of laborers who descended upon the town. The streets were still dirt and turned to mud when the James River, which ran through Richmond, flooded.

The town had started to fill with taverns and gambling houses. Crime and prostitution had become huge problems for the local residents. Most of the slaves in the South lived on plantations. The hundreds, and later thousands, of slaves who lived in Richmond, working in factories or the shipyards, though, enjoyed unprecedented freedom that worried the local residents. The tobacco business, the backbone of industry in Virginia, was better than ever, utilizing thousands of slaves. All of this, plus the population flood and mix of black and white residents made Richmond one of the most unique cities in America, an odd place to hold a ratification convention and an unusual stage for one of the nation's most historic moments.

The delegates to the Virginia Convention were among the most important political figures in the country and included several men who would later go on to political prominence, such as James Monroe and James Madison, future presidents, and John Marshall, future chief justice of the U.S. Supreme Court. Among the others were Patrick Henry, the state's five-time governor and one of the most fiery orators in the country. There was aging Edmund Pendleton, the irascible George Mason, Governor Edmund Randolph, former governor John Blair, Edward Carrington, Judge George Wythe, former governor Benjamin Harrison, and James Innis.[358]

Among those not present was Richard Henry Lee, who begged off because he always became ill when visiting Richmond (many said he had been too hurt by the Federalist attacks on him to show up), and Thomas Jefferson, in Paris. Washington did not attend because he was trying to remain above politics and prevent anyone from thinking he was in any way trying to become the new nation's first president.

The convention was scheduled to be held in the state capitol building, a wooden, ramshackle, barn-like structure just fifty square feet in the center of town. It was such an undistinguished building British army troops under Benedict Arnold overlooked it when they torched the city in 1778. The building was too small for a convention of any real size, though, and on the second day the assembly moved to the Academy of Sciences and Fine Arts, built by the French to cement relations with Virginia, referred to by all as "the New Academy." The brand-new, twenty-four-month-old "New Academy" was a two-story high, ornately appointed building with a spacious auditorium and large gallery for spectators. It sat on Broad Street between Eleventh and Twelfth streets on a square, opposite the Monumental Church.

The titular chairman of the Virginia convention was the aging Edmund Pendleton, one of the justices on the Virginia Supreme Court, but the chair of its Committee of the Whole, which actually ran proceedings of the convention, was George Wythe of Williamsburg, sixty-two but in strong health, a perfect choice for both the Federalists and the Anti-Federalists. He was perhaps the most qualified man in the state to chair what appeared to be a raucous convention. Wythe had served for years as the mayor of Williamsburg, a member of the state legislature, and as a county court judge in Elizabeth City County. He was also one of the three chancellors on the state's Chancery Court, the final judicial arbiter of all civil matters in the state. He had been Thomas Jefferson's mentor at William and Mary College, where he served as the nation's first professor of law.

The chancellor, who spoke several languages including Greek and Latin, had signed the Declaration of Independence and served as a delegate to the Continental Congress and the Constitutional Convention in Philadelphia. In those places he had become close friends with the leaders of the different states. And, too, there was his long-standing friendship with George Washington. He was not elected chair for those reasons. He was given the post because of his years as a parliamentarian and then speaker of the state legislature. Those jobs gave him the skills to oversee a convention in which delegates held diametrically opposite views and in which heated debates and harsh disputes were certain to develop.

Wythe impressed all at the Philadelphia Convention. One delegate wrote, "He is confessedly one of the most learned legal characters of the present age. No man, it is said, understands the history of government better than Mr. Wythe nor [does] anyone understand the fluctuating conditions to which all societies are liable better than he does."[359]

Wythe was a relatively quiet and nonthreatening man, an aging founder and judge who had no political or personal goals of his own. He was a scholar who was a combination of the new American democracy and the democracies of ancient Rome and Greece; people had nicknamed him the "American Aristedes."

There was something charming in his appearance, wrote nineteenth-century historian Hugh Grigsby. "He had reached his sixty second year; yet as he moved with a brisk and graceful step from the floor to the chair, his small and erect stature presented a pleasing image of a fresh and healthy old man. As he sat in the chair, he appeared to be bald; but his gray hair grew thick behind, and instead of being wrapped with a ribbon, as was then and many years later the universal custom, descended down his neck and rose in a broad curl...he was arrayed in neat and simple dress...a single breasted coat with a standing collar, a single breasted vest and a white cravat buckled behind."[360]

Wythe did not seek the role or even run for a delegate spot. The leaders of the mini-convention held in Yorktown to select two candidates for that region insisted that Wythe and John Blair, another veteran state legislator, be chosen by acclamation over the men who were running. There was a roar of approval and the two other candidates stepped down.

The voters in Yorktown, en masse, rode to Williamsburg to inform Wythe and Blair of their selection. Wythe was in the first floor study of his home that fronted on the village green, tutoring a student, when the noisy crowd arrived on his front lawn and the leader, Judge William Nelson, knocked on his door. Wythe opened it and peered out at the throng, a startled look on his face. Nelson told him what happened.

"Will you serve!" shouted dozens of men in the crowd. "Yes, serve! Serve!" yelled others.

"Mr. Wythe was quite agitated," wrote the student he had been with, Littleton Tazewell. "Every muscle of his face was in motion, and when the good old man, standing on the steps, his bald head quite bare, attempted to speak, tears flowed down his cheeks in copious streams."

Wythe accepted, muttering to Nelson, "How can I refuse?"

The multitude roared again and left, marching down the lane toward the home of John Blair, who also agreed to go to Richmond.[361]

When Madison first arrived in Richmond, he was not happy. He had heard rumors for months that Virginia was pro-Constitution, then anti-Constitution, then pro-Constitution. Washington, who had been furiously corresponding with and meeting people at his home at Mount Vernon, had been telling him that the convention would be split right down the middle. Washington's nephew Bushrod Washington, a legislator, in fact, wrote him from Richmond as early as December 7, 1787, that "I am sorry to inform you that the Constitution has lost so considerably that it is doubted whether it has any longer a majority in its favor."[362]

Each day, arm in arm, Patrick Henry and George Mason, the heads of the opposition, walked from the tavern, The Swan, where they stayed for the duration of the Convention, to the New Academy. They were a dignified duo; each said "Good morning" to all of the Virginians who addressed them each day.

Mason possessed enormous amounts of "Roman energy and wit," according to one of his biographers. He had "once raven hair white as snow, his stalwart figure, attired in deep mourning, still erect, his black eyes fairly flashing…his voice deliberate and full." On his daily walk to the hall with Henry, Mason greeted anyone he met, friend or foe, with distinction. "[He] was remarkable for the urbanity and dignity with which he received the courtesies of those who passed by him," wrote a biographer.[363]

It was not George Mason, but Patrick Henry that all looked to as the most important man in the upcoming convention. How well would he do?

In New York each morning, federal treasury notes rose and fell, the price related to how Virginia would vote. The *Virginia Independent Chronicle* published a 1783 letter by George Washington to the executives of each of the American states at the end of the Revolution, calling for a strong federal government. The next day John Brown, in New York, wrote a Kentucky delegate in Virginia that he had heard all of the Kentuckians were opposed to the Constitution. He told him that Congress was getting ready to bring Kentucky in as a new state and delicately suggested that their delegates in Virginia should approve the Constitution to ensure a safe future for their area. Around June 4 or 5 Anti-Federalist newspaper editor Eleazar Oswald of the *Philadelphia Independent Gazetteer* arrived in Richmond, black patch over his eye, with letters for numerous delegates from Pennsylvanians who rejected ratification. He left for Philadelphia a few days later carrying their responses. Richmond was a city of news and tumult, hurried arrivals and departures, as the convention approached.[364]

Gouverneur Morris told Hamilton all looked grim. He wrote, "Matters are not going so well in [Virginia]…as you well know, certain dark modes of operating on the minds of members which like contagious diseases are only known by their effects."[365]

The convention had the help of the continued publication of essays from *The Federalist* collection, which helped the pro-Constitution group. The convention started when George Mason insisted on having the entire Constitution read and debated, clause by clause. Madison was startled. A clause-by-clause debate had taken place at most of the other state conventions and he had hoped to repeat that process in Richmond, after a tough battle. Now the leader of the Anti-Federalists championed it. Madison agreed, right away, because he knew that no one in the country was better than he at defending anything clause by clause. It was his greatest strength.

Governor Randolph, seen as one of the prominent Antis, arrived full of determination on the first day of the Convention. He always impressed those who met him. A delegate to the Philadelphia Convention had described him as "a young gentleman in whom [people] unite all the accomplishments of the scholar and the statesman...He has a most harmonious voice, is a fine person, and [has] striking manners."[366]

Madison and other federalists had been working on Randolph to change his mind for months.[367]

Randolph recounted all of his objections to the Constitution, highlighted by the lack of a bill of rights. The governor told the delegates, though, that they had no real government under the Articles of Confederation and that no one in the world respected the United States. Something more was needed. "[Our] commerce lagging, produce falling in value, and justice trampled under foot. We became contemptible in the eyes of foreign nations; they discarded us as little wanton bees who had played for liberty but had no sufficient solidity or wisdom to secure it on a permanent basis and were therefore unworthy of their regard," he said. "Without adequate powers vested in Congress, America cannot be respectable in the eyes of other nations. Congress ought to be fully vested with power to maintain justice and promote harmony and public tranquility among the states..."[368]

It was a surprising and powerful speech. One of the leaders of the Anti-Federalists had switched and others in his group would surely change their minds, too. "Mr. Henry has been answered by Mr. Randolph most fully," wrote one delegate in a newspaper. "The astonishment of the opposition was greatly excited" by the speech, wrote another in a letter reprinted in nearly thirty American newspapers.[369]

"The Govr [sic]…has thrown himself fully into our scale," Madison wrote triumphantly.[370]

The middle-of-the-roaders were stunned at Randolph's change of heart. Randolph had not only refused to vote for the Constitution in Philadelphia, but published a letter in numerous newspapers defending his stand. He was still against it, everyone believed. "His present conduct [was] consistent with that letter and the letter with his refusal to sign," declared James Monroe.[371]

The governor's defection startled the Antis. "We are alarmed," wrote one.[372]

And then, on that same day, word arrived from Charleston that South Carolina, earlier seen as one of the states destined to turn down the Constitution, had approved it. The Federalists were off to a flying start.

"Henry and Mason made a lame figure and appeared to take different and awkward ground. The Federalists are a good deal elated by the existing prospect," Madison wrote Washington that night. He added, though, that he was not overly optimistic and had to work harder on courting the delegates from Kentucky.[373]

Washington was a better political strategist than Madison, and offered Jay a deft analysis of the situation in Virginia. He wrote, "Mr. Randolph's declaration will have considerable effect on those who had hitherto been wavering. Mr. Henry and Col. Mason took different and awkward ground and by no means equaled the public expectation in their speeches, the former has probably receded somewhat from his violent measure to coalesce with the latter—and that the leaders of the opposition appear rather chagrined and hardly to be decided as to their mode of opposition..."

Washington told Jay that Madison and others were working on the Kentuckians. "The beginning has been as auspicious as could possibly have been expected..." he coldly calculated.[374]

George Mason spent most of his time calling for a bill of rights. Madison rose to debate him. Madison looked brilliant in a blue and buff suit, ruffles at the ends of his sleeves, his hair pulled back in a queue, powdered white. He wore a single-breasted coat, a strait collar doubled. He had put on weight and looked heavier than usual. Madison had become, over his eight years in Congress and years in the state house, a fine debater. His low voice both hurt him and helped him. Its lack of power made it difficult to hear him, but it also made the people in his audiences pay far more attention to everything he said. He was an exemplary debater, well prepared. Madison knew all of the key people in the room and how to speak to them.

He had prepped hard for these debates. Madison had read everything he had in his home on politics, written out pages and pages of notes, and prepared well for the encounter for weeks. In addition, he and others had worked together to plan an attack on the Anti-Federalists, to organize the convention, to get Governor Randolph to change his mind, and to blunt the oratorical thunder of Patrick Henry.

Madison had studied for so long, and so hard, that he confided to friend Edward Coles, later the governor of Illinois, that the work in writing out his notes for the debates, and participating in them, "almost killed him."[375]

Madison told Mason, Henry, and the others that there was no need for a bill of rights because the men elected to Congress would honor the rights of the people at all times. "Let me observe that as far as the number of representatives may seem to be inadequate to discharge their duty, they will have sufficient information from the laws of particular states, from the state legislatures, from their own experience, and from a great number of individuals; and as to our security against them, I conceive that the general limitation of their powers, and the general watchfulness of the states, will be a sufficient guard."

The convention ended for the first day with Madison's afternoon remarks. He went directly to the Swan Tavern, where he had rooms, and wrote George Washington to let him know everything that had happened. He told him he was hard at work. He wrote that "every kind of address was going on privately to work on the local interests and prejudices of that [Kentucky delegation] and other quarters." Washington then sent off as many letters as he could, every day, to Federalist friends around the country, as well as a collection of notes to Madison and others at the Virginia convention.[376]

Washington was not satisfied. He wrote that the Federalists entered the convention with, they presumed, a twenty-vote majority. He said that margin had been exceeded on the first day, but that attacks from the Anti-Federalists in the coming days would reduce it.[377]

The debates were acrimonious, fueled by opinion and personal animosity. Mason, a leader in the Revolutionary movement for twenty years, opposed the sweeping powers given the Federal government at the Philadelphia convention. He did not understand how any government could function if it could simply pass new legislation to permit its leaders to take new actions. "[Under it] Congress may grant monopolies in trade and commerce, constitute new crimes, inflict unusual and severe punishments, and extend their power as far as they shall think proper; so that the state legislatures shall have no security for the powers now presumed to remain to them, or the people for their rights."

That government was a runaway train, accountable to no one except its leaders. Mason's campaign against the clause had been picked up by dozens of Anti-Federalists throughout the lengthy autumn and winter parade of state conventions. Mason was opposed to the "general welfare" clause of the Constitution, too, arguing that it set up the possibility that Congress and the president could take away the rights of the people if they felt threatened.

George Mason was a good public speaker and had a witty and wry way with his words. As an example, in discussing his anger over Jay's proposed Spanish treaty that closed the Mississippi to navigation whenever Spain proposed to do so, he jokingly called it "a very sound argument indeed, that we should cheerfully burn ourselves to death in hopes of a joyful and happy resurrection." Now, nearly a year later, Madison wrote that Mason was outrageous in his crusade to quash the Constitution.[378]

In Virginia, Madison resurrected his arguments from *The Federalist* to win passage of the new government. He had written in *The Federalist* that men were not angels and therefore government was necessary. In Virginia, he pounded away at that same theme, adding, to refute Mason's charges that the national government would become corrupt, that "internal controls on government would be necessary" and that, in the end, the government had to control itself as much as it had to control those it governed. He amplified that even more, reminding all that in a large assembly, like the House of Representatives, the divergence of opinion would create a workable majority to run the country, not the other way around.

He had to work hard to defend Hamilton's refutation of the bill of rights as "dangerous" and Hamilton's stand that "a nation without a national government is, in my view, an awful spectacle. The establishment of a Constitution, in time of profound peace, by the voluntary consent of a whole people, is a prodigy to the completion of which I look forward to with trembling anxiety."[379]

Madison was adamant about a three-branch federal government and no bill of rights, and would never give in on his positions. He wrote, "Every one of clear comprehension understood the binding effect of the final yea or nay."[380]

Henry was the unquestioned leader of the opposition because of his oratorical prowess and, as former governor and longtime legislative leader, his fame and political skills. "Mr. Henry is the great adversary who will render the event precarious. He is, I find with his usual address, working up every possible interest into a spirit of opposition," a worried Madison wrote Jefferson that winter.

Madison realized, too, that despite his efforts and those of the local Federalists in Richmond, and within the convention hall, people's opinions would be formed by what they heard, and Henry gave people much to hear. He added, "I am told that a very bold language is held by Mr. Henry and some of his partisans."[381]

Madison should have been happy with the returns, which seemed to give the Federalists a slight edge in the vote. The Federalists had supported a popular group of candidates—judges, well-known merchants, and Revolutionary War heroes, such as William Darke.

Patrick Henry had arrived in Richmond with the plain eloquence that always surrounded him. The fifty-two-year-old former governor traveled into town in a simple carriage, dressed plainly, on the same morning that Pendleton arrived. Henry was tired from the trip, but ready for the fight.

Henry's bombast was nothing new to the delegates at the Convention. One of Patrick Henry's weaknesses, though, was that in his melodrama he often paid little attention to what he actually said, more concerned about the overall effect of his words. He was extremely repetitive, paying no notice to his prior references, and that repetitiveness became grating as he spoke—hours at a time. Madison was counting on these long-winded speeches.

Henry had a long life in Virginia politics as an assemblyman and governor and now looked a bit worn-out. He wore glasses now. The

Virginia leader had lost most of his hair and wore a wig, which he twirled on his head when he was excited about something he said. He was slightly stooped over and walked slower as the years went by. He still had his wonderful voice and a grand personal persona, though, and looked forward to speaking at the convention.[382]

His defenders idolized him. He appeared in those debates, his early biographer St. George Tucker said, as "the fine image of Virginia seated on an eminence and holding in her hand the balance in which the fate of America was weighing…the variety of arguments which Mr. Henry generally presented in his speeches, addressed to the capacities, prejudices, and individual interests of his hearers, made his speeches unequal…"[383]

St. Jean de Crevecoeur wrote that the convention was all about Patrick Henry. "All the talents of Mr. Henry made use of to break and split the union…should Henry triumph, be assured that this highly anti-federal state will refuse [the Constitution] also."[384]

Henry was not just a fine politician, but a superb actor. When confronted by the president of Hampden-Sydney College in his home county about why he decided not to attend the federal convention that wrote the Constitution and, instead, stayed home to criticize it, Henry's eyebrows raised, a twinkle formed in his eye, his lips turned into a slight smile, and he responded to the minister, "I smelt a rat!"[385]

Madison never let go of his suspicions about Henry and thought so much of his love of Virginia over country that he believed that in the furor over Jay's efforts to let Spain navigate the Mississippi, Henry would side with Spain. "Mr. Henry, who has been hitherto the champion of the federal party, has become a cold advocate and, in the event of an actual sacrifice of the Mississippi by Congress, will unquestionably go over to the other side," Madison had written to Washington a year prior to the Constitutional Convention.[386]

Madison and the Federalists began a letter-writing campaign to denounce Henry, claiming that his call for a bill of rights was a mere excuse for his determination to wreck the Constitution because he did not like the new government. Madison blasted Henry, writing Randolph at one point before the convention that "his licentiousness of animadversion, it is said, no longer spares even the moderate opponents of the Constitution."[387]

Henry talked and talked. He gave speeches on eighteen of the twenty-three days of the Convention; some lasted an hour, some three, and one reportedly ran on for seven. He was a nonstop torrent of words, a great verbal train.

Henry started off on the very first day of the Convention, rising in his full splendor. What followed would be three weeks in which he could take center stage nearly every day, the sole object of attention, speak for as long as he desired, and use every word and phrase in his verbal artillery to sink the new government. He was a one-man show, and his advocacy frightened James Madison.

Henry started right away by challenging the first words in the preamble of the Constitution, "We, the people…" Henry asked why it did not say "We, the states…" and was off on a long first-day speech.[388]

He never stopped to take a breath, his voice rising and falling, his head snapping back and forward, his hands and arms waving for effect as he continued. He asked what were the problems that brought about the end of the Confederation? One riot in Massachusetts? "Disorders have arisen in other parts of America, but here, sir, no dangers, no insurrections or tumult, has happened—every thing has been calm and tranquil. But notwithstanding this, we are wandering on the great ocean of human affairs. I see no landmark to guide us…"[389]

Then, in careful strokes, he painted a land of two Americas, one run by the states and the other run by the federal government. The federal sheriffs will come and ask the farmer for a federal tax and if they cannot procure it, he said, they will run to federal administrators, who will in turn race to federal judges, and they will ultimately collect those taxes. He railed against a president whom, he said, could easily become a king, a Congress that did little to help the people, and, everywhere, corruption. "I see great jeopardy in this new government...[The Constitution's features] are horribly frightful. Among these deformities, it has an awful squinting, it squints toward monarchy and does not this raise the indignation in the breasts of every true American?"[390]

He argued bitterly in wonderful, moving language, that Congress could simply pass new tax laws that states could not overturn and that the president and the Senate could, without consulting anyone, start wars that could last for years, take the lives of thousands of Americans, and cost millions of dollars. He said of congressmen that "they may carry on the most wicked and pernicious of schemes under the dark veil of secrecy."[391]

Madison was waiting for that attack and told Henry then, as he told others, that the secret to good democratic government was that its ability to control the people gave it the strength to succeed in its own halls.[392] He reminded all, too, that under the Articles the powers of the states had been separate from those of the federal government and that was true under the Constitution; they did not have to fear federal trampling.[393]

And what was the purpose of government? It was to ensure the happiness of the people, not the government. "The war is between government and licentiousness, faction, turbulence, and other violations of the role of society to preserve liberty. Where is the cause of alarm?" he asked. He believed, too, that the Constitution should not be continually criticized, but revered. "Public opinion of the United States should be enlightened; that it should attach itself to their governments as delineated in the great charters, derived not from the usurped power of kings, but from the legitimate authority of the people, and that it should guarantee, with a holy zeal, these political scriptures from every attempt to add to or to diminish from them."[394]

Henry was back again the second day at full throttle, arguing that criticism of the Constitution was not disgraceful, but patriotic. He defended the current government. He said, "The Confederation… carried us through a long and dangerous war: it rendered us victorious in that bloody conflict with a powerful nation: it has secured us a territory greater than any European Monarch possesses: and shall a government which has been this strong and vigorous be accused of imbecility and abandoned for want of energy?"

It wasn't just his words that made Henry such a great speaker; it was every one of the dozens of little mannerisms of his hands, arms, head, eyes, and body posture—the way he inflected his voice and raised his eyebrows. Madison told a friend later that whenever he rose to rebut Henry, the former governor would pause in his words, or shake his head, or strike a gesture before uttering a word, and, in that single second, wipe out everything Madison had said in an hour.[395]

Henry insisted, "The first thing I have at heart is American liberty and the second thing is American Union."[396]

Henry had oratorical gifts that were beyond the grasp of most men. The speaking prowess of the most important public officials in the country—governors, congressmen, and generals—paled in comparison to his flourishing style. Edmund Randolph, who listened to him often, claimed that it was an indefinable crudeness that made Henry so powerful when speaking to a crowd, a style though, that appealed to large crowds.

Henry always managed to be standing alone, arms waving, fingers pointing, eyes fixed directly on those he addressed, oblivious to applause or support as he drove on with his argument. William Wirt, later the attorney general of the United States and a noted speaker himself, called Henry's style "true eloquence." He had "a mixture of sensations which a dramatic versatility of action and of countenance produced" and spoke in torrents of words interrupted by long pauses that heightened the crowd's yearning for yet more torrents. He laced his speeches with references to people and places, filled his stories with anecdotes from scriptures and moved from subject to subject easily, his passions rising as he did, and rarely referred to notes. He combined the strengths of a polished public speaker with those of an excited revival preacher and the result was mesmerizing, even to crowds that had listened to him for an hour or more—and remained excited about whatever he said. "His lightning consisted in quick successive flashes which rested only to alarm the more," Wirt said.[397]

Henry insisted, day after day, that experience showed the new federal system would not work and that a national government could not protect the people.[398]

All of the Federalists feared Henry and his soaring speeches. St. Jean de Crevecocur called Henry "nefarious and highly criminal."[399] St. George Tucker, a friend and professor at William and Mary who was there, admitted that Henry had no focus as he leapt from topic to topic. "If he soared at times like the eagle, and seemed, like the bird of Jove, to be armed with his thunder, he did not disdain to stoop like the hawk to seize his prey but the instant he had done it, rose in pursuit of another quarry."[400]

The Anti-Federalists loved him. Judge Edmund Wilson wrote of Henry that "while he was speaking, there was a perfect stillness throughout the House, and in the galleries. There was no inattention or appearance of weariness. When any other member spoke, the members and the audience would in half an hour be going out or moving from their seats."[401] Another man added that "whenever he rose, a deathlike silence prevailed, and the eager listeners did not fail to catch every syllable he uttered."[402]

On day two of the convention, Henry was on his feet and at full speed, speaking for more than an hour and shaking the roof of the New Academy with his brashness and bellow. Madison waited until he had concluded, listened to the loud and long applause, and then rose. People did not expect oratorical pyrotechnics from James Madison and they received none. They sat back and listened to a low-keyed but highly effective defense of the Constitution. Madison, notes with him, answered the charges. Most were impressed by what he said and the way that he said it. Madison was content to let Henry roar. He would make his case like a fine lawyer, point by point, argument by argument, building up his speech with irrefutable facts and details. He was considered "the main pillar" of the Federalists in the Virginia Convention and was so knowledgeable about the new government that other Federalists had asked him to brief them on the Constitution so they could know what arguments to use when debating it themselves.[403]

Unlike the blustery Henry, Madison began speaking so quietly that a reporter who took shorthand notes on the entire convention for publication wrote that many could not hear his first sentences, stood, and walked closer to him. After a few moments, his voice rose and he proceeded to explain why he was supporting the Constitution and then went on, point by point, always speaking in a low voice, to reject Henry's attacks on the document and the proposed new government.

He told the crowd that the new government was neither a federal or confederate institution, but a hybrid of each. He added that "it is unprecedented…we cannot find one express example in the experience of the world. It stands by itself…"

"We ought sir," he said, looking at Henry, "examine the Constitution on its own merits solely; we are to enquire whether it will promote the public happiness…in this pursuit, we ought not to address our arguments to the feelings and passions, but to those understandings and judgments which were selected by the people of this country, to decide this great question by a calm and rational investigation…"

He then began a succession of answers to Henry's objections. Henry had insisted that the United States had a good government under the Confederation. If so, asked Madison, why was a federal convention held, with every state except Rhode Island present, to form a new one?

Next, he turned Henry's call for a bill of rights upside down. He asked how, if Henry thought ratification by three-quarters of the states was too many, could he propose a bill of rights approved by just a majority of voters? Madison made a long and solid argument in favor of the need for a strong federal government, reminding Henry and the others that for years a single state, Rhode Island, had clogged the progress of the national government, which required unanimity from all thirteen states for the passage of any legislation. "It has obstructed every attempt to reform the government…has repeatedly disobeyed and counteracted the general authority," Madison said. "Would [Henry] agree to continue the most radical defects in the old system because the petty state of Rhode Island would not agree to remove them?"

Hamilton, too, had excoriated the democratic ideas of Rhode Island. "What is her legislature but the picture of a mob?" Even the Antis agreed with him. New York's Melancton Smith scoffed at Rhode Island. "If there were in the world but one example of political depravity, it would be [Rhode Island]."[404]

One Rhode Islander, acknowledging the low esteem the nation held his state, wrote sarcastically in the *Lansingburgh Northern Centinel,* "It is with pleasure I inform you, that all honest men in Rhode Island (who, alas, are not very numerous) are anxious for the adoption of the new constitution…"[405]

Madison then turned his defense to the national militia, which would be called up to fight wars against foreign powers or put down civil insurrections. "Without a general power...to repel invasions, the country might be overrun and conquered by foreign enemies...our liberties might be destroyed by domestic faction and domestic tyranny be established," he said.

He noted that the United States had been so weak during the Revolution that the only way victory had been achieved was through an alliance with France. Could the country go on, with no standing army, relying on different European powers and, in return, give away money and land for that help?

Madison tore apart Henry's praise of the Confederation government run by the Swiss for years as a fine example for the United States. Here, Madison's years of research made his defense of the Constitution and new government invaluable. He simply knew everything and could, without hesitation, refute any argument. He called the Swiss "one of the vilest aristocracies that ever was instituted" and gave very little power to the people.

He angrily denounced Henry's strong contention that the new government would take away all power from the states and the people. "Powers are not given to any set of men, they are in the hands of the people; delegated to their representatives chosen for short terms, representatives responsible to the people and whose situation is perfectly similar to our own; as long as this is the case we have no danger to apprehend," he said, adding that the Constitution enumerated federal powers and left all other powers to the states.

He disagreed with Henry's general criticism of federal taxes and his wails that the federal taxman would be chasing each citizen. Madison slowly and carefully pointed out that federal taxes would only be charged when the country was in a crisis, such as a war, and needed the money. All nations operated on that same basis for national taxes, he said, and the tax ended when the crisis ended. "How is it possible a war could be supported without money or credit? And would it be possible for the government to have credit without having the power of raising money? No, it would be impossible for any government to defend itself," he said, and added that to have thirteen state militias team up to make a national army, with volunteer generals, was not workable.

Exhausted from his work, Madison fell ill that night and remained in bed for the next two, crucial days. When it was time, the next day, for him to once again answer Henry, people realized he was not there.

Chairman Edmund Pendleton rose slowly, laying his wooden crutches aside. It was a dramatic moment. The idea of the aging Pendleton defending the Constitution in Madison's place, of standing and not sitting, unaided by his crutches, and giving a rousing good speech to blunt Henry and Mason, was moving. He defended the Constitution and particularly its opening line of "We, the people..." that had offended Henry, who preferred "We, the States..."

Pendleton refuted all of Henry's major attacks. He dismissed the call for a bill of rights, reminding Henry and his friends that Britain's Magna Carta had no "bill of rights" but had served that nation well for nearly six hundred years because it was "the foundation" of British liberty, with laws and amendments added over the years. America could do the same. And, he argued, a bill of rights written now would limit any rights that could be added later.

He attacked Henry's insinuation that Virginia could survive as an independent nation or in league with a southern confederacy, arguing that their single state could not fight a war by itself and would suffer, as an independent entity, in an economic depression.[406]

Madison had been quite ill, "laid up with a bilious attack," as he told all, and unable to read or write.[407] He did not leave his room for forty-eight hours, eating and drinking little and making every effort to rest. He was back, reduced in spirit but eager for the debates, on June

7 to hear Mason. His enemy Mason rambled in his discussions yet again, with little genuine emotion, influencing few. "If Col. Mason is really the great man I expected, his cause must be bad indeed, or my senses gone…" wrote a surprised Alexander White, a war veteran, at the convention.[408]

Brissot de Warville, a French reformer in Richmond for the convention as a spectator, wrote that Madison was too ill to return to the debates. "He had, when I saw him, an air of fatigue; perhaps it was the effect of the immense labors to which he has devoted himself for some time past. His look announces a censor, his conversation discovers the man of learning, and his reserve was that of a man conscious of his talents and of his duties."[409]

Mason offered an amendment to end the slave trade because, he insisted, the new federal government would pass laws to tax the southerners on their slaves, forcing their emancipation. An excited Henry jumped to his feet, eyes wide, pointed at his friend, and chortled, "They'll free your niggers!"[410]

The southerners had a great and growing fear that the northerners would eliminate slavery somehow, now or in the near future. Federalist George Nicholas rose to refute their concerns, explaining that the growth in the United States was in the South and Southwest, slave areas, and that all the new states and new people in those areas would protect slavery.

On June 9, Henry's arguments no longer seemed rational. In a long-winded, bellicose speech that became more heated as he continued, he called George Washington a dictator during the Revolution, angering many. He said that Congress would tax Virginians to death, that the Federal army would build forts everywhere, subjugating America for the president. He made numerous broad accusations against the proposed government. He went over his charges again and again. He reminded all that civil war would come if the new government was approved. Repetition followed repetition.

Henry did not mind continually repeating himself. He told the assembly on June 12 that "important truths lose nothing of their validity or weight by frequency of repetition."[411]

Henry was weary, too. He was tired of being pummeled by numerous Federalists on charges that as governor he permitted an innocent man to be hanged without a trial, a charge that was not true.[412] In fact, Henry rarely answered any of the personal attacks upon him made by the overly zealous Federalists, but he suffered from them.[413]

Throughout Richmond at the end of that first week, there was a buzz, pro and con, about the debates inside the New Academy. "Each side pretends to count a majority in their own favor," wrote Robert Morris, in Richmond during the state convention, unable to determine which side was ahead.[414]

Madison, who counted heads every day, saw the race for ratification as a dead heat. "We make but slow progress, the parties are pretty nicely balanced," he wrote one man, adding that the hot weather and the upcoming legislative session might mean an adjournment that he thought would kill the Constitution. He wrote Washington that "it is probable the majority on either side will not exceed 3, 4, 5, or 6."[415]

A few days later, an even glummer Madison wrote Rufus King that the vote would be close and that, in the end, the decision would be made by the delegates from the western counties, who all seemed against any new government. "The vote of Kentucky will turn the scale," he said. "The majority of either side will be small." Madison reiterated that feeling to Hamilton and Washington, writing Hamilton that "if we lose it, Kentucky will be the cause" and Washington that "the business is in the most ticklish state that can be imagined." The Kentuckians, who lived on the far side of Virginia, with the Ohio and Mississippi rivers on their borders, were terrified that a foreign power would shut down the Mississippi to their commerce.[416]

Gouverneur Morris, in Richmond for the debates, was just as downhearted on June 13. He wrote Hamilton that "matters are not going so well in this state as the friends of America could wish…"[417]

Peter Singleton, too, writing from Kempsville, Virginia, on June 10, saw a dead heat on the Constitutional vote. A week later, the vote seemed so close that Madison wrote his father that he thought the Federalists would win, but if they did, it would only be by a handful of ballots.[418]

The national sense of the importance of the debates grew throughout Richmond. Each day, every seat in the gallery was filled, very early, as long lines of people formed to be admitted. Those not seated stood outside and discussed the debates. There were so many people in and around the New Academy that delegates had difficulty making their way through the crowds.[419]

Anger ran so high that on June 12, Virginian Tom Macon was shot in the head and nearly killed in a duel with fellow tobacco planter William Fontaine following an argument over the state convention and the Constitution. On hearing the news, Patrick Henry, who knew the men, gasped to his daughter, "Poor Tom Macon has a ball lodged in his head in a duel with Wm. Fontaine…"[420]

Henry's men were making headway. Senator William Grayson assured Antis around the country that they had eighty votes out of the required majority of eighty-five and that eight persons were still undecided. He wrote that "we have got 10 out of 13 Kentucky members, but we wanted the whole…this is an important point and which both sides are contending for by every means in their power."[421]

Henry continued to scorn the Federalists and said they would end the Virginia judiciary, which he much admired. He finished with a few more oratorical flurries, with more logical, detailed, planned answers from Madison.

Henry made powerful arguments, but each time he did so, Madison stood and ably answered him. Madison was constantly on his feet, arguing back and forth with others. Altogether, he spoke 161 times in the Convention, 25 percent more than Mason and more than twice as often as the third busiest speaker, Governor Randolph. Young delegate John Marshall, a hero of the Revolution, who would one day become chief justice of the Supreme Court, refuted Henry, too.[422]

Madison took the floor on June 11 to argue against the charges of Henry that the new federal government, because of its size, would soon become hopelessly corrupt. History showed that was not true, Madison said, and pointed to England. "Who are the most corrupt members of Parliament? Are they not the inhabitants of small towns and districts? Have we not seen that the representatives of the city of London, who are chosen by such thousands of voters, have continually studied and supported the liberties of the people and opposed the corruption of the crown?"

He again turned Henry's argument against the strong federal government upside down. Madison said, "The people will be attached to their state legislatures from a thousand causes; and into whatever scale the people at large will throw themselves, that scale will preponderate."[423]

Henry rose and continued to bluster. His repetitions continued and his acolytes grimaced when he launched into yet another attack on the Constitution. He was, as Madison had secretly hoped, losing more ground each time he spoke. He was giving the assembly too much verbal brilliance. How much oratorical thunder could anyone tolerate? "The purse is gone. The sword is gone, and now the last barrier, the judiciary, is about to fall. Old as I am, I may yet have the appellation of rebel, for as this government stands, I despise and abhor it!" Patrick Henry roared.

Federalists leapt to their feet to denounce Henry. Adam Stephens, a war veteran, got the nod from George Wythe. "If the gentleman does not like his government, then let him go and live among the Indians!" said Stephens, to the cheers of many.[424]

Henry then called for a vote to include the bill of rights in the Virginia Constitutional approval. He argued that a Constitution without a bill of rights was not a constitution at all.

Day after day, in the hot New Academy hall, James Madison had defended the Constitution he had written against all attacks. He was convinced it was a good system and that despite its radical structure and unprecedented goals, was the best form of government men had yet devised. He had done a far better job than Patrick Henry in advancing his form of government. "Mr. Henry's declamatory powers" were "vastly overpowered by the deep reasoning of our glorious little Madison," wrote a man from Richmond.[425] Another Madison defender wrote a poem:

> *Madison among the rest,*
> *Pouring from his narrow chest,*
> *More than Greek or Roman sense,*
> *Boundless tides of eloquence.*

Madison let Henry plunge on, hour after hour, day after day, until even his own supporters tired of him. He had permitted Henry and his friends to set up an either/or scenario for the future of the United States—disunion and civil war or a federal government not to be trusted. All right, Madison suggested, who then, would really vote for disunion and civil war?[426]

He was generally admired by both sides for his knowledge and his work, but what members of either side did not realize was that he was quite sick with a fever throughout the entire convention. His two-day absence had weakened him considerably. He knew that if he left the defense of the new government to others, and stayed in bed in his room, to get better, he would risk having the Virginia Convention vote down the new government. He had to go back to the Convention, day after day, and work hard despite his illness. He wrote George Washington toward the end of the convention, "I find myself not yet restored and extremely feeble."[427]

On June 23, at the end of three turbulent weeks of debates and arguments, Henry's proposal that his bill of rights be added to the ratification package was scheduled for a vote. Henry was at full throttle that day, when he began to talk in the morning, his language heated and his temper even hotter as the summer day continued. He was at his full bombastic heights, delivering perhaps the best speech of his life, an oration that might have won over many Federalists to his cause and defeated the Constitution easily.

Then, suddenly, from out of nowhere, just before 2:00 p.m., a horrific thunderstorm hit Richmond. Booming thunder tore through the skies above the town and rain poured down from the heavens, flooding the streets. Fierce winds banged open windows with a fury. After several moments of the pounding rain and thunder, dozens of bolts of lightning struck the city. Huge balls of hail accompanied the flashing, frenzied lightning, slamming into the roofs and sides of buildings, frightening all. One bolt of lightning hit the building next door to the New Academy, setting it on fire. At the same time that the fire raged next to it, threatening to engulf it, too, the New Academy was pounded by hail and rain. The hall full of concerned delegates seemed under attack by heaven itself. Dozens ran to the windows to watch the storm and all were fretful when the structure next door began to burn.

Henry, at full throttle in his speech, his verbal thunder inside matched by the real thunder outside, did not know what to do. The wily Pendleton, the chairman, did. He stood up, clung to his chair amid the wild fury of the storm, and ordered the convention recessed for the day. He urged delegates to leave the building as speedily as possible and retreat to their lodgings and seek safety. They did so immediately.

Richmond was quiet and peaceful the following morning, after the storm blew out of Henrico County and headed east. So was Patrick Henry. Overnight, he had lost most of his oratorical fervor. He finished his speech in the morning with tepid language and little emotion, his energy drained by the storm. The delegates remembered little of what he said the day before and the moment was lost. It might have been the moment that Henry could have gathered enough votes to defeat the Constitution, and now it was gone.[428]

"Is this government necessary for the safety of Virginia?" Governor Randolph asked out loud in one of his final speeches that day. It was. He reminded them that the state was under constant attack by Indians, sought mostly foreign markets for its tobaccos, and daily saw hundreds of newly arrived immigrants seeking jobs and housing. "In case of [a military] attack, what defense can we make? Our export trade is entirely in the hands of foreigners. I believe that, as surely as there is a God in heaven, our safety, our political happiness, and existence depend on the union of the states…" he said. Now, after all of the conventions had left the federal union up to Virginia, he told the audience that it was "a single question of union or no union…When I see safety on my right and destruction on my left…I cannot hesitate to decide in favor of the former."[429]

Mason did not agree. He continued to insist on the inclusion of a bill of rights and protested that the new president of the United States would be a worse monarch than King George III ever was. Mason argued that the president could be elected every four years and serve a lifetime in office. As such, he could become a puppet of a foreign power or a tyrannical head of America. He scoffed when delegates said

Washington would be the first president and he could be trusted.[430] What about future presidents?[431]

Madison benefited from several peculiar turns in the convention, especially the seeming inability of Henry, Mason, and company to unite. The Federalists had been firm in their good points since the previous September, but the Anti-Federalists always seemed to make up their objections as they went along, during the conventions in each state. Henry, Mason, and friends were doing the same. They did not have a list of printed objections, did not promise a ready set of amendments, objected to the Constitution only on general terms, and were not led by men other than the constantly lecturing Henry. In Richmond, the Federalists had Madison and a half-dozen other leaders who held the party line on the Constitution from the first day of the Virginia convention to the last. And in New York, they had the rest of the Triumvirate.

Madison and the Federalists also benefited from a secret. New York Governor George Clinton had mailed Randolph a letter, which he received in the middle of May, stating that New York's Convention would call upon Virginia to agree to hold a second, general federal convention to start the ratification process all over again. Randolph showed it to his Council of State. They advised him to send copies to the members of the General Assembly, due to arrive at the end of June, and members of the ratification convention. Knowing how explosive the letter could be, Randolph simply put it away and did not show it to anyone until after the ratification convention ended. What would the convention delegates have done if he had read them the letter? They might have adjourned. They might have waited before voting to see what New York would do. They might have voted for a second convention. Randolph did not want them to consider any of those choices and put the letter in a desk drawer—and left it there.[432]

At the very end of the Convention, two delegates from Kentucky announced that they were switching allegiances from Anti- to pro-Federal cause. Still, the other twelve Kentucky votes remained a mystery. As late as June 22, Madison fretted about the vote. He counted heads every day but could not make any predictions.[433] He had a premonition on June 24, though, when the delegates voted down inclusion of the bill of rights, 88–80. It was a sign that perhaps the pro-government forces would win, after all.

In the end, Madison stood firm against a bill of rights as part of the Virginia vote on the Constitution, but very publicly told Henry and Mason that he would do all that he could to make certain that a bill of rights was passed as soon as the new federal government took office. "We shall freely, fairly, and dispassionately consider and investigate your propositions, and endeavour to gratify your wishes," he said.[434]

The lengthy debate over the bill of rights throughout the country, and the continual objections to an overly strong federal government by so many people in the large states, had finally convinced Madison that some sort of collection of amendments to the Constitution was necessary. "A bill of rights will be a good ground for an appeal to the sense of the community [in a crisis]" he wrote.[435]

The shrewd Madison also supported the eventual passage of amendments to ensure Virginia's approval of the Constitution, writing Rufus King that "the opponents will bring forward a bill of rights with sundry other amendments as conditions of ratification and in case of disappointment will probably aim at an adjournment. Some apprehend a secession…[We could pass] a recommendation of a few amendments to be pursued in the constitutional mode. This expedient is necessary to conciliate some individuals."[436]

Nevertheless, Madison saw an extremely close vote and, right to the end, predicted that Kentucky's fourteen delegates would determine whether or not the Constitution would pass. Randolph made the same prediction to friends he wrote or spoke to in Richmond.[437]

As the delegates prepared to vote in Richmond, they did not know that New Hampshire ratified on June 25, the same day they voted. News of that event filtered down the East Coast slowly. French diplomats in New York knew and townspeople throughout Connecticut and Massachusetts knew, and rang church bells upon the news because New Hampshire's approval meant that the needed nine states had ratified. The delegates in Virginia, nearly four hundred miles further south of New York, were unaware and cast their votes, they believed, as the ninth and deciding state.[438]

Across the country, people worried over what would happen in Virginia. The arguments over the Constitution and the new government had engaged America for nine long months. They had been resolved in all of the eight states that had held conventions so far, with just one more state apparently needed. There would be lengthy celebrations if Virginia approved the Constitution, but what would happen if the delegates there rejected it, as they might, despite approval in New Hampshire, that was unknown in Virginia? Could the new United States really be formed without Virginia?

No one worried about that prospect more than George Washington. At Mount Vernon, just days before the vote, he wrote his trusted friend the Marquis de Lafayette that God had a vote in Richmond, too. "I do not believe that Providence has done so much for nothing. It has always been my creed that we should not be left as an awful monument to prove 'that mankind, under the most favourable circumstances for civil liberty and happiness, are unequal to the task of governing themselves'..."[439]

Madison's final defense of the Constitution and the proposed government was short but brilliant. He did not become entangled in all of his voluminous notes and arguments, but made a simple and compelling case. He started by reminding people that the United States had become the wonder of the earth. "Nothing has excited more admiration in the world than the manner in which free governments have been established in America," he said. "For it was the first instance from the creation of the world to the American revolution, that free inhabitants have been seen deliberating on a form of government, and selecting such of their citizens as possessed their confidence, to determine upon and give effect to it."

Then, he asked why "this has excited so much wonder and applause?"

He answered: (1) How could Virginia turn down a government that had been approved by eight other states and probably would be approved of by four more? (2) Virginia could not stand alone as its own country or team up with one or two other states as a confederation and (3) The Constitution, in its three branches of government, provided for a good government and, importantly, a government that assumed some powers but left all others to the states.

On the final day of the convention, June 25, the highly respected Wythe was asked to step down from the Committee of the Whole chairman's desk by Madison to read the draft of the final, pro-Constitution resolution. He was supposed to get the delegates to approve the Constitution with his speech. The Federalists were nervous because Wythe was not a polished public speaker. Wythe had served Virginia in many capacities, as a delegate to the Continental Congress, a delegate to the state legislature, and a judge, but in political debates he often bored listeners with interminable stories of European history and readings from Greek and Latin scholars.

But that day George Wythe was as forceful and persuasive as any of the delegates. He stood in the well of the New Academy, read the resolution, and then told the assemblage in as plain language as he could find that the American Revolution was necessary to free the country from an oppressive monarch and Parliament in England. Now, a strong federal government was needed, within the framework of the Constitution, to guide the brand-new country through the problems it was sure to encounter.

He spoke in a quiet voice, so low that some of the delegates could not hear everything he said. He explained carefully that the Constitution was certainly not a perfect document and that, as many in the hall had argued, loudly, it had numerous flaws. However, he insisted, the chaos of the last five years was proof that a new and different government was needed. The beauty of the document, he said, was that the Constitution would have amendments added from time to time to make it even better. It would change as the government changed and the people changed. It would be pointless to vote it down now and never give the Constitution, and American democracy, the change to flourish.[440]

His short, impressive, and well-reasoned speech was greeted with applause. He had presented the Federalists case with great strength, and yet in a simple way, and seemed to have appeased some of the borderline Anti-Federalists. "It may well be that Wythe's adherence to the Constitution may have given the margin necessary for ratification," Edmund Pendleton told friends.[441]

When the leaders of both sides had finished their summary speeches, Wythe called the votes slowly in the chamber and a clerk added them up. The vote was close from start to finish, but in the end the Federalists earned a slender victory, 89–79; twelve of the fourteen Kentuckians voted against it. There was a sustained eruption of joy from the Federalist delegates and their supporters in the gallery in the New Academy. They believed Virginia had become the ninth and final state to pass the Constitution and created the brand-new federal government, the great new experiment in the world.

When the final vote ended, Patrick Henry, the great loser in the convention, remained optimistic. The passage of the Constitution did not upset him and neither did the attacks on his beliefs and character throughout the grueling three-week ordeal. The sterling orator shook hands with all the delegates he could reach on both sides and pledged his support to the new government. He was a professional politician and would work with this national government as he had worked with the British Crown, the colonial legislature, and the government under the Articles of Confederation.

Nine Anti-Federalists, including Henry and Mason, joined eleven Federalists two days later, on June 27, to write suggested amendments to protect individual rights. George Wythe was one of the leaders. He simply recreated the rights guaranteed under the 1776 Declaration of Rights in Virginia and added three more protected rights. The committee quickly adopted the suggestions.[442]

Mason was still angry, and unable to let the defeat pass as easily as Henry and most of the remaining delegates. He called for a meeting of the Anti-Federalists and wrote a manifesto for them to sign to show their disdain for the outcome of the convention. The Anti-Federalists had finished their fight, though. They had no desire for yet another round. They talked Mason into withdrawing the manifesto and went back to their rooms to pack their bags and return home.

Mason was still bitter. There was a Constitution now in Virginia, but no protection for the people.[443] A weary Madison understood Mason's feelings. He wrote, "Some of the leaders [of the opposition], as might be imagined, have a keen feeling of their disappointment."[444]

There was jubilation throughout Virginia at the news of the passage of the Constitution. George Washington, who had worked so long and so hard behind the scenes with the Triumvirate, was ecstatic. He abandoned his usually reserved style of writing in telling Benjamin Lincoln, in Massachusetts, how happy he was. "No one can rejoice more than I do at every step taken by the people of this great country to preserve the Union—establish good order and government—and to render the nation happy at home and respected abroad. No country upon earth ever had it more in its power to attain these blessings than United America. Wondrously strange then, and much to be regretted indeed would it be, were we to neglect the means, and to stray from the road to which the finger of Providence has so manifestly pointed... By folly and misconduct (proceeding from a variety of causes) we may now and then get bewildered, but I hope, and trust, that there is good sense and virtue enough left to bring us back into the right way before we shall be entirely lost."[445]

By the morning of June 28, the Virginia Convention was over. Everyone except James Madison was headed home to recuperate from the strenuous three-week ordeal in Richmond. Madison's work was not yet done, however. He was in a carriage headed toward New York City, where he would rejoin Congress and do what he could to help Hamilton and Jay, in Poughkeepsie at the dismal New York Convention, turn around the overwhelming Anti-Federalist delegate majority there of nearly 70 percent. He had written a letter describing the passage of the Constitution and sent it off to New York by courier rider as soon as the vote had been carried in Virginia. The rider was probably in Poughkeepsie already with the dramatic news as Madison's carriage raced northward.

It did not matter that ten states had now ratified; there could be no United States without New York. The Constitution had to pass in the sleepy, little Hudson river port hamlet of Poughkeepsie.

# NEW YORK: THE FINAL ROUND IN THE TINY VILLAGE OF POUGHKEEPSIE

The presses attack and defend the [Constitution] with spirit; whether it will be adopted or not must rest with the conventions: I wish to see some government, for I declare I am sick of anarchy...

—Ebenezer Hazard, Postmaster General of the United States

New York in 1788 was one of the most unusual states in America. It was huge, over 29 million acres, yet, with its 340,120 residents it was only fifth in population, behind Virginia, Pennsylvania, North Carolina, and Massachusetts. Almost all of the people lived in New York City or in small towns along the banks of the Hudson River just north of it; just twenty thousand lived on the vast western frontier lands. The unbalanced population was caused by New York's longstanding and controversial upstate manor lord system, under which a small number of wealthy men were given gigantic land grants by the king. They leased their land to others with high rents; few moved there.

Geographically, New York was two separate regions. The city of New York was the most densely populated in the country, with 33,131 people living on what is today the lower quarter of Manhattan Island (Philadelphia, with 28,522, was second, Boston third). The counties around it, which make up the boroughs of New York City today, were reasonably populated, as were Long Island, Westchester, and Dutchess counties. Along the Hudson River were numerous villages and the city of Albany, with 10,000 residents. Montgomery County, which covered the entire western half of the large state, had few residents.[446] The New York City area residents were the richest in the state and paid more than 60 percent of the state's various personal income and business taxes.[447]

There was considerable resentment between New York City residents and their neighbors upstate, whom some New Yorkers derisively referred to as "a set of ignorant Dutchmen." The two areas were wholly unlike each other and their differences had grown since the Revolution.[448]

The state had been immensely patriotic during the Revolution, when it suffered deprivations at the hands of the British. New York City was occupied by the British army for seven years of the war, as were other New York towns. Prior to its defeat at Saratoga, Burgoyne's army occupied and marched through upstate New York. The British navy shelled several communities on the banks of the Hudson. New Yorkers, under war governor George Clinton, never lost faith in the Revolution, though, prompting George Washington to admire its people and to tell the governor that New York "considering the situation, has done everything that could be expected of it."[449]

Yet New York had its problems with the Confederation government after the war. It never paid all of the taxes it owed and constantly criticized Congress, which sat in New York City, for permitting Vermont, then part of New York, to consider forming its own state.

New Yorkers raged for years that Congress did not order British troops out of the five forts it ceded to the United States at the end of the war. In 1783, Congress needed money and leveled a national tax on all the states. Each agreed to pay it except New York, which voted it down in 1786, at the height of a national depression. Since under the laws of the Confederation all national tax laws had to be passed by each state, the tax bill collapsed when New York rejected it, sending the nation deeper into its financial crisis. The state was torn apart by different factions, geographic, economic, and political. The city areas had all the money and power, but the rural areas had as much clout in the state legislature.[450]

After the defeat of the national tax, one newspaper writer said that "thanks to New York, none will have the hardiness to deny that the federal government trembles to its basis and threatens ruin by its fall."[451]

The disputes became so incendiary that in 1784 New York threatened to secede from the United States and become its own country.

And then there was the state's enormously popular governor, Clinton. The multitalented Clinton was a middle-class farmer from upstate's Ulster County. He was a giant of a man for the time, over 6 feet tall, with rugged good looks and a simple, charming style. In 1777, when he was thirty seven years old, he stunned New Yorkers by defeating the powerful and wealthy Philip Schuyler for governor in the first election under the new state constitution. An irritated Schuyler said that Clinton's background did not entitle him to be governor, but in letters to friends and to Clinton himself he lauded him for his skills. Clinton was "virtuous and loves his country, has abilities and is brave," Schuyler wrote John Jay. He told Clinton himself that he would do all he could to help his administration. "Your virtue and love of my country and that friendship which I have always and with great truth professed, are also many inducements to [success]."[452]

Clinton was not a glib public speaker or an intellectual, and he disdained campaigning. Though not a good politician, he managed to get elected governor in the beginning of the war and was reelected every three years in the twelve years since his first inauguration. He was one of the most popular figures in early American political history.

His success was due to patriotism, military heroism, and a simple desire to help New Yorkers live as well as they could in the turbulent times during and after the Revolution. Hamilton, who feuded with Clinton, hated him and wrote that "his passions are much warmer than his judgment is enlightened." Even his friendly biographers admitted that he was not terribly smart, did not speak well in public, and did not even learn to read and write until he was an adult.

How did he maintain his power and popularity? He had been in the assembly since 1760, elected at age twenty. He had been the minority leader at age twenty-eight and sent by the assembly as a delegate to the Continental Congress in 1775. When the war began, he left his farm and joined the army, quickly becoming a general, and served two years before his election as governor. He ardently supported independence, became friendly with General Washington, and did all he could to supply the army with troops, supplies, and state funds. He was, as one man wrote, "plain, but dignified, his conversation easy, shrewd, sensible, and commonly about matters of fact" and a man who loved his state and its people and would do anything to help them.[453]

But there was also, beneath all of that, a clever man who knew how to get what he wanted. A surprised Schuyler, when he lost the first governor's election to him, cannily wrote that Clinton "has played his cards better than expected."[454]

George Clinton was so popular that after the war, when most states cut the governor's power, New York increased his. Legislatures elected most governors during the war and in the postwar years, but New York entrusted that to the people. One historian wrote that

Clinton was "the idol of the common folk, of the little Whig farmer and mechanic" but he was admired by the wealthy, too. "New York follows, of course," his leadership, wrote one man.[455]

Clinton left the introduction and passage of bills to his legislature, permitted counties and villages to run themselves with little state interference, and did not meddle with the state courts. He was anxious to spend his time just administering New York.

He was a pleasant man. Abigail Adams Smith wrote her mother of Governor Clinton, "We are treated here with great politeness, civility, and friendship."[456]

There were factions in New York going back to the tenant riots in the 1760s, when thousands who rented lands from the wealthy protested what they saw as an unfair leasing system. The farmers and the city dwellers in New York had always been at odds; the workers and those in the large shipping industry had their differences. Federalists and Anti-Federalists aligned against each other in the battle over the Constitution was just the latest skirmish. As in most states, the rich and powerful were Federalists and the middle-class farmers and laborers who feared a powerful federal government run by the wealthy were the Anti-Federalists.[457]

In all of the states, local issues had joined the national issues in the debates over the Constitution, and in New York it was the three-year fight over the national tax. It came to symbolize the reluctance of the state to cede its power and money to a national government.

That reluctance was highlighted, vividly, at the Philadelphia Constitutional Convention, where two of the three New York delegates, Robert Yates and John Lansing, six-term State Assembly members, quit and returned home in a huff, leaving Hamilton alone. Both left, they said, because the Constitution usurped the liberties of the people. That lack of interest was shown again a few months later when New York voted to hold its Constitutional ratification convention. The motion carried by just three votes in the Senate and only two in the Assembly.[458]

New Yorkers, particularly the upstate farmers, were in no hurry for a new American government. In fact, during the Revolution, many people in the state said they feared an overly nationalistic United States government as much as they feared England, which was at war with them.[459]

Most of the newspaper editors in New York, like those in the other states, agreed that the old Confederation government had to go and a new one had to be designed to replace it, but what kind of new government? "The American language has been worn thread-bare upon this subject, the most nervous and emphatical expressions that its genius will afford, having been repeatedly culled by writers from one extremity of the United States to the other, to demonstrate the absolute necessity of federal power," wrote a man in the *New York Journal* on December 14, 1786, long before the New York convention.[460]

Everybody in New York realized the importance of the new Constitution that the state convention would consider, no matter what its final form. One man wrote that "it will be a revolution in government, accomplished by reasoning and deliberation, an event that has never occurred since the formation of society and which will be strongly characteristic of the philosophic and tolerant spirit of the age." Another said that "the eyes of friends and enemies, of all Europe, nay more, of the whole world are upon the United States."[461]

That work began in tumult while the Philadelphia Convention was still going on when Hamilton heard that Governor Clinton opposed the Constitution. Instead of talking to him about it when he saw him, writing him or, better yet, saying nothing at all until the ratification convention in New York, the short-tempered Hamilton fired off a nasty letter to newspapers, unsigned, that blasted Clinton.[462]

Hamilton's actions did not surprise anyone. Many saw him as arrogant. William Pierce of Georgia, who met him at the Philadelphia Convention, wrote that "his manners are tinctured with stiffness and sometimes with a degree of vanity that is highly disagreeable."[463]

Hamilton alarmed all at the Philadelphia Convention when he called for a far more powerful national government than the delegates had designed, one in which the president would appoint all state governors and in which the United States would have a standing national army and the states were forbidden to have any militia. He indicated, too, that he thought the United States might even be better off with a monarchy. Of course, this was not surprising, his critics ranted, given his elitist view of the world. Hamilton had written that "the perpetual charges which have been rung upon the wealthy, the well-born, and the great have been such as to inspire the disgust of all sensible men."[464]

Hamilton wrote in his notorious July 21, 1787, newspaper letter in the *New York Daily Advertiser* that in several different instances, Governor Clinton had denounced the Constitution and the federal convention in Philadelphia. Hamilton said that Clinton had secretly told friends that the Confederation had been a success and simply needed some improvement. Hamilton asserted Clinton had said a new federal government would not only be ineffective, but would confuse the people.

The governor of New York was therefore an Anti-Federalist and a dangerous man who had "declared the union unnecessary," according to Hamilton. He argued that for Clinton to undermine the convention was "unwarrantable and culpable in any man" and that he was trying to deny New Yorkers "the blessings of heaven." He added that such "conduct in a man high in office argues greater attachment to his own power than to the public good."[465]

Two months later, Hamilton attacked Clinton again. "Though the Governor has not publicly declared himself, his particular connection and confidential friends are loud against it..." he wrote, adding that there was "no saying what turn things may take when the full flood of official influence is let loose against [the Constitution]..."[466]

Hamilton had little respect for anyone opposed to the Constitution and could not understand their views. Each, to him, was someone gnawing at it to bring success to himself, and not the country. When he returned from the Philadelphia Convention he wrote that "the influence of many inconsiderable men in possession of considerable offices under the state governments who will fear a diminution of their consequences, power, and emolument by the establishment of the general government and who can hope for nothing here—[and] the influence of considerable men in office [who need to be] playing a part in a convulsion for their aggrandizement will oppose [it]."[467]

Clinton had remained quiet for months, but in late September 1787, writing as "Cato," he attacked Hamilton and his Federalist friends in a surprisingly well-written essay. He did not say that he was an Anti-Federalist, but told readers to deliberate "on this new national government with coolness; analyze it with criticism and reflect on it with candor." Clinton added that citizens should beware of a powerful government. "If you are negligent or inattentive, the ambitious and despotic will entrap you in their toils, and bind you with the cord of power from which you and your posterity may never be free." He summed up his feelings by telling New Yorkers that it was "better to be where you are for the present, than insecure forever afterwards."[468]

Hamilton, writing as "Caesar," fired back. He accused Clinton of trying to create disorder among the people with his criticism of the Constitution and told him that his objections were hurting the chances for George Washington to become president and warned that Washington might "be solicited again to accept the command of an army."

Cato angrily responded that an "American Fabius" was to command an army to impose this new government that he said was "founded in usurpation" and that the Constitution's "principles and exercises of them will be dangerous to your liberty and happiness."[469]

The feud would go on for a long time. An entire year later, in February 1789, Hamilton, using a pseudonym, would charge that Clinton as a Revolutionary War general had retreated from battles and that any praise of his military skills was mere "rant and romance."[470]

The trio constantly told delegates throughout the country that Washington was going to be the first president. How then could they worry about the fate of the new government under the national hero? They knew that in the new government he would always do the right thing, just as he had in leading American forces throughout the Revolution. Washington wrung his hands each time his name was used in this manner. He did not want to be the president, he repeatedly told Madison, Jay, and Hamilton. He wrote Hamilton, "It is my great and sole desire to live and die, in peace and retirement, on my own farm" and added that any false talk of him as president would make "the world and posterity accuse me of inconsistency and ambition."[471]

Clinton produced a long string of articles, again as "Cato," printed in most of New York's newspapers, that established the basic platform of the Anti-Federalists' crusade, all sparked by Hamilton's personal attack on him in the newspapers. These articles, which began to appear in October, were very persuasive. As soon as Hamilton read the first, he knew that something was required to answer them and began to write *The Federalist.*

Friends of both jumped into the debate, with supporters of Governor Clinton howling that little else could have been expected from Hamilton, whose ambition had no bounds. The people "tremble under an apprehension of becoming dupes to exalted ambition and they see with deep concern, those men who profess to the fathers of their country endeavoring by mean arts to detach the affections of the people from everything which bears the name of Federal," seethed one.

Other defenders of the governor argued that even if he did criticize the Constitution, what was wrong with that? Only Hamilton was allowed to enjoy freedom of speech? And, too, who was Hamilton to criticize anybody? That just showed how the leaders of the new government would act.[472]

The Anti-Federalists argued that even if the new government did work well in the beginning, bad management would eventually ruin it. The Federalists countered that the government would work so well that bad management could be easily overcome.[473]

Anti-Federalists blasted Hamilton a week later when he admitted that he had written the anonymous letter attacking Clinton. Hamilton was seen not only as Clinton's enemy, but the enemy of all the Anti-Federalists in the United States. One man wrote, "The conduct of several leading men, among us, has, of late, given the friends of liberty much uneasiness." Another referred to Hamilton as "Tom S——t" in a nasty rebuttal. The Antis saw him as a self-centered nationalist who cared little for the states, counties, and villages of America.[474]

Others used the Hamilton attack to begin the anti-Constitution campaign of many New Yorkers, who began to scrutinize its clauses, demand a bill of rights, and, as in every other state, complain that it was designed for the wealthy or, as one newspaper writer put it with great nastiness, "an aristocratic junta who appear determined, by their writings, to silence and traduce every person who will not subscribe to every part of their political creed." Others were even more caustic, writing that the people "will never consent to have a constitution crammed down their throats."[475]

Hamilton, reeling from the criticism, asked Washington for help. The general was alarmed by the Clinton–Hamilton feud. "When the situation of this country calls loudly for unanimity and vigor, it is to be lamented that gentlemen of talents and character should disagree in their sentiments for promoting the public weal," he scolded his former aide.[476]

While Clinton, like so many, wanted a bill of rights in the Constitution, he was not a leader of the Anti-Federalists and his name had not appeared on the lists of any Anti-Federalist organizations. In his public statements and private letters, he never avowed any great disdain for the Constitution. Hamilton's attacks, though, instantly made him an Anti-Federalist champion. The real Anti-Federalists embraced him, then, as their new leader and thanked Hamilton for putting the popular governor on their side.[477]

Hamilton was not well-liked outside of New York City and he had enemies within the city boundaries, too. Hamilton spoke in tones that were sometimes difficult and often seemed to ramble as he talked about a subject. He rarely acknowledged the other side in any debate, who saw him as overconfident to the point of cockiness.

New York, like Massachusetts and Virginia, had seen itself as a large and powerful state that functioned as its own country prior to and during the Revolution. Its governor led the choir of political figures who thought that way. Why give up that power and autonomy now and become just one of thirteen equal states? Much of Clinton's widespread popularity was due to that stand.[478]

Another very heated, and lingering, issue concerned the Tories who had supported the British during the war. Several thousands fled New York and moved to Canada and England before the war ended and local governments had seized and sold their homes and lands. Charges were being pressed against others. Jay and Hamilton constantly defended the Tories, charging that Americans looked bad in the eyes of Europeans with their excessive condemnation and punishment of them. Jay wrote that, "an undue severity toward them would be…unjustifiable. They who incline to involve that whole class of men in indiscriminate punishment and ruin, certainly carry the matter too far. It would be…unmanly revenge, without a parallel, except in the annals of religious rage, in times of bigotry and blindness."

Hamilton even defended Tories in cases brought against them, agreeing with Jay's stand. Their defense of the Loyalists brought public anger against the pair.

Finally, there was the paper money issue, which had caused splits in many states and caused Rhode Island to ignore the Constitution completely. The wealthy were in favor of paper money that they could use to drive the value of their goods up and their costs down. The working farmers and laborers loved hard money—gold and silver—and insisted that it was needed to stabilize the struggling post-war economy.

So, by the time the Constitutional fight arrived in the spring of 1788, New York had been split into two distinct factions on several issues, plus the longtime geographical differences between those who lived in New York City and those in upstate counties.

The number two Anti-Federalist in New York was lawyer Melancton Smith, who grew up in Dutchess County and later moved to New York City. The well-read, respected, and experienced Smith had served in New York's Provincial Congress, the Continental Congress, and as a member of New York's wartime committee to detect conspiracies and arrest and imprison British spies. Yates was a delegate to the Philadelphia federal convention and, it has been claimed, the writer "Brutus." He was also a member of several different wartime committees in the state, the state legislature, a delegate to the state Constitutional Convention, and one of the justices of the state supreme court. He was joined in his Anti-Federalist views by John Lansing, Jr., the mayor of Albany and a former speaker of the New York Assembly and member of the Continental Congress.

Most New Yorkers viewed the Constitution unfavorably. The members of the Triumvirate knew that. Madison wrote in October 1787, when he returned to the city, "This state has long had the character of being anti federal. Most of the respectable characters are zealous on the right side. The party in power is suspected on good grounds to be on the wrong one."[479]

George Washington lamented the Anti-Federal shift in New York since the Revolution and worried how it might affect ratification.[480]

The Antis in New York carefully portrayed the Federalists as rich, snobbish aristocratic villains out for their own enrichment at the expense of the common people. It was put dramatically in a lengthy satirical lambasting of the Constitution by "Curtiopolis," published in several newspapers in the winter of 1788. He wrote that "the happiness and existence of America being now suspended upon your wise deliberations; three or four sly aristocrats having lashed the public passions like wild horses to the car of legislation and driving us all in the middle of political clouds of error into that ditch of despotism lately dug by the convention…"

Smith, the Anti leader, made much the same argument when the convention began, demanding fewer aristocrats and more middle-class representatives in Congress. The Antis all agreed with the *Federal Farmer,* who wrote that a government run by the aristocrats was not a good one; men from all walks of life had to be in the government to insure freedom. The *Federal Farmer* wrote, "Every order of men in the community according to the common course of election, can have a share in it—professional men, merchants, traders, farmers, mechanics etc., to bring a just proportion of their best informed men…into the legislature."[481]

❧

The Federalists were convinced they would sweep the elections for Convention delegates and one of the reasons for that supreme confidence was what they read in the New York City newspapers every day. Just about all the papers there were pro-Federalist and even the Anti-Federalist paper printed dozens of pro-Constitution essays.

The Federalists had misjudged the state's press, though. New York had eleven newspapers, five of them published in New York City. Most were Federalist papers and filled their columns with the essays of *The Federalist*, by Publius, and other pro-Constitution writers. The New York papers dominated the state in volume of essays, too. The *Albany Gazette* published twenty-five essays, as an example, but the *New York Journal*, in New York City, published more than 150 and also printed dozens of essays that had previously been published in other papers. The essays written for the New York papers were superior to those printed upstate by Anti-Federalist journals.

The pro-Federalist residents of New York had no trouble obtaining newspapers and many read two or three each week, but upstate residents who lived far from the few towns that published newspapers rarely read them. Many people who lived in upstate towns that did have newspapers did not read them either. The national government was also involved in a mail system change at that time that made the delivery of newspapers very late or never.

The New York City newspapers were loaded with essays and letters about the Constitution. Newspapers produced nearly one thousand essays on the Constitution fight and thousands of letters from readers on the battle. Many New York essays were serious and contemplative, such as *The Federalist* or, on the Anti side, the *Letters from a Federal Farmer*, "the best of anything that has been written" against the Constitution, admitted Virginia Federalist Edward Carrington.[482] Many were wildly written, unorganized, and ineffective. Some were humorous, such as one that decried the seemingly endless essay-writing by asking readers, "Do not you see the Aristocrats, Monocrats, Demagogues, Pedagogues, Gogamagogs, Brobdingnags, Conspirators, and Federal Hobgobolins, are preparing to govern you, to enslave you, enthrall you, and bemuse you…"[483]

The city was home to seven newspapers, three of them dailies—the *Daily Advertiser*, the *Morning Post and Daily Advertiser*, and the *New York Journal and Daily Patriotic Register*. The city's only Anti-Federalist newspaper, the *New York Journal*, appeared as both a daily and a weekly, with reprinted articles from all the leading Anti-Federalists in the country. To prove he was an independent journalist and not a political figure, editor Thomas Greenleaf also published thirty-five of *The Federalist* essays.

Others carried on attacks by one essayist upon another, such as the disputes between "The Examiner" and "Democritus." "Democritus" wrote, "A monkey has more unexceptional claim to reason than the 'Examiner' to elegance or satire" and "The Examiner" snapped back that "as to that sniveling blockhead Democritus, his drunken performance does not demand a reply…"[484]

"The Examiner" chased all of his critics. On Christmas Eve 1787, he first assailed "Brutus" for "his windings, twistings, turnings, flacings, wearings, and tearings. His political knowledge, which is the basis or lowest region of his intellects, appears as a vail sparkling with infernal fire, in some cases black as smoke and in others pale and livid as a corpse." Then, in the next sentence, he went after "Democritus." "I really pity the situation of that poor devil Democritus, who is stark staring mad. My advice is that he be sent in the next packet to England and confined in Tothill-fields' Bridewell [prison]."[485]

A man whose nom de plume was "Roderick Razor" poked fun at everybody, referring to Democracy as "Stocracy" and referred to his learned political friends as Squire Sour Crout and Squire Clip Purse Van Clink de Gelt. Another writer called political enemies "Orang Outangs, blockheads, numbskulls, asses, monkeys, sheep, owls, and lobsters" and ended his newspaper column by writing that "every person who differs from me in belief is an infernal villain."[486] Another writer, an Anti-Federalist, wrote a very sarcastic "Political Creed of

Every Federalist," in which he poked fun at the national stands of the Federalists. He concluded by writing, "I believe that to speak, write, read, think, or hear any thing against the proposed government is damnable heresy, execrable rebellion, and high treason against the sovereign majesty of the convention. And lastly, I believe that every person who differs from me in belief is an infernal villain. AMEN."[487]

One writer called the work of all the Anti-Federalists a "low business" and said he was appalled by "the vile, dirty arts certain great characters in this state have had recourse to and are still making use of, to prejudice the honest uniformed part of the community against the new federal system of government…" and said they were "a species of villainy beneath our avowed enemies." Another called them "Yahoos."[488] This was typical of the low level of respect for the Antis in what had become a pro-Federal flood in the press.[489]

The massive newspaper war created a firestorm of public opinion, a battle that lasted in the papers for seven months. It also made clear to newspaper readers what the different arguments for and against the Constitution were. This press war began on May 24, 1787, just before the Federal Convention began, and did not let up until the Constitution was voted upon in New York State. Most of the pro-Constitution essays sounded like the article written by the editor of the *New York Packet* on January 1, 1788. He wrote, "The year 1788 would probably be the memorable era, in which would be erected a government, unprecedented in the annals of mankind—capable of perpetuating the liberties of America, maintaining her glory as a nation, preserving her from the attacks of anarchy, opening her lenient bosom as an asylum for the distressed of all nations, and the last resort of FREEDOM."[490]

Some of the best essayists on the controversy often denounced some of the worst. Governor Clinton, as "Cato," decried the scurrilous writing about such a momentous subject. "It is easy to foresee that the present crisis will form a principal epoch in the politics of America, from whence we may date our national consequence and dignity, or anarchy, discord, and ruin; the arguments made us of by a certain class of political scribblers; I conceive calculated (instead of throwing light on the subject) to deceive the ignorant but perhaps honest part of the community and to misguide the thoughtless and unweary..." he wrote in the *Poughkeepsie County Journal* just before Christmas 1787.[491]

In addition to the hundreds of essays, both sides routinely printed pro- and Anti-Federalist poems and wrote simple songs that people sang, pro and con, throughout the country about the Constitution.[492]

Newspapers were considered so essential for both sides that when the first Anti-Federalist committee was organized in February 1788, its leaders unsuccessfully tried to lure a New York City printer northward to the Albany area to publish a large, heavily funded Anti-Federalist newspaper there to blunt the power of the pro-Federalist press.

It was similar to everything the Antis did—too little and too late. When Hannah Thompson, a wealthy Philadelphia woman, heard of the newspaper idea, she wrote a friend that the Federalists had handed out their buttons, hats, and coats months before. Now the Antis were trying to catch up. "Ye transactions glided quick o'er frozen rivers and beaten tracks of snow..." she sneered at their delay.[493]

Even without their own newspaper, the Anti-Federalists upstate were very busy that February. After the Albany meeting and construction of a state organization, the Antis formed numerous county and community groups, with large rolls of members, to fight the Federalists. They were pleased with their work. One Federalist said of the Antis that "they use every art and strain every nerve to gain their points & if the Federalists do not exert themselves (which they never have done, nor ever will do sufficiently) they will be beaten."[494]

Some of the Anti-Federalist meetings, at which copies of the Constitution were burned to the roars of the crowd, drew as many as six hundred people, most of whom signed up as members. Different county and village groups held meetings, corresponded with each other, and forwarded pamphlets and newspaper clippings to each other. The Antis increased their campaign to dismiss the Constitution by reminding residents of the upstate counties that the rich manor lords had been raising their rents over the last year and engaging in other disputes. Those wealthy manor barons were, or course, Federalists. They let everyone know, too, that former Federalists had joined their cause after being slighted socially, such as not being invited to a party at the homes of the Schuylers or other wealthy families. The Antis campaign was so organized that at the end of the month, Anti-Federalist leader Abraham Yates could write that, "Anti-Federal business is carried on in (Dutchess) County and, so they tell me, in Ulster, Orange, and Westchester with spirit…and by the reports we have lately had federalists are in greater doubt about their success in the county of Albany."[495]

The Antis' success in organizing everywhere except New York City worried Hamilton, Jay, and Madison. Their success at reminding people of the importance of amendments to protect the personal rights of the people left out of the Constitution hurt, too. Young DeWitt Clinton, eighteen, Governor Clinton's nephew who would go on to become governor himself later, wrote in his series of essays that the heart of democratic government was the jury trial and it was missing in the Constitution.[496]

This hurt the efforts of the Triumvirate. Madison wrote that New Yorkers were "hostile to everything beyond the federal principle." Jay wrote Washington that "the Constitution still continues to cause great party zeal and ferment among us; and the opposition is yet so formidable that the issue appears problematical." Knox wrote that although he believed that both sides would perhaps have the same number of delegates in the New York convention, Federalist claims of a majority would not be true. In fact, a worried Knox said, "The issue will depend greatly on the industry of the different sides. I am apprehensive that the Anti-Federalists will be the most indefatigable."[497]

They were. They organized committees and persuaded hundreds of people to work for them in the upstate counties where they thought they had a chance of defeating the Federalists to elect delegates. They worked honorably most of the time and dishonorably some of the time, such as when they circulated a rumor, which was published in newspapers, that Jay was a secret Anti-Federalist. Other rumors they started were that after the elections, the Federalist Congress would name Washington king and that Long Island would be renamed German Flatts in exchange for the votes of Germans there. Prince William Henry of Canada, they told people, might be brought down by the new government to serve as a regent. They worked hard at getting people to convince their friends to vote Anti-Federal and to publish broadsides that they nailed to trees and the walls of buildings.[498]

The Federalists did the same. They, too, persuaded prominent people in each city and village in the state to write letters and visit friends to persuade them to vote Federalist in the elections for delegates. They convinced a grand jury in Albany, after it finished listening to a case, to hold a press conference to announce its support of the Constitution. The remarks were then published in numerous newspapers.[499] But they sometimes played dirty, too, circulating published rumors they knew were wrong.

The Federalists were a well-oiled machine in the New York metropolitan area, but had organizational problems upstate. Several of the wealthy manor lord families that controlled politics there split among themselves and leadership collapsed. At the same time, their tenants began to revolt against them. An Anti leader exulted in that dispute, writing that the tenants were "wonderfully poisoned against all the manor lords."[500]

Both sides arranged town meetings in different communities, with the Antis following the Federalists to capture their audience. On occasion, these meetings drew sizable crowds and sometimes as little as seven people. Local officials would convince leading Federalists or Anti leaders from around the state to visit and give speeches.[501]

The Antis cleverly took advantage of voting rules to place some of their leaders into county elections where the Antis held their strongest bases. Sam Jones and Melancton Smith, as an example, New York City residents for years, ran in the Anti stronghold of Dutchess County upstate. The Antis did not want to take any chances that their leader, Governor Clinton, might lose, so they ran him in safe Ulster County, where he had a good chance of election.[502]

The Federalists accused their enemies of ranting, but most of the pamphlets and newspaper columns written by the Anti-Federalist leaders were intelligent criticisms of the Constitution and the areas of vagueness that were in it. They were written by some of the most sophisticated public figures in the state. What exactly did the vice president do? How did one distinguish between federal and state taxes? How powerful was the new president going to be? Did he declare war or did Congress? They attacked weak areas and raised important questions. Brutus and Clinton, as Cato, when read thoroughly, were pristine examples of political writing. Their criticism was well aimed and demanded answers. Who really would run the country, Congress or the president? How could the framers of the Constitution not think that as the country grew, and it would, the problems of government would multiply and the current proposed form of government might not be able to handle them? Would there be a bill of rights?[503]

And they were not cowed by Federalist demands that this Constitution was needed because, historically, European and ancient nations that had governmental structures similar to the Confederacy had failed. "Tredwell" told the Federalists that any government, democracy or monarchy, can turn tyrannical, especially those with no personal protection for the rights of the people. He singled out the government of Holland, which many Federalists admired. "The arbitrary courts of Philip in the Netherlands, in which life and property were daily confiscated without a jury, occasioned as much misery and a more rapid depopulation of the province before the people took up arms in their own defense than all the armies of that haughty monarch were able to effect afterwards…the end or design of government is, or ought to be, the safety, peace, and welfare of the governed."[504]

Both sides were convinced that they had done good work in educating the voting public about their hopes, and fears, of the new government. The Anti leaders were sure they had made their case.[505]

There was so much talk about the Constitution that it even ended gossip between young girls. One Boston girl wrote her girlfriend in New York, "Patience, Patience! The dogs take the new constitution. It robs us of all those endearing sentences of chit chat with which our letters used to be replete and which we always classed among our choicest treasures."[506] A New York woman complained that there was little social life in her city. "The minds of all ranks of people appear affected with the situation of this country. A general anxiety for the event suspends the love of pleasure. All the men are immersed in politics and the women say 'life is not life without them.' I tell them it's all a mistake, but they won't believe me."[507]

Just prior to the elections, the Antis tried to scare the people about the Federalists. Wrote one, "On the one side with the dark secret and profound intrigues of the statesman, long practiced in the purlieus of despotism and on the other, with the ideal projects of young ambition, with its wings just expanded to soar to a summit which imagination has painted in such gaudy colors as to intoxicate the inexperienced votary."[508]

This worried Jay, who told Washington one week prior to the statewide elections that "the opposition is so formidable that the issue appears problematical."[509]

Jay had come down with a severe case of rheumatism in the middle of November, after he had written just a few essays for *The Federalist*. He was incapacitated for nearly three months, complaining to George Washington that he could not get rid of a constant pain in his left side.

He recovered by the beginning of springtime, but was then nearly killed in an April 1788 riot sparked by one of the strangest incidents in American history—the grave robber melee. For years, doctors who taught medicine in New York had paid grave robbers to exhume corpses and bring them to their homes for use in anatomical studies in their classrooms. There had been several public protests against the practice, one following a man's discovery that his wife's body had been stolen just two days after her death and autopsied in a classroom. The riot began when another man saw the severed arm of a stolen body through a hospital window. He recruited a mob of people that attacked the hospital, holding several medical students hostage. They were released to the mayor, who kept them in a city jail overnight for protection.

On the following day, the mob stormed the jail. The entire city knew of the incident and Governor George Clinton called out the militia. A friend rushed into Jay's house and recruited him for the students' defense. As he arrived at the jail, he was joined by the governor, the mayor, several councilmen, Revolutionary War hero Baron Von Steuben, and others. A second troop of militia arrived on horseback. The rioters threw heavy stones at the defenders, hitting many, including Jay, and the militia men unsheathed their muskets. Shots were fired, four people were killed and numerous people on both sides badly injured by musket balls, stones, sticks, and other objects hurled in anger.

Jay was cut badly about the head and, severely bloodied, was taken to his home where he was cared for by his wife and, shortly afterwards, a doctor. The badly battered Jay was "grievously wounded," bleeding profusely from two large holes in his forehead, according to friends, and remained bedridden and immobile for several weeks. He did not get much work done on Federalists' efforts to get their men elected as delegates to the convention, leaving that to Hamilton.[510]

His lengthy time in bed did enable him to reflect and to write his *Address to the People of the State of New York*, a forty-page pamphlet written as well as any of *The Federalist* essays. The pamphlet called for unity among New Yorkers and Americans. They had to realize, he wrote, that the Confederation had to be disbanded and a new government instituted. The Constitution, he argued carefully, was the best solution for the present and the future. Its strength was that it allowed for amendments, for years to come, which could change it as times were altered. Whatever problems people had with it now could be corrected later, as long as most of the people agreed. Its ability to change reflected its support of a government that would change as the people changed, a true democracy. In careful language, he brought both sides together. He wrote that New Yorkers had to unite with those in other states "as a band of brothers; to have confidence in themselves and in one another...[and] at least to give the proposed Constitution a fair trial, and to mend it as time, occasion, and experience may dictate."[511]

The moderate pamphlet seemed to please all, including many Anti-Federalists in the state, whose opinion it changed. Washington was impressed and told Jay it would have as much influence on the opposition as the Federalists. "The good sense, forcible observations, temper, and moderation with which it is written cannot fail...of making a serious impression even upon the Anti-Federal mind where it is not under the influence of such local views as will yield to no argument—no proofs."[512]

Bedridden, Jay never gave up his faith in the Constitution, but he always thought it would pass in New York for practical, not theoretical, reasons. He simply assumed that if everybody else approved it, New York would have no choice but to do the same, telling George Washington in early February 1788, that "the influence of Massachusetts on the one hand, and of Virginia on the other, renders their conduct on the present occasion very interesting…"[513]

Politicians urged other politicians to campaign harder. David Gelston, of Suffolk County, wrote John Smith, "For shame, you must stir yourself meet your friends somewhere—agree upon a good list— hold them up—persevere—even to the end—characters you know—go through the county—don't lie idle." Those men who campaigned promoted the cause earnestly. Judge Thomas Treadwell in Suffolk County described "the dreadful consequences that will follow this adoption of the Constitution in as high colors as the prophet Daniel did the distress of the Babylonians previous to their destruction."[514]

Candidates campaigned with Messianic zeal. One man wrote of Phillip Van Cortlandt, an Anti candidate from Westchester County, that he ran "as out of a Gothic Cloister, and the air so strongly impregnated with federalism has infused into his nostrils the aromatic, his whole frame infected with the contagion has called him forth to action and has transported him from extreme inaction to increasing exertion."[515]

The Antis in upstate were diligent. They sent out thousands of lengthy, persuasive circular letters to the residents of different counties—more than two thousand letters to the residents of Albany County alone—nailed hundreds of broadsides to trees and buildings, and filled every newspaper they could find with incendiary letters targeting the Federalists. They induced prominent people who lived upstate to join them and send out their own letters. The Antis wrote circulars that were mailed every two weeks from March until June and throughout the upstate counties hosted weekly meetings to gain new converts to their cause. The Antis printed copies of *The Federal Farmer* and distributed them throughout the upstate counties to counter the distribution of *The Federalist*. Sometimes candidates dropped out at the last moment, throwing county races into confusion.[516]

The Antis' campaign scared the Federalists. One wrote, "No man can behold the insidious efforts of the anti-federal party without disgust and indignation. They are straining every nerve; conjuring up imaginary phantoms, to delude those people…[prominent Antis here] are like the witches in Macbeth, dancing around the cauldron of sedition, each throwing in his proportion of spells for the confusion of his country…"[517]

The Antis planned to take advantage of new election laws in New York that hurt the wealthy. Now, all men could vote without land and wealth restrictions, permitting the small farmers and their workers to cast ballots alongside working-class laborers. Polling places were now set up in each village, not just the county seat, making it easier for working people to cast their ballots. The secret ballot was instituted just for the vote, permitting people to finally cast a vote without other individuals who could do them harm knowing how they voted. All of this helped the Antis.[518]

On election day, the Federalists won in New York City and nearby counties by huge numbers (all of the Federalists received between 2,300 and 2,735 votes, with the highest Anti-Federalist, Governor Clinton, winning just 134 there).[519] But the Anti-Federalists swept through most of the upstate counties, in some places by very wide margins, giving them two-thirds of the delegates and an overwhelming victory. Both sides charged voter fraud; several people were arrested for it.[520] Most candidates were elected in their home counties, but, as in other states, some ran in safer counties. Governor Clinton elected to run in both New York City, where he lost, and in Ulster County, where he won handily, along with his brother. One Anti-Federal judge wrote that never had there been such campaigning.[521]

In some contests to choose the sixty-one convention delegates, the Federalists were surprised by their defeat, especially Albany County, where they expected to win. Their ticket won 2,618 votes there, losing to the Anti-Federalists, who won 4,670.[522]

In the elections, the Anti-Federalists swept the upstate counties and even carried suburban New York City counties, such as Queens, where the Federalists, overconfident, had not campaigned very hard. They won some counties easily (sweeping Ulster using a committee of correspondence that conducted a massive letter-writing campaign) and took the cliffhangers, too, such as Suffolk, where the vote was extremely close.[523]

The Federalists were stunned by the elections. They had expected more of a 50–50 split. Hamilton was crestfallen at the result of the delegate elections. He wrote Madison, equally astonished at the Anti-Federalist landslide, that he feared "eventual disunion and Civil War."[524]

He had support in that fear. The editor of the *Virginia Independent Chronicle* wrote in May, "If the proposed government does not take place, or one similar to it, I expect that some Oliver [Cromwell] will start up and give laws to this new world. The eastern states appear ripe, loaded as they are with a heavy domestic and foreign debt, their commerce drooping, manufactures at a stand, little money among them, and heavy taxes that must be paid—all conspire to make them desperate and ready to attempt anything…"[525]

Around the country, Federalists received the New York election results with alarm. "New York looks black," wrote John Vaughn in Philadelphia.[526] James Kent disagreed. He wrote of the newly elected delegates that they were "the most splendid constellation of the sages and patriots of the Revolution which I had ever witnessed."[527]

Abigail Adams fretted over the result. She wrote her son John Quincy that most were "very doubtful" of passage in New York.

"The Governor of the State is said to be opposed to it and some say he has taken all means to prejudice the country people against the adoption."[528]

The Antis were ecstatic. One wrote that "the number of Antis astonish the Federalists and they look on their case as desperate."[529]

A glum Hamilton wrote that "the elections have gone wrong." He was still determined, though. "Having started it, I did not choose to give up the chase."[530]

Jay was more optimistic than his friend Hamilton. He noted that while the Antis had a large majority, they were split. They did not all oppose certain parts of the Constitution, demand a bill of rights, or denounce a strong federal government. Perhaps, he thought, some of the thirty-eight Anti delegates could be persuaded to change their minds.

Their leadership was questionable, too. Jay wrote Washington that "it is doubtful whether the leaders will be able to govern the party. It is not...certain that the greater part of their party will be equally decided or equally desperate." And, too, he thought that many Antis had come to the same conclusion that he had—too many Americans were greedy for money and power and that stood in the way of effective government. He wrote, "The spirit of private gain expelled the spirit of public good, and men became more intent on the means of enriching and aggrandizing themselves than of enriching and aggrandizing their country."[531]

The Antis believed that the virtue of the people would overcome governmental obstacles; the Federalists believed just as firmly that the people were not virtuous, that "men were not angels" and needed restrictions. James Wilson wrote, "If [the people] should now be otherwise, the fault will not be in Congress, but in the people...that for a people wanting to be themselves there is no remedy."

Madison threw up his hands over the character of the people. He wrote, "No theoretical checks, no form of government, can render us secure. To suppose that any form of government will secure liberty or happiness without any virtue in the people is a chimerical idea."[532]

What was certain, given the overwhelming majority of Anti-Federalist winners, was that only the persuasive efforts of Jay, Hamilton, and their colleagues would bring victory in Poughkeepsie. Tench Coxe, in Philadelphia, wrote, "The course of things at New York has proved very unfavorable unless the virtue, knowledge, and abilities of the friends of the Constitution in that convention work such conversions as were effected in Massachusetts."[533]

To those across the country, it was a grand, dramatic occasion. None appreciated the drama more than George Washington, watching the scene unfold from his veranda overlooking the Potomac River in Virginia. He wrote the Marquis de Lafayette in May, "The plot thickens fast. A few short weeks will determine the political fate of America."[534]

In New York, the Antis did not fall for the trap the Triumvirate had set of assuring everyone that Washington would be the beloved first president. One critic under the pseudonym of Philo-Publius II held up the popular ancient Greek leader Pericles as his model to show his disdain for the rumor and for Washington. Philo wrote that Pericles took charge of the Greek government and ran it into ruin, wrecking the privileges and power of the governing court, promoting aristocrats wherever he found them, and then leading Greece into an unpopular war. In an obvious comparison to Washington, he added, "Pericles was, nevertheless, a man endowed with many amiable and shining qualities, and, except in a few instances, was always the favorite of the people."[535]

"Cato" complained that it did not matter who was president, the Constitution was written to protect him from any punishment for performing badly. "His infallibility," he claimed, "pervades every part of the system."[536]

Foreign diplomats saw the defeat of the Constitution as inevitable. One wrote, "Although no one knows what will happen in [New York], it is asserted that the Governor and his party, which is the strongest, are violently opposed to the plan..."[537]

Hugh Hughes thought the lopsided victory of the Antis had put the Federalists in their place. He wrote, "There has not been a time since the revolution in which the well born who are the leaders of that party have felt and appeared so uninfluential, as they feel and appear at this time and place. How the mighty have fallen...taught their high blown imaginations a lesson of humility."[538]

The Anti Fedcralists had not only won an overwhelming majority, but they had beaten down the hated aristocrats, whom they abhorred. They were proud of that victory.[539] But the Antis knew, too, that although they had won two-thirds of the seats in the convention, they had not won them by an overwhelming majority. Some Federalists, such as Jay, won by just as wide margins in New York City as Anti leaders such as Clinton and Smith won upstate. Overall, the Antis won the New York vote by just 12 percent (the Federalists won 9,741 of the 22,088 known votes), a sound victory, but certainly not an overwhelming triumph.[540]

Hamilton knew that. He wrote Madison when the New York convention began that "our adversaries greatly outnumber us" and their leaders had been "pretty desperate" in their bragging about victory. But, he added hopefully, "the minor partisans have their scruples and an air of moderation is now assumed."[541]

The Federalists constantly appealed to these moderates. State Chancellor R. R. Livingston, on the very first day, said that "I trust, sir, there are many gentlemen present who have yet formed no decided opinion on the important questions before us and who (like myself) bring with them dispositions to examine whatever shall be offered and not to determine 'til after the maturest deliberations..."[542]

Other Federalists around the country, such as Coxe in Philadelphia, wrote pamphlet-length essays addressed "To the New York Convention" that were first printed in their home states, then reprinted in New York newspapers and then delivered to the Antis in Poughkeepsie. These were countered by the distribution there of lengthy Anti-Federalist essays.[543]

The Federalists unleashed last-minute criticism of their foes as often as they could. Richard Platt sneered on the day that delegates left for the convention that the Antis there would be up to their "rascality."[544]

The Antis resented being the Antis, too. The Federalists had conveniently hung the "Anti-Federalist" nametag on all of them long ago and that's how they were seen—wrongfully so, they insisted. Massachusetts's Elbridge Gerry later wrote that the Antis wanted a national government and Constitution, too, just a different kind. He added that the Antis were unjustifiably called "Anti-Federalists." He wrote, "They were in favor of the federal government and the others were in favor of a national one; the Federalists were for ratifying the Constitution as it stood and the others, not until amendments were made. Their names ought not to have been the Federalists and Anti-Federalists, but the Rats and Anti-Rats."[545]

The Antis felt, too, that they were victimized by the Federalists, "those who are for cramming down the new Constitution by force, fraud, and falsehood."[546]

# NEW YORK: INTO THE STRETCH

The New York convention began at the courthouse in Poughkeepsie, chosen as the capital city of the state when the British army occupied New York City in the American Revolution. The town, seventy-five miles south of Albany, was a mile west of the Hudson River and home in 1788 to three thousand people. The spacious courthouse was as new as the government being debated in its halls. It had been built just a year earlier. Home to the state legislature, the courthouse was a handsome two-story stone building topped by a cupola. The hall of the building held the sixty-five delegates comfortably, along with balcony seating for two hundred spectators. The Federalist delegates stayed nearby, mostly at Hendrickson's Inn, and the Antis resided at Poole's Inn.[547]

The Federalists boldly proclaimed victory while silently dreading defeat. They needed to stall the vote as long as possible, hoping that the conventions in New Hampshire and Virginia would bring them success and the critical ninth state to ratify. Victories in those two states, or in either, could turn the tables on the Antis and make

New York's decision not to adopt the Constitution, but to join or ignore the new United States, a more serious choice. To do that, Jay and Hamilton urged the convention to debate the Constitution paragraph by paragraph. They encountered no objections from the Antis. Hamilton breathed a sigh of relief and told Madison that "a full discussion will take place, which will keep us together at least a fortnight."[548]

In Poughkeepsie, the Triumvirate set up goals: (1) Turn Melancton Smith, the Anti leader along with Clinton, into a friend; (2) Show that the old government could no longer work and that this one, even with its problems, was much better; (3) Convince all that regardless of their views, New York should not wind up being the only state to vote "no" and, if nine had ratified, the only state not to join the union—they assumed North Carolina would vote yes and that Rhode Island would go its own way; (4) Remember that in all of the pamphlets and broadsides, and public speeches, none of the Anti-Federalists had ever said they did not want a new and better national government. Their debate was over the composition of it.

And they wanted to reassure the Antis that their common goals, a government that represented all, were the same. "All power is derived from the people," said New York Chancellor R. R. Livingston, "[Antis] consider the state and the general governments as different deposits of that power."[549]

The Antis insisted that was not the case, that they were not simply arguing for a bill of rights, but a government in which the states maintained significant power. They all quoted Montesquieu, who argued that the larger the government, the more opportunity for corruption and oppression.[550]

Hamilton and Jay began to lobby the Antis as soon as they arrived in Poughkeepsie. The Federalists were an impressive group. Jay was the foreign secretary of the United States; Hamilton, a Congressman and war hero. They were joined by R. R. Livingston, the state's chancellor, Richard Morris, the chief justice of the state supreme court, and James Duane, the mayor of New York City.

Sometimes their lobbying worked and sometimes it did not.

On the positive side, the Federalists had the sociable Jay. The highly respected foreign secretary had worked with Clinton and his brother throughout the war and served with Melancton Smith on the conspiracy committee; Smith and he were both members of the manumission society. Jay knew most of the other Anti-Federalists from his work in the war or as foreign secretary; many had dined at his New York mansion. Now, he used these connections to help the Triumvirate.

Jay and Hamilton talked to the Anti-Federalist delegates as soon as they arrived, or had other Federalists do so, trying to change their minds. After a few days, the defiant Antis took refuge in their hotel.

Most of the Antis disliked Hamilton. "You would be surprised" at his personality, wrote Charles Tillinghast. "Did you know the man… what an amazing Republican Hamilton wishes to make himself be considered. But he is known." They worried about the friendly Jay. "His manners and mode of address would probably do much mischief, were the members not as firm as they are," wrote Tillinghast.[551] One Federalist complained that "our opponents keep themselves at much distance from us, and we cannot collect any of their sentiments, either out or in doors, by any means whatever."[552]

The Constitution supporters brought copies of *The Federalist* with them, along with other Federalist pamphlets, such as Jay's *Address to the People of New York*, which were distributed and had a great effect. Newspaper columns had been clipped out and passed around at Poughkeepsie.

A rider circuit had been arranged between Poughkeepsie and both Virginia to the south and New Hampshire to the north so that word of victory in either state there could be brought to New York immediately. It was part of the overall rider network the Triumvirate had formed months earlier as part of their lobbying schemes.

Hamilton wrote New Hampshire friends, "Send an express to me at Poughkeepsie. Let him take the shortest route to that place, change horses on the road, and use all possible diligence. I shall with pleasure defray all expenses and give a liberal reward to the person."[553]

The Antis finally discussed a plan to have the Anti-Federalist groups in each state work together at this final convention. Melancton Smith wrote to the heads of the Antis in New Hampshire and Virginia and suggested that joint cooperation would enable all three to defeat the Constitution. In Poughkeepsie, Smith wrote that "the necessary alterations can be affected and all the apprehensions of danger from the new government removed, if your state and ours could unite in sentiments respecting amendments and act in concert in measures to bring them about."[554]

The letters were written so late that the one dispatched to New Hampshire arrived after that state had ratified and the one to Virginia was never found. At the same time that Smith and the Antis foundered, the Triumvirate ran an elaborate system of riders and horses throughout the country.

The initial debate was led by Smith on the side of the Antis and Hamilton for the Federalists.

While not liked, Hamilton was seen as a formidable opponent. Said one delegate, "He generally spoke with much animation and energy and with considerable gesture. His language was clear, nervous, and classical. His investigations penetrated to the foundation and reason of every doctrine and principle which he examined, and he brought to the debate a mind filled with all the learning and precedents applicable to the subject."

Another delegate marveled at him. "What a noble field this young man had for his ebullient parts! It would almost persuade me to be in love with a Republic against my better judgement."[555]

Melancton Smith had no great regard for Hamilton, writing that "he speaks frequently, very long and very vehemently—has, like Publius, much to say not very applicable to the subject."[556]

Smith was a plain-looking man. He possessed a large head with an ordinary face. His hair was long and curled up at the ends. He did not powder it. While he enjoyed none of the soaring qualities of Hamilton, Smith was an impressive speaker. He knew how to state his case and did so with simplistic force. Perhaps his greatest quality was that he was looked upon favorably by all of the Federalists as well as the Antis. Everyone in Poughkeepsie had enormous respect for him. Federalist James Kent said he was "a man of remarkable simplicity and of the most gentle, liberal, and amiable disposition," adding that those who argued with him had to be careful.[557]

And Smith, at least, was not completely opposed to the Constitution. He was keeping an open mind. A reporter wrote of one of his talks in the first days of the convention that he possessed "a spirit of patriotism, mind open to conviction, with a determination to form opinions only on the merits of the questions, from those evidences which should appear in the course of the investigation."[558]

And, added to Smith's sense of patriotism, was the Antis' belief that since there was no bill of rights, the freedom of the people was not protected. "Apprehension of [the union's] dissolution ought not to induce us to submit to any measure which may involve in its conse-quences the loss of civil liberty," said John Lansing Jr. of Albany."[559]

The debates in Poughkeepsie were lengthy, but the arguments were simple. Richard Morris put the issue best. He said, "An energetic federal government is essential to the preservation of the Union; and that a constitution for these states ought to unite firmness and rigor in the national operations, with the full security of our rights and liberties. It is our business, then, to examine whether the proposed Constitution be agreeable to this description…"[560]

The Federalists turned to the republics of Europe and ancient Rome and Greece to show that democracies had worked in the past and elsewhere, and then the Antis jumped on them, pointing out how those same systems had failed repeatedly.[561]

Hamilton told delegates that they had been entrusted with a special task, the development of a stable government. "It is necessary that we apply an immediate remedy and eradicate the poisonous principle from our government. If this be not done…we shall feel, and posterity will be convulsed by, a painful malady…" he said, and added that their deliberations were "the most important study which can interest mankind."[562]

Their debate opened on June 20, when Smith took the floor of the crowded chamber, teeming with several hundred spectators in the balcony, the building's windows open for ventilation. Smith denounced the Federalist argument that since the Confederation government had failed, the proposed new government was necessary. Smith blunted that argument rather easily, telling the delegates that he was in favor of a stronger union but not certain the proposed government was the right one. "Defective as the old confederation is, no one could deny but it was possible we might have a worse government. But the question was not whether the present confederation be a bad one, but whether the proposed Constitution a good one."[563]

Smith reminded all that they had a momentous task before them. He said, "The investigation is difficult, because we have no examples to serve as guides. The world has never seen such a government over such a country. If we consult authorities in this matter, they will declare the impracticability of governing a free people on such an extensive plan."[564]

Smith then enumerated the weaknesses of the Constitution, starting with the omission of the bill of rights, calling it "a beast dreadful and terrible, and strong exceedingly, having great iron teeth—which devours, breaks in pieces, and stamps the resident with his feet."[565]

One of the most powerful and effective arguments that Hamilton and Jay adopted from the start in their New York campaign was that the Anti-Federalists were against a single national union, which they were not. They also argued falsely that the rejection of the Constitution would not only lead to civil war, but perhaps result in the British again taking over the United States and putting a relative of the king in charge as a monarch, a spurious claim at best.

The pair embraced this view because they understood that while the people might argue over exactly what form the new government should take, everybody wanted to preserve the nation they had fought for in the Revolution. To suggest, again and again, that the country might plunge into war and be divided into three or four separate republics alarmed the people and hurt the Anti-Federalists efforts—unfairly so.

Hamilton argued, "In the course of a few years, it is probable that the contests about the boundaries of power between the particular governments and the general government and momentum of the larger states in such contests will produce a dissolution of the Union."[566]

Jay again predicted continual wars between different confederations carved out of the thirteen states—including a war between north and south over slavery—if one united country could not be formed under the Constitution.

Hamilton then rose and spoke for more than an hour, delivering an impassioned speech that Governor Clinton called "a second edition of Publius well delivered." Hamilton savaged the Confederation, telling delegates heatedly that its "weaknesses were real and pregnant with destruction." He bragged about the Constitution and explained carefully that while it might not solve all of the country's problems, it solved most. He reminded the delegates, as he did again and again in his carefully planned speeches, that the states had enormous powers that could never be overridden by any federal government.

Unable to finish without attacking Clinton, Hamilton then charged that the governor was in Poughkeepsie not to help the country but to wreck it. Clinton jumped to his feet when he finished and assured delegates that was not the case and that Hamilton's accusations were unjust. "I am really at a loss to determine whence he draws his inference. I declare that the dissolution of the union is, of all events, the remotest from my wishes. I wish for a federal republic. The object of both of us is a firm, energetic government, and we may both have our country in view, though we disagree as to the means of procuring it."[567]

Hamilton defended himself and launched into a lengthy recitation of the points he had made as Publius; the Antis saw it as simply more talk without purpose. He went over, at length, the checks and balances system and the sharing of power between the federal and state governments. He again defended the representative system of government and argued heatedly that because such a system did not work in ancient republics did not mean it could not work in the United States.[568]

He defended the often-attacked "aristocratic government" that the Antis feared would take over and ruin the country. Carefully selected men would be elected and that small group would control Congress. Hamilton rebutted that concern, as Madison had been doing for months, by arguing that the House and Senate could overturn each other's decisions and so could the president. The system of checks and balances would prevent an aristocracy. Besides, he said, in an election anyone could win, not just an aristocrat. "The people should choose whom they please to govern them," he said.[569]

Chancellor R. R. Livingston added that the Antis saw a "phantom aristocracy" and continually labeled "men of merit" as aristocrats and said that the Antis preferred the "rogue and robber" to the aristocrat.

Smith jumped up to object to that depiction of the Antis' idea of a good congressman.

Smith also objected to Hamilton's lashing of the middle and working class in his speeches. Hamilton said, "The advantage of character belongs to the wealthy. Their vices are probably more favorable to the prosperity of the state than those of the indigent, and partake less of moral depravity."[570]

Smith contended that the small number of senators was unfair, that it would enable the "natural aristocracy" to take those seats, cutting out the representatives of the "middling class." Hamilton countered by saying that the different types of congressmen would insure protection for all of the classes.

The arguments continued for days, each side refuting the other. Personal animosities grew deep. Simple debates turned into heated arguments. The Federalist speakers were overly harsh on their Anti-Federalist foes, doing nothing except to increase their defiance. Instead of merely taking umbrage at the legislatively elected senate as a way of assuring good senators, Anti speakers denounced it as an avenue of corruption. One man saw the Senate isolated from the people by "an impenetrable wall of adamant and gold, the wealth of the whole country flowing into it" and ignorant of the will of the people, who lived far away. Of the disputes, the *Maryland Gazette* wrote that the debates had taken a "warm turn."[571]

The Antis feared corruption at all levels of the larger government, which they said offered more avenues for bribery and coercion. Jay disagreed. He told the assembly that under the old Confederation someone only had to bribe three states to block passage of a bill; under the proposed government many more would have to be bribed. He argued, "On the score of corruption, we have much the best chance under the new Constitution; and that, if we do not reach perfection, we certainly change for the better."[572]

The Antis, often led by Smith, charged that the federal government would grow into a monolithic structure, located far from the people, that ran the country with no input from the state governments, despite what Hamilton said. He again fumed, as did other Antis, that there seemed to be little point in discussing questions concerning the Constitution in that the Federalists were intent on passage of the document without changes.

The two sides argued back and forth on a number of issues. Smith wanted to know why there was a standing army in the first place if the president was never going to use it? What about taxes? Wouldn't the new plan call for all of the people's taxes going to the federal government and not the states?

The Constitution was attacked, and defended, by dozens of people. One reporter there wrote that the debates were held by the finest minds in America.[573]

The Antis became more entrenched in their opposition to the Federalists' cause. They did not understand why, if the old Confederation was not working well, it could not simply be amended. They paid no attention to Hamilton's lengthy speech in which he pointed out that it was not just the American Confederation, but all European confederations, too, for two thousand years, that had failed. They ignored Hamilton's plea that the federal convention had done the best job possible. They dismissed him when he fervently argued, "Let a convention be called tomorrow; let them meet twenty times—nay, twenty thousand times; they will have the same difficulties to encounter, the same clashing interests to reconcile."[574]

They paid little heed to his plea that the states would always have power.[575]

Hamilton sent Madison frequent notes. He gloomily told his friend in late June that the Federalists were having great difficulty. "Our arguments confound, but do not convince," he wrote. William Duer, a former congressman and New York City political figure, wrote

Madison that Clinton was having a profound effect on the debates and might wreck the Federalist cause.[576]

A historian wrote that Hamilton seemed overmatched, that it was "a Homeric battle, Hamilton against a host. His mind like an ample shield, took all their darts with verge enough for more."[577]

All were impressed with Jay when he rose to talk in his single speech of the debate part of the convention. The upstate men who had never met him or heard him speak, but who had read with pleasure his pamphlet, *Address to the People of New York*, were impressed. "[Jay] had the most peculiar knack of expressing himself I ever heard. Fancy, passion, in short everything that makes an orator, he is a stranger to, and yet none who hear but are pleased with him, and captivated beyond expression."[578]

Jay went out of his way to be conciliatory every day. He would stop in midsentence and ask the Anti-Federalist with whom he was arguing if, in fact, he was stating the man's objection correctly, and then, assured that he was, nod and go on. Unlike Hamilton, he was modest, thereby encouraging everyone who despised Hamilton, enhancing Jay's stature. Most importantly, again and again he told the delegates that he knew that he was not always right. "We did not come here to carry points. If the gentleman will convince me I am wrong, I will submit. It is from this reciprocal interchange of ideas that the truth must come out," he said. The opposition appreciated that modest view.[579]

Far more clearly than Hamilton or any other Federalist, Jay assured the delegates that the powers of Congress and those of the states would be separate and obvious. Congress would never encroach upon the states and the large legislatures in most states, and their powerful governors would prevent that. He talked about national taxes that might be placed, reminding all that the national congress could not tax revenue that now was paid to the states. The national government, he said, would take care of national matters, leaving everything else to the states.

During the final week of June, the delegates at the New Hampshire convention, in its second term after an earlier adjournment, ratified the Constitution. As planned, riders employed by the Triumvirate galloped southward, carrying the news to Poughkeepsie, where it arrived three days later and was announced. Church bells rang throughout all of the cities in the United States when news of New Hampshire's ratification arrived in June of 1788. [580]

The news might have promptly ended the New York Convention, but Chancellor Livingston could not let it go without a swipe at the Antis. He stood up in the courthouse and practically accused them of being treasonous now for insisting that the ratification needed to be discussed. He said they were against the national union. John Lansing Jr. jumped to his feet and shouted at Livingston, branding any charge that anyone in the chamber was against union was "utterly false." The moment had been lost.[581]

Livingston's derisive remark angered all of the Antis and reminded them how much they detested Hamilton, too. Governor Clinton told John Lamb that he wrote him a letter while "the great little man [was] employed in repeating over parts of Publius to us..." And no one appreciated Hamilton's smug criticism of Melancton Smith, that Smith "copiously declaimed against all declamation..."[582]

The Antis railed against Hamilton's defense of the wealthy, whom they despised. "If [Smith] will look around among the rich men of his acquaintance, I fancy he will find them as honest and virtuous as any class in the community. He says the rich are unfeeling; I believe they are less so than the poor," Hamilton had said, and went further, arguing that the poor were more ambitious than the rich, all comments that angered the Antis.[583]

This, of course, equaled Hamilton's own view of them, especially Clinton. Hamilton later wrote, "I do not recollect a single measure of public utility since the peace for which the state is indebted to its chief magistrate..."[584]

Hamilton always tried to paint him as the villain, writing nearly a year later, "Is there a man in America who has more early, more decidedly, or more pertenaciously opposed that constitution than the present Governor?"[585]

The Antis realized that as the convention wore on, the popularity of both Hamilton and Jay had grown with the crowd that gathered each day to view the proceedings. Hamilton played to the crowd, constantly appealing to them when he felt attacked on the floor. On July 12, as an example, he objected to something and then turned to the crowd.

One newspaper reporter there wrote, "He described in a delicate but most affecting manner the various ungenerous attempts to prejudice the minds of the convention against him. He had been represented as an ambitious man, a man unattached to the interests and insensible to the feelings of the people; and even his supposed talents had been wrested to his dishonor and procured as a charge against his integrity and virtue. He called on the world to point out an instance in which he had ever deviated from the line of public or private duty. The...appeal fixed the silent sympathetic gaze of the spectators, and made them all his own."[586]

The Antis shrugged off the New Hampshire vote and continued to insist on a bill of rights for passage and increased their anger at the Federalists. "The news from New Hampshire has not had the least effect on our friends at this place," wrote the governor.[587]

The approval of New Hampshire was supposed to force the Antis to change their minds, but none did. Now New York had to decide whether it wanted to be a part of the United States or become its own country, with its own taxes, foreign relations, and army. This new country might be cut in two, with New York City seceding and forming its own state. This had been something Hamilton had worried about since his election as a delegate. He wrote Madison on June 6, "A separation of the southern district from the other part of the state, it is perceived, would become the object of the Federalists and of the two neighboring states." He also feared that a break up of New York would bring about a civil war.[588]

The Federalists, losing, looked to the Virginia vote. Many were certain adoption there would surely mean adoption in New York. Merchant John Pintard wrote that it would "influence our Copperheads [Antis]."[589]

Henry Knox was so certain that Virginia's verdict would carry the day in New York that he wrote, "If she will adopt the Constitution, all things will be easy notwithstanding the crooked policy of this state..."[590]

As the debates continued, many Antis became angrier at Hamilton and Jay. One snapped in debate, "This government is founded in sin and reared up in iniquity; the foundations are laid in a most sinful breach of public trust and the top stone is a most iniquitous breach of public faith and I fear if it goes into operation we shall be justly punished with the total extinction of our civil liberties."[591]

The Antis saw the issue as a fight between two sides, each as bitter as the other, and could not reach a resolution. Moderates fumed that both sides needed to compromise. One wrote, "Let those who call themselves Federalists lay aside a little of their arrogance and instead of abusing, endeavor to convince their fellow citizens of the necessity of embracing the constitution as it stands..."[592]

The Triumvirate used every argument they could. Hamilton even delivered a speech showing how New York State had paid more money than other states in taxes to the Confederation and how under the new government their residents would only pay an proportionate share.

"Why do [Antis] affect to cherish this political demon and present it once more to our embraces. [Why] recommend the ruinous principle and make it the basis of a new government?"[593]

At 3:00 a.m., July 2, the Triumvirate's rider from Richmond arrived in New York City with the momentous news that Virginia, too, had approved the Constitution—and without a bill of rights. Church bells started to ring as soon as he dismounted with the news and tolled until dawn, when their sound was replaced with the sounds of batteries of twenty-four pound cannon being fired in joyful celebration throughout the city.

The *New York Independent Journal* rushed the official Virginia confirmation notice into its pages as a supplement. No one could fail to notice the supplement, in which the Virginians loudly proclaimed that they only voted for it because the bill of rights, whose freedoms they enumerated, was promised to be added later. It was also approved, they argued, because a clear division between federal and state powers was guaranteed.[594]

William Livingston took the packet early in the morning and galloped as fast as he could to Poughkeepsie, where he delivered the news to the chamber of delegates. It caused cheering from the Federalists and a parade of happy townspeople marched around the courthouse several times, joined by a small band. Inside, though, the Antis were as little affected as they had been by the ratification in New Hampshire. Now every state except New York (and Rhode Island, written off as a lost cause) had approved.

The Antis had dug in and nothing was going to change their mind, or so it seemed. The vote in Virginia had changed the situation, though. Now not only did the Federalists have the ninth and deciding state, New Hampshire, but they had Virginia, too, where the fight had been so contentious. Now, it was New York, all by itself, against the rest of the nation.

Jay and Hamilton saw the vote in Virginia, delivered by Madison's rider, as enormous good news. Jay wrote, "The constitution constantly gains advocates among the people and its enemies in the convention seem to be much embarrassed."[595]

But the news meant little. One man wrote to a newspaper, "We (in vain) expected that the ratification of Virginia would have a very serious effect on the minds of the anti-federal party, and would have constituted so forcible an appeal to their apprehensions, that it would have compelled them to adopt a system different from that destructive one they seem intent on pursuing…"[596]

The Federalists knew that now they had to get the Constitution passed on their own, with no argument that everybody else had approved, but they did not know what they needed to do beyond everything that they had already tried. The Antis were adamant in what they wanted. Governor Clinton told the assembly on June 17 that his idea of a good national government was one that could protect the rights of the states while at the same time protecting the union. Clinton argued, too, that the great divide between the two sides was not the bill of rights, but states' rights and the power of the federal government over the states. And so they sat and did nothing, waiting for a move by the Antis, who also sat, waiting for the Federalists.

And then the Fourth of July arrived.

There were toasts everywhere to celebrate the independence of the United States and to urge the people at the New York Convention to hurry and finish their business so that the new government could be assembled. Every city had Fourth of July parades and celebrations. Hundreds of letters praising the United States on its anniversary were printed in newspapers.[597]

The Federalists and their opponents in the New York Convention ended their debates on the Fourth to celebrate by watching a small parade in Poughkeepsie, listening to the booming of cannon salutes, and joining in joint celebratory feast where those who had argued so strongly against each other dined and drank. Together they cheered what they had accomplished in the American Revolution. Many of them had fought in the war or worked with the leaders of the army.

The sociable Jay, one of the most sought-after party guests in New York City and any foreign capital he visited, thrived at these parties. He moved from room to room, table to table, engaging the Anti-Federalists in small talk that made them like him even more. He was, as he sought to be seen, a good man trying to help them to do the right thing. At one point, he sat with Smith, and the Anti-Federalist and Jay talked at length about their bitter disputes in the convention. Jay told Smith, "We must find the road to compromise without gutting the Constitution."

"We must get guarantees first, though," Smith said, starting the old Anti-Federalist argument. Jay stood, a wide smile on his face, looked down at Smith and said, "At least let us try." Then, as he walked away, he patted Smith gently on the back in a very friendly way that assured Smith, and all that observed the gesture, that they would all do the right thing in the end.[598]

There were other reasons for hope that the Constitution would be approved. Newspapers writers throughout the country applauded the proposed new government and denounced the Antis of New York, of whom they were tired now that ten states had ratified. One man in Brooklyn, New York, wrote, "May continual disappointment and never dying remorse pain, poverty, and contempt ever attend those Anti-Federalists who through motives of interest, stand opposed..."[599]

The Antis were sick of the newspaper denunciations of them.

There were dreaded signs, too, that the violence that many had predicted over the Constitution had begun. It occurred in Albany, New York, where the Federalists and Anti-Federalists held July 4 parades. Both sides clashed, with swords, bayonets, clubs, and stones. The Federalists drove a group of Antis into a private residential home and then stormed in. During the melee that followed, one Anti-Federalist was killed and eighteen were wounded. Twelve Federalists were wounded. The incident shocked everyone as news of it spread over the next week.[600]

On July 11, John Lansing Jr. introduced a series of personal liberty amendments, to be seen as explanatory, recommendatory, or conditional. The Federalists, as always, balked at their introduction. They were still completely opposed to a bill of rights despite all of the support the bill of rights had obtained in every state. The convention appointed a committee of seven volunteers from both sides to study the amendments, with Jay leading the Federalists. Hamilton, though, realizing his unpopularity, did not join the committee. Without him, the committee engaged in bitter debate over the wording of the personal liberties amendments. "Conditional" was the key word; New York's Antis wanted to approve the Constitution, but only with the bill of rights. They insisted on it. The leading voice in the committee was Jay's; he argued for compromise and merely a recommended bill of rights, which he promised he would have instituted by the new government as soon as it was formed.

Many of the New Yorkers against the Constitution did not believe that the Triumvirate would give them a bill of rights later, as they promised. They wanted it spelled out in print and signed by all. One Anti wrote that their promises were "fairy tales."[601]

They had to look no farther than Hamilton, who scoffed at the idea of a bill of rights. He wrote, "I go further and affirm that bills of rights…are not only unnecessary in the proposed constitution, but would even be dangerous."[602]

But the drama of the Convention had its effects on the stubborn Hamilton. Toward the very end of the acrimonious debates, he took the floor and, the eyes of all on him, stunned the assembly by actually apologizing for his "vehemence" and admitting that he was an aristocrat and an ambitious man and was sorry if his remarks or attitude had offended anyone. He said, "I have no design to wound the feelings of any one who is opposed to me."

He knew that he was unpopular and went on to say that the delegates "reckon me amongst the obnoxious few." He said that one day his own family might suffer from his ambition. He reminded them all, though, that his behavior was simply his nature and asked for forgiveness.[603]

His apologies reminded the delegates how effective he had been with his arguments. James Kent wrote that he was "prompt, ardent, energetic, and overflowing with an exuberance of argument and illustration. He generally spoke with much animation and energy and with considerable gesture." His harangues, Kent said, "combine the poignancy of vinegar with the smoothness of oil."[604]

The committee broke up and the issue tumbled onto the floor, where the personal liberties bill was voted as "recommended." The convention, wrote Dewitt Clinton, was "in crisis" at that point.

Jay took the lead. He rose in the chamber and reminded the delegates that a rejection of the Constitution now meant that the convention would have to adjourn and it might not reassemble for another year. By then, the new federal government would be in place, all of its offices filled and all of its business in motion. New York, he threatened, would be left out in the cold. Why not simply pass the "recommended" bill of rights now and help the new American government get started?

The Antis paid no attention to Jay and one demanded a vote for adjournment of the entire convention, but it was defeated. Melancton Smith offered an amendment to Jay's ratification resolution that tempered it a bit, but still made a bill of rights conditional. Governor Clinton begged the delegates to approve the Smith amendment, pleading that "the proposition is a reasonable one that contains nothing that can give offense or that can prevent its being accepted [by Congress]. I could only be induced to this from a strong attachment to the union, from a spirit of conciliation and earnest desire to promote peace and harmony…" the governor said.[605]

The delays aggravated all. One reporter wrote that "we cannot discover the least feature in these momentous debates by which an adequate idea can be formed of its final result."[606]

Antis around the country saw the muddle as hopeful. "I am well informed [the convention] will annex a bill of rights to a conditional ratification, which will remove all our objections," wrote Gerry of Massachusetts.[607]

Hamilton, too, was perplexed. He wrote Madison, "There is so great a diversity in the views of our opponents that it is impossible to predict anything. Upon the whole, however, our fears diminish."[608]

There was enormous pressure put on the Antis at this point. Since May, when Jay began writing to George Washington about it, there had been veiled threats by anonymous people that if the Antis turned down the Constitution, the lower counties of the state that made up metropolitan New York City would secede, form their own state, and join the United States. They would leave Upstate New York not only as its own country, but a nation with no revenue from New York City. This possibility had been mentioned often in Poughkeepsie.

Several newspapers had written about it. The editor of the *Pennsylvania Gazette* warned that if she did, New York "would be placed between the upper and nether millstone, and find herself an alien among her father's children…" Jay had repeatedly told the Anti delegates that as a New Yorker he knew for certain that the city planned to do so if the Convention failed. It was a powerful argument.[609]

And, too, the Antis living in New York City pressured the Anti delegates to approve the Constitution because if New York turned it down, Congress would leave New York City, taking the entire federal government with it, and reopen somewhere else. New York City would lose all the attendant prestige, jobs, and income that Congress gave it.

Jay had written Washington that he thought some of the Antis were starting to change their minds. He explained that "the party begins to divide in their opinions" and now many favored voting in favor if amendments were guaranteed later. "These circumstances afford room for hope."[610]

And then, on July 23, to put more pressure on the Antis, the Federalists staged a huge, colorful daylong parade and other festivities in New York City to celebrate the approval of the Constitution by both New Hampshire and Virginia, giving America a new government. The parade, led by a large float designed as a ship and called the *Hamilton*, drew a teeming crowd of thousands of jubilant spectators. The parade signaled Anti delegates in Poughkeepsie that approval had been given and they were going to be left on the doorstep by themselves if they did not approve, too.[611]

And it was obvious that steps were already underway in Congress to quickly hold elections and construct a brand-new government. Everyone in the country suspected that George Washington would be president and that he would appoint his close friends, Hamilton and Jay, to help him run the country. Why make Hamilton and Jay mad at New York by turning down the Constitution now, at the very last moment?

A new plan was proposed, giving New York the right to secede if their amendments were not passed within a certain period of time when the government was formed, but Hamilton, anticipating that proposal, read a letter from Madison that stated under no circumstances could New York be allowed in the Union under that plan. Madison wrote that the idea made the amendments conditional. "The

Constitution requires an adoption in toto and forever," he wrote abruptly. The new plan died.

A nervous Madison waited in New York as the vote approached in Poughkeepsie. "It seems by no means certain what the result there would be," he wrote Edmund Randolph in Virginia, adding that he was sure that approval would only come with an agreement to add the bill of rights.

He and others were growing weary of ratification, too, and eager to get the new government into place—as soon as New York ratified, if it ratified.[612]

Would it? Many believed that the New Yorkers, as tired of the rancorous debates as the men in New Hampshire had been, would adjourn, delaying and possibly wrecking the entire process. "The New Yorkers are determined to have their frolic," wrote one congressman.[613]

Foreign diplomats simply assumed that the two-thirds majority of Antis in the New York Convention killed the vote for ratification. "In [New York] the opinion of the Anti-Federalists is positively in favor of separation. They are claiming that it is advisable for them to form a separate government and not involve themselves for a long time to come in the affairs of Europe..." wrote Comte Moustier of France, who was unhappy about such an outcome and added that "without Virginia and New York the new government will exist more in name than in fact."[614]

After more wrangling in Poughkeepsie, an Anti delegate proposed that the "condition" term be replaced with "in confidence" that amendments would be passed. All liked that switch. Jay, by now the overriding voice of the Federalists and a man who had won the respect of all, told the delegates with great diplomacy that the Antis had to now be pleased because "they have carried all their amendments." He told the Federalists that they should be happy because "we have adopted such measures as will bring us into the union." He said that both parties should be glad that "we have the highest possible prospect of a convention for amendments—we are now one people all pledged for amendments."[615]

As a bow to their opponents, the Federalists importantly agreed to include a circular letter to the states, written by Jay, asking all of them to join with New York in a second convention to design a bill of rights. Jay may have done so out of pressure from the Antis. He also knew there would probably be no second convention. Madison had assured him that there were forces at work within Congress and the country to put the new government into office very quickly. There would be no time for a second convention, but his agreement on the circular letter pleased all of the Antis, whose respect for Jay had grown immensely throughout the convention.

The Federalists outside the convention were furious with the circular letter, but agreed to go along in order to get the constitution ratified. "This will set everything afloat again," fumed George Washington in Virginia over the second convention notion.[616]

The ratification vote was taken on July 25, which happened to be Governor Clinton's forty-ninth birthday. Many of the Antis had changed their minds, led by their leader, Melancton Smith. He had been in touch with several Anti-Federalists across the country to whom he pleaded that he was torn. They advised him to vote for the Constitution and press hard for the bill of rights during the very first year of the new government. On the day of the vote, Smith, as a signal to all, walked across the room, sat down next to Alexander Hamilton, announced that he had changed his mind, and voted for the Constitution.

Smith had become the hero of the convention. Following his conversion to the Federalist cause, eleven other Anti delegates switched their votes, too, joining him, giving the Constitution approval by a slender three vote margin, 30–27 (four fiercely Anti delegates had left the Convention earlier and did not vote, perhaps creating the difference).[617]

The circular letter that the Antis had so fervently hoped would result in a second convention failed. Several states rejected the idea outright and it died.

Why did twelve Anti delegates change their minds and vote for the Constitution, despite being rebuffed in efforts to have a bill of rights as part of it? It was simply the best policy at the time to jettison the useless old Confederation and start a new government, with a bill of rights promised to America by the Triumvirate, individuals whom most of the Antis now saw as men of their word.

Gilbert Livingston, an Anti who switched and a member of New York's prominent Livingston family, put it best. He said on the day of the vote, the key factor was the passage of a bill of rights and its recommendation in the Constitution they had passed was "considering our present situation with respect to our sister states, the wisest and best measure we can possibly pursue..." Smith may have felt that the debating over the way the bill of rights would be presented may have at least forced the Federalists to agree to it—for the time being. Many Antis agreed with him; events and personalities, rather than strident beliefs, meant the difference in affirmation.[618]

In the end, it was the work of the Triumvirate's Hamilton and Jay that carried the vote for the Constitution. Jay's connections to just about everybody in the courthouse, convivial charm, status as foreign secretary, and his conciliatory *Address to the People of New York State* convinced the Antis that he was genuinely interested in their point of view and would work with Hamilton and others to get a bill of rights passed.

Hamilton's speeches and off-the-floor arm-twisting were hailed by many. "He argued, he remonstrated, he entreated, he warned...till apathy itself was moved, and the most relentless of human things, a preconcerted majority, was staggered and broken," said the Reverend John Mason later.[619]

Would the vote have been different if New Hampshire and Virginia had not yet affirmed the Constitution? If anyone else besides Hamilton and Jay had led the fight for the Constitution? If the Antis had not been put under pressure from their colleagues in New York City? If New York City men had not threatened to secede from New York State? If Hamilton had not been so energetic? Or Jay that charming? If the four Anti delegates had not left? If the convention had not been held with the Fourth of July taking place in the middle of it?

No one will ever know. New York did ratify the Constitution, the Congress and new government remained in New York City, and steps were taken quickly to elect and organize the new government of the United States.

Observers were stunned by the victory. The Federalists "seemed throughout the course of the whole transaction to have been on the brink of failure," wrote Joshua Atherton to John Lamb later.[620]

Many were simply happy that the eight-month-long drama had ended. R. R. Livingston of New York was one. He "wished that all opposers would be quiet and settle their minds and be composed and heartily join the federals and promote the happiness of the states in general, the great object of the whole, which pray God grant."[621]

George Washington was thrilled. He wrote a correspondent from Great Britain, Sir Edward Newenham, that because of the Confederation, "we have not yet been in a situation fully to enjoy those blessings which God and nature seemed to have intended for us—But I begin to look forward, with a kind of political faith, to scenes of national happiness, which have not heretofore been offered for the fruition of the most favored nations…we [now] have the unequalled privilege of choosing our own political institutions and of improving upon the experience of mankind…a greater drama is now acting in this theater than has heretofore been brought on the American stage, or any other in the world. We exhibit at present the novel and astonishing spectacle of a whole people deliberating calmly on what form of government will be the most conducive to their happiness..."[622]

Foreigners breathed a sigh of relief at the final approval in New York. One Brit, Andrew Allen, wrote to an American that the Constitution "gives unity to the different and otherwise discordant interests of the states...less liable to be thwarted or controlled in their operations by the narrow and partial schemes of factious demagogues."[623]

Following numerous celebrations, Madison, Hamilton, and Jay were sent hundreds of letters from all over the United States congratulating them for shepherding the Constitution through each of the state conventions. The feelings of most Americans could best be summed up in a letter sent to Madison by his friend, former Virginia governor John Page. He wrote, "I congratulate you on the brightening prospects of our affairs, and the success of your wishes and patriotic labors—they are crowned with success and to your immortal honor...I have always attributed to you the glory of laying the foundation of this great fabric of government."[624]

The United States was born.

# AFTERMATH

The Triumvirate's work did not stop at the ratification of the Constitution. James Madison, Alexander Hamilton, and John Jay became three of the most influential men in the early history of the United States. Through their efforts as politicians and administrators, the men, with Washington, John Adams, Thomas Jefferson, and others, established the United States as a successful independent nation and as an emerging world power.

## James Madison and the Bill of Rights

The slight Virginian had promised Patrick Henry, George Mason, and others that he would work hard to have a bill of rights passed in Congress. Now he had to do so. If the Federalists ignored the Antis yet again, the firestorm could wreck the new government. Madison also knew, after a long and difficult year of conventions, that a large percentage of the people in the country favored a bill of rights now, not in the future. The more Madison thought about it, the more he believed that, in fact, the bill of rights had to be approved immediately. What better way to get the brand-new government off its feet than passage of the bill that would secure the support of all the government's critics?

Madison planned to oversee the passage of the Bill of Rights as a U.S. senator from Virginia, but Patrick Henry and his crafty political associates ruined that dream, and quickly. Henry, still angry at Madison over the state convention, worked hard to defeat him in the state legislature's election for the state's two U.S. Senate seats. Henry's men, Richard Henry Lee and William Grayson, were picked; Madison ran third. Thwarted there, Madison then ran for Congress. Henry again tried to have him defeated, convincing the popular James Monroe, the war hero and the man who would one day be the nation's fifth president, to run against him.

Madison knew that to defeat Monroe, his friend, in their district, which covered eight counties, he could not simply sit back and shake hands on election day. He had to do something he loathed—campaign for office. State legislator Hardin Burnley wrote him, "I know that this has not been your usual practice, and am certain that it will be very irksome to you, but your friends hope that you will make some sacrifices of this sort however disagreeable they may be."[625]

Madison's main plank in his campaign was his newfound support for the bill of rights. That campaign consisted of writing letters to political figures and Baptist ministers, some published in Virginia newspapers. He wrote one minister, "The first Congress meeting under [the Constitution] ought to prepare and recommend to the states for ratification the most satisfactory provisions for all essential rights, particularly the rights of conscience in the fullest latitude, the freedom of the press, trials by jury, security against general warrants, etc."[626]

Madison defeated Monroe in a close race by carrying his own county by a huge margin.

As a member of the very first House of Representatives, Madison quickly became one of the best congressmen and a political bridge between Congress and his friend, President Washington. In New York, he was able to team up with the other members of the Triumvirate and to see them often. Washington had named Hamilton the secretary of the treasury and Jay the first chief justice of the United States Supreme Court. Madison's friend Jefferson was named the first secretary of state upon his return from Paris and was happy to find his good friend Madison in town with him.

Madison plunged into his new job. He went to work on the bill of rights when he arrived. He had kept the copies of the suggested amendments from the different state conventions—in his own hand and in newspaper stories—and, in little time, wrote a generalized bill of rights with twelve amendments.

The insistence of many for the right to own guns to protect themselves and to join militias was phrased: "A well regulated militia, being necessary to the security of a free State, the right of the people to keep and bear arms, shall not be infringed." Over the centuries, courts have upheld the amendment as it stood, but in June 2008, the U.S. Supreme Court ruled that Americans could keep arms without any connection to militias.

He told Congress that a bill of rights was needed to guarantee personal liberties to the people right away. He knew that there were other reasons to pass it, too: that its passage would be a huge step in the patching up of the disputes between the Federalists and Anti-Federalists, that it would ingratiate Congress with the newspapers, which were calling for a bill of rights. He told his Federalist friends it would show the Antis, and the rest of the country, that the Federalists were not interested in a tyrannical, nationalistic government that preyed on the people.[627]

On June 8, 1789, Madison spoke for nearly the entire day on the need for the bill of rights in the House of Representatives. He carefully described each of the twelve amendments and discussed their individual as well as the collective goals. He noted, too, that he believed that an additional reason to pass the bill was to encourage county and state courts to use the Bill of Rights to not only protect citizens, but to curb the power of the federal government. He told Jefferson that autumn that he had always favored a bill of rights, but not one that created an imbalance of power. The overwhelming call for a bill of rights at the ratifying conventions had changed his mind, too. He wrote at the end of them that "a great many of our constituents are dissatisfied."[628]

Now, with this groundswell of public support for the bill of rights, he felt he had to go along.[629]

There was still grumbling from some Federalists, but the House and Senate passed the twelve amendments that September and sent them to the states for ratification. Ironically, the state that caused the greatest delay because of its lengthy debates was Virginia, whose Anti-Federalist leaders had been so insistent on it in the 1788 state conventions. Finally, in December 1791, the Bill of Rights, whittled down to ten amendments by the states (one more became the twenty-seventh amendment later), became law and has stood since then as the foundation of American liberties.[630]

In Congress, Madison worked for states' rights underneath the federal umbrella, spent much time with the president conveying the feelings of Congress to him, and studied bills the administration offered and the bills of others in the House and Senate. He was one of the guiding hands behind the country's first tariff bill on foreign goods, which raised needed revenue to pay for the new U.S. government.

Congressmen admired Madison's hard work, intelligence, and growing ability to work with others to get things done. Fisher Ames, who would split with him later, was one of his strongest supporters in the first Congress. Ames said of Madison, "He is a studious man, devoted to the public business, and a thorough master of almost every public question that can arise, or he will spare no pains to become so, if he happens to be in want of information," adding that many congressmen simply sought his advice and explanation on bills to save themselves work.[631]

The friendship between Madison and Alexander Hamilton that was brought about by the Triumvirate's work on the ratification campaign began to crumble in 1790 when Hamilton introduced his plans to revamp the finances of the United States, with the full backing of President Washington. Part of that plan was for the federal government to assume the more than $70 million in state debts acquired throughout the Revolution and the intervening years and pay them off. Another part was the creation of the Bank of the United States to provide needed funds for the U.S. government. It would be funded by investors purchasing stock in it. Madison was opposed to the plan, despite his Federalist leanings, because he thought it weakened the financial foundations of the states. He worked hard to defeat it in Congress, where its passage wavered daily. Many of the opponents saw Hamilton's plan as a means for the federal government to grow into an all-powerful financial monolith.

To get the bills passed, Jefferson intervened in a memorable dinner with Hamilton. Jefferson could get several southern congressmen to change their votes and approve Hamilton's financial plans if the U.S. government would, in return, agree to establish the nation's permanent capitol along the northern bank of the Potomac river, in what would be a special federal district, named after George Washington, called the District of Columbia. It was located in what was then the middle of the country, on the banks of a large river that provided excellent shipping service to the ocean and would serve as nexus between northern and southern legislators. This plan would mean moving the government out of New York, and turning down efforts to bring it back to Philadelphia, but it would also be a good location for the national capital and, importantly, assure passage of Hamilton's financial plans.

It worked, even though Madison did not change his vote. The financial plan was approved and the U.S. government moved to Washington, D.C. The cost was high, though. The entire battle over the capital, the bank, and other issues, plus a growing personal animosity between those who supported and distrusted the federal government, left great bitterness between Hamilton and Jefferson and Hamilton and Madison, a bitterness that even Washington could not smooth over. Jefferson resigned from the cabinet and, with Madison, created a political party, the Jeffersonian Republicans, devoted to states' rights. At the same time, Washington and Hamilton created the nationalistic Federalist Party. The two parties, which adapted new names over the years, changed American politics forever.

The anger and disputes between the two parties grew quickly, pitting Hamilton against Jefferson, and his friend Madison. Bitterness followed, and Hamilton and Jefferson constantly lashed out at each other publicly and privately and at cabinet meetings, with Washington unable to make any peace between them despite heroic personal efforts. Each wrote attacks on the other in newspapers, or had friends (such as Madison) do the same.[632] The only thing they all agreed upon was that their friend George Washington, who seemed to contemplate retiring as president after his first term, should run again.

They encouraged Washington to remain in office and he did, once again elected unanimously.

In 1794, Madison's life changed forever. Aaron Burr introduced the quiet, forty-three–year-old lifelong bachelor to Dolley Todd, a vivacious, twenty-five-year-old Quaker widow from Philadelphia. The pair were smitten with each other. Madison had never been completely in love before and felt like a teenager in the relationship. In Dolley, he rediscovered his youth. In Madison, Dolley found a mature and loving companion for herself and her young son.[633]

Marriage to Dolley changed the sense of importance in Madison's life. John Adams was elected president in 1796, and Jefferson vice president. Madison saw it as a good time to retire from politics to work as a planter at Montpelier, finally, bringing his young wife and brand-new son there to begin their new life together.[634]

Despite his best efforts, the life of a planter seemed dull after nearly twenty years in government. He had to work so hard that he wrote few letters and his famous correspondence with dozens of men who were key figures in American life evaporated. At Montpelier, isolated from the rest of Virginia, he saw few public figures. Madison traveled little. His father was old and dying. Madison told everyone that he enjoyed his life with his new wife and the frequent visits from Vice President Jefferson, but after several years, he yearned for a chance to return to public life.

That opportunity arrived in 1800 when Jefferson was elected president by the House of Representatives after he and Aaron Burr were tied in the presidential contest in the electoral college. Jefferson asked his old friend Madison to be his secretary of state. Overnight, Madison became one of the most powerful men in the country. Ironically, Jefferson's close election in the House brought about an unexpected new unity in the country. In a stirring inaugural address, Jefferson told America that on that day, "We are all Republicans; we are all Federalists..."[635]

Jefferson and his friend Madison seized the reigns of government in a capital city that was still being built. The Executive Mansion [White House] was not even completed when Jefferson moved in.[636]

The duo of Jefferson and Madison seemed made for each other. One Washington social leader of the day, Margaret Smith, wrote, "Never were there a plainer set of men and I think I may add more virtuous and enlightened than at present forming our administration." She added that Madison "cannot fail in inspiring good will."[637]

Madison had come back into the government, in part, to fulfill his dreams of creating a united country. He had written that governments were created "to cure the mischiefs of faction" and now he had another, and better, chance to cure them himself.[638]

Madison threw himself into a job that had become increasingly responsible as the young nation had grown over eleven years. Now, as secretary of state, he had to deal with numerous crises: the Barbary States in the Mediterranean were seizing American ships and seamen and holding them for ransom; Napoleon Bonaparte eyed Louisiana; the French had been forced out of Haiti in a slave revolt; American ships, captains, and ship owners found themselves constantly embroiled in international law disputes as American shipping grew in size around the world.[639]

On the personal side, Madison had to defend himself against attacks that he was naming only Federalists to the 80 jobs he controlled as secretary of state and was interfering in the 316 jobs that Jefferson controlled as president.

The hardworking Madison paid little attention to his critics, however. With the president, he labored to help turn the United States into a world power, diplomatically fighting in the Caribbean, the Mediterranean, London, Paris, Moscow, and other capitals.

His wife Dolley dramatically enhanced Madison's position at home. Since Jefferson was a bachelor, he asked Dolley to serve as the nation's official hostess at the White House, running dinners, receptions, and parties and appearing as the glamorous and much-admired hostess. Her popularity was enormous and reflected well on her husband, the quiet man who stayed in the background at White House affairs while she shone at the center of them.

The jewel of Madison's terms as secretary of state was the purchase of the vast Louisiana Territory from Napoleon in 1803. The French emperor was sick of the Caribbean and North America following the slave revolts in Haiti; he also needed money to continue his European wars. He was eager to sell the Louisiana Territory, which comprised one-third of what would eventually be the United States, plus the city of New Orleans, for just $15 million, or a penny per acre, a price Madison considered a bargain. Madison did not negotiate the sale (that was done by Minister to France Robert Livingston and special envoy James Monroe) but he approved it and recommended it to Jefferson, who agreed immediately. The president soon sent Louis and Clark on a lengthy expedition to explore the Louisiana Territory and lands that went all the way to the Pacific Coast. While they did that, Jefferson and Madison began negotiations to buy Florida from the Spaniards and possibly purchase all of Texas, too.

Jefferson's first term in office ended in 1804 with his easy reelection in a country that was quite happy with the performance of the president and his administration, especially Secretary of State Madison. Troubles with England would develop in 1807 and 1808, however, and linger when Madison became the nation's fourth president in 1808.[640]

## John Jay, America's First Chief Justice

George Washington had known John Jay for slightly over twelve years when he became the nation's first president. Jay and his wife Sarah were frequent dinner companions of the Washingtons throughout the American Revolution during the winters the Continental Army was camped in New Jersey. He was fully aware of Jay's work for the Revolution, the Continental Congress, and the courts of New York, as well as his personal campaign for ratification of the Constitution. He saw Jay as a man who was loyal to the goals of the Revolution and the new government, a trusted friend and, most importantly, a lawyer and judge who could set the nation on the proper course as it grappled with the unprecedented legal complexities of the new Constitution. Because of the war and his work in the government for the Confederation, Jay had not actually practiced law in ten years and had not presided over court actions in that period of time. The president, though, wanted a chief justice who could devise a new system of laws and, even more importantly, who had the respect of all the people, not just judges and lawyers. That was Jay.

Everybody respected Jay and many wanted Washington to make him the secretary of state, because he had been secretary of foreign affairs in the Confederation government and had considerable diplomatic experience. That was problematic for Washington, though, because he needed to put Thomas Jefferson, who also had substantial diplomatic experience, into an important office and that would be as head of the State Department. The new president's dilemma was happily solved when Jay asked Washington to be the chief justice of the first U.S. Supreme Court. With great relief, Washington agreed and appointed him chief justice in the spring of 1789.[641]

He wrote Jay of his new job, "The love which you bear our country, and a desire to promote general happiness, will not suffer you to hesitate a moment to bring into action the talents, knowledge, and integrity which are so necessary to be exercised at the head of that department which must be considered as the keystone of our political fabric."[642]

Jay understood that he had to move carefully as the first chief justice. Every decision he handed down, or anything he said, would be used as legal precedent for hundreds of cases that would come to the court over the years. His first views on the law and the relationship of the branches of the federal government, and the relationship of the federal government to the states, would be set in stone.

Realizing that, and certain, like the president, that the new government had to establish itself quickly, and to be a government always responsible to the people, he took bold steps as chief justice. From his first few decisions until his last, he let everybody know that the new federal government's powers always superceded those of the individual states. He also ruled that there were many powers of the states that were separate from those of the federal government and had to be left alone. His decisions hinted that in any battle between the power of the federal government and the states, the federal government would always win. This view, that gave so much authority to the federal government, was underscored ten years later by the landmark decisions of Chief Justice John Marshall.[643]

Jay set other precedents. In 1793, George Washington asked Jay and the Supreme Court to consult with him on what the federal government should do in its relations with England and France, engaged in a war. Washington wanted to issue a neutrality proclamation and avoid conflict, but sought legal advice. Jay told the president that the role of the Supreme Court was to decide cases and make law, not to serve as consultants. They did not meet with him.

Jay was so emphatic of the role the federal government had to establish in its first years that he often went over, in great detail, the purposes of the three branches of government in his charge to juries and as a preamble to his decisions as the chief justice, a practice later dropped.

In addition to sitting in New York for Supreme Court decisions, the six justices had to travel to other states to hear cases there as "circuit court" judges. This lengthy and difficult travel took up months of Jay's time each year, but it was the only way that the court could come to the people. The cities in these areas held special parades for the justices when they arrived and reporters wrote that Jay was inspirational in all of his judicial proceedings, giving the people a positive view of the Supreme Court and the new government. Jay refused to stay at the homes of local politicians, who always invited him, in order to retain his objectivity as a justice.

He saw his role as a justice who brought the federal government to the people and enjoyed it, even though it took him away from his wife and family for long stretches of time.

Jay's work in determining the paths the Supreme Court would follow for years was appreciated later by generations of Americans, but not at the time. After four years as chief justice, Washington called upon him to travel to England to serve as a negotiator for a new treaty to keep the United States out of a war between England and France, to end disputes that had remained since the end of the Revolution, and to strengthen America's financial credit with England.

President Washington issued a proclamation of neutrality when war broke out between France and England that angered the French. At the same time, the British began seizing American merchant ships bound for French ports, along with their passengers and sailors, refused to give up their forts in the American Northwest, as promised at the end of the Revolution, charged Americans higher rates for goods than British citizens, insisted on payment of prewar debts by Americans, left the boundary between Canada and the United States nebulous, refused to advance the United States credit, and stirred up rebellion toward the Americans among American Indian tribes.

Jay's treaty with the British failed to resolve some disputes, but it called for the evacuation of their American forts, allowed the British to collect American debts, and granted even credit to Americans as well as the British. It solidified trade with England, a major step, ignored the French and their claims of U.S. allegiance, and kept the United States out of that war.

Jay thought he had done a creditable job and that, acting on public instructions from Secretary of State Edmund Randolph and secret instructions from his old friend Hamilton, he had greatly enhanced the position of the United States on the world stage.

However, many Americans did not want to pay their prewar debts, now nearly twenty years old. Many sided with the French and believed the United States should enter the war on their side. More thought that the treaty was a surrender to England, the recent enemy, and seethed about it. The nation was so evenly split, the treaty barely passed in Congress and was signed with great reluctance by President Washington.[644]

The treaty was Jay's last work in the federal government. Jay had been working for the national government, in one way or another, for twenty years. He was getting tired. As chief justice, Jay spent nearly six months of each year traveling with another justice to different towns and cities in the northeast to hear cases on "the circuit" and felt very lonely. He loved his wife and sons deeply and missed them when his judicial swings took him way from home for months at a time. He had taken time off from his court duties for his treaty work in England.

Looking for a more stable life, and work closer to home, Jay ran for governor of New York in 1792. He lost a close, and disputed, election to George Clinton and continued on the Supreme Court.

In 1795, his international prestige greater and the politics of New York even more complex than in 1792, Jay was elected governor while he was negotiating Jay's Treaty in England. He left the Supreme Court for the governor's post, happily so, when he returned from England. His departure, and growing criticism of the circuit-riding structure of the highest court, brought about dramatic changes. In 1801, under the Judiciary Act, Congress kept the Supreme Court in Washington and created six regional circuit federal courts, staffed by three judges each.

Just five years later, Jay became embroiled in crisis and controversy again when the presidential election of 1800 took place. No one gained the needed votes to become president in the electoral college and the election was thrown into the newly elected House of Representatives.

Hamilton tried to persuade Governor Jay to side with him in a scheme to have New York's previous congressmen, not the new ones, cast the votes, which Hamilton thought would decide the election. Jay argued that he could not put political parties over the good of the country and permitted the new congressmen to vote in what turned out to be the election of Thomas Jefferson.

A Supreme Court opening emerged in 1800. John Adams, as respectful of Jay as Washington had been, wrote him and asked him to return as the Chief Justice. He had Secretary of State John Marshall send Jay the note. Jay turned him down, intent on retiring from public life. His wife's health was also poor, and Jay wanted to spend more time with her. Jay, then fifty-six, also told the president, "My best work is done. I've earned a rest."[645]

Adams, to the surprise of many, then nominated Marshall, who went on to be one of the greatest chief justices in American history.

Jay was urged to run for governor again. Refusing, he retired to his family home in Bedford, New York, in 1800 following twenty-six years of service to his country. He was eager for a quiet life with his wife Sarah, forty-three, and his five children. In 1802, Sarah Jay died.

The former chief justice, who missed his wife very much, never remarried. Jay spent twenty-seven more years in retirement, with little connection to public life, and died in 1829.

## Alexander Hamilton's Great Gamble

By the time the Constitution was ratified in 1789, Alexander Hamilton had solidified his position as one of the most influential men in the country. The veteran aide to George Washington in the Revolution left the service in 1782 and completed law school. A few months later, he was elected a delegate to the Continental Congress from New York State, at age twenty-five. He served there until the Constitutional Convention in 1787. His work in the Triumvirate to write *The Federalist*, revealed after the conventions ended, and the passage of the Constitution gained him even more recognition and respect.

Over the years, Hamilton maintained his close friendship with Washington, who saw his young former aide as both a political and economic genius. He made him the secretary of the treasury in his first cabinet in the summer of 1789, certain that young Hamilton would be able to put the United States's finances on solid ground in the early days of the Republic. He also saw Hamilton as a friend and loyalist who would give the president substantial political advice and always be true to him, regardless of what crisis developed in the new country.

The job was a gamble for Hamilton. To accept it, he had to venture into national politics and also suffer a steep reduction in salary. He did so eagerly. "In undertaking the task, I hazarded much, but I thought it an occasion that called upon me to hazard," he said.[646]

It was also a chance for Hamilton, who had planned the new government for so many years, back to the winters of the early years of the Revolution, to help Washington create a new United States.

Hamilton did everything Washington had hoped he would. As a political adviser, he continued to help Washington write his formal papers and speeches, as he had done throughout the Revolution. He gave him prudent advice on running the country and establishing the president as a powerful national leader. He sided with him in cabinet debates, stood by his side in national and international political disputes, and always reminded people that the general was the very best possible president the young nation could have.

The greatest work of Hamilton, the father of eight by the time he assumed his cabinet post, was in finances. The United States had never established any credit, had no real revenue, no collectable taxes, and, throughout the war and under the Confederation government, was always bankrupt and enjoyed little respect from either foreign countries or its own people.

One big problem was the national debt. The states owed some $77 million. Hamilton proposed that the federal government assume all of the debts the states owed to the national government and any debts owed to foreign governments. To pay it, and to have funds for the operation of the new national government for years, he proposed a series of taxes on foreign goods that were sold in the United States and homegrown goods, too. This not only meant millions in yearly revenue for the government but enabled American craftsmen to sell their products cheaper than those from overseas, giving them a solid financial standing.[647]

These projects were opposed by Madison and Jefferson, states' rights advocates, but, following months of acrimonious debates in and out of Congress, Hamilton won them over by assuring them that the nation's capital would move out of New York and later Philadelphia and be permanently established on the shores of Virginia's Potomac River in Washington, D.C.[648]

Part of the tax plan Hamilton proposed included a domestic tax on liquor produced in local distilleries throughout the states. Liquor producers in Pennsylvania balked at this and refused to pay taxes. They saw it as an unnecessary tax on their business and a trampling of states' rights. Several pleas by Washington himself failed to get the whiskey distillers to pay their taxes. Hamilton then advised President Washington to utilize his Constitutional authority as commander in chief of the U.S. military forces and take an army to Pennsylvania to put down the tax rebellion. Washington, in uniform, took Hamilton, also in uniform, and a volunteer army into Pennsylvania, but the tax rebels gave up before there was even a confrontation. The affair not only solidified the government's ability to collect all taxes, but also resulted in an enormous increase in public admiration for the president for his willingness to confront the rebels.

Perhaps Hamilton's greatest achievement as the secretary of the treasury was the establishment of the National Bank, patterned after the Bank of England. He persuaded Washington to propose the bank even though there was no language in the Constitution to do that. Hamilton argued, as did Madison and others, that there were "implied powers" in the Constitution that permitted it. Washington agreed and proposed the bank, which Congress passed. The bank not only gave the United States money, credit, reserves, and the ability to borrow money, but greatly expanded the strength of the president under the "implied powers" phrase. Hamilton had done a superb job of establishing the finances of the United States.[649]

Throughout the early years of the Washington administration, Hamilton enjoyed great success but he also reminded people, on this national stage, how inflexible his views were, how little he was willing to compromise, and that, while a revolutionary who filled his speeches with phrases about power and the people, he truly did believe in an elitist government run by the few well-to-do, over the many middle and working class citizens.[650]

Hamilton and Secretary of State Thomas Jefferson began to disagree in cabinet meetings over the assumption of debt, then the taxes, then the location of the nation's capital. Their arguments became more intense as the months went by, with Madison siding with his close friend Jefferson. Each dismissed pleas by President Washington to work together for the good of the administration. Their feud was not just professional, but personal.[651]

Finally, the war between the French and British in Europe brought the two secretaries to a collision. Hamilton favored a policy of neutrality, which Washington adapted, certain that the brand-new United States was simply not equipped to fight a war of any kind. Washington wanted Hamilton to travel to London and negotiate a new treaty with the British to end that country's antagonistic hostilities toward the United States, but opposition by Jefferson stopped that assignment and the president sent John Jay instead.

By that time, Hamilton's heavy-handed diplomatic tactics, which included much backroom bargaining and political deals, had started to annoy people. Rufus King, of Massachusetts, who worked with him to get the Constitution passed, became one of many critics. He told Hamilton that "great and good schemes ought to succeed on their own merits and not by intrigue or the establishment of bad measures," but Hamilton ignored him.[652]

During Washington's first term, Hamilton grew into a devoted nationalist, determined to expand the powers of the federal government and to convince the states to see the benefit of a strong union.[653] Jefferson was just the opposite, determined to lessen the national government's grip on the public and the states. "The natural progress of things is for liberty to yield and government to gain ground," warned Jefferson, who, with Madison, started the Jeffersonian Republican political party, a well-organized group that gave birth to America's two party system.[654]

The debut of the new party politics also brought about substantial changes in the U.S. media. The two brand-new parties, Republicans and Federalists, now purchased controlling interests in the weekly newspapers in different cities and used them to launch scurrilous attacks on the other party and its leaders. Hamilton and Jefferson both came under considerable fire from the newspapers controlled by the other.

Angry and unable to work with Jefferson, Hamilton resigned as secretary of the treasury in 1795, midway into Washington's second term; Jefferson also resigned. Hamilton returned to his legal practice in New York City. That same year, Jay left the Supreme Court and became the governor of New York. It was the end of the Triumvirate.

Even though he was out of office, Hamilton continued to have great influence in the government, and the second president, John Adams, named him Inspector General of the Army in 1798 in case the United States went to war with France. He had named Washington the head of the army for the war, which never began.

Hamilton, as arrogant as ever as a private citizen in the eyes of many, backed Charles Pinckney over President John Adams in the election of 1800, with Thomas Jefferson and Aaron Burr also running. He wrote a scathing denunciation of Adams intended only for the eyes of certain party leaders, but Burr published it as a public document and it created a political firestorm.

The Electoral College could not pick the president, with Jefferson and Burr tied for first and John Adams third. The election was thrown into the House of Representatives. Hamilton then abandoned Pinckney and urged the House to select his archenemy, Jefferson, as president in order to reunite the divided country. He also sided with Jefferson to get back at his enemy, Burr. The House elected Jefferson president; Burr and his supporters were angered by Hamilton's actions.

Four years later, Hamilton worked against Burr when Burr ran for governor of New York. His successful opposition to Burr once again gained him many enemies. He wondered how he had begun his public life as the admired right-hand man of General Washington and wound up the center of so much criticism. He wrote near the end of his days that, "Mine is an odd destiny...this American world was not made for me."[655]

Burr, furious that Hamilton's work had denied him both the presidency and the governorship, challenged him to a duel in Weehawken, New Jersey. There, he shot Hamilton dead on July 11, 1804.[656]

Hamilton's passing saddened the country. Following his death, Gouverneur Morris said of him, "He, more than any other man, did the thinking of the time...it seemed as if God had called him suddenly into existence, that he might assist to save the nation." Chief Justice John Marshall, who had known him for years, insisted that among all the Founding Fathers, none supported the Constitution more than Hamilton, who had done so much to see it approved by each state. And Fisher Ames wrote that "the name of Hamilton would have honored Greece in the age of Aristides."[657]

Jay had retired from public life in 1800, returning to his family estate at Bedford to care for his ailing wife, and Hamilton was killed in 1804. That left James Madison, the secretary of state, as the only member of the old Triumvirate still in the government. Madison, who enjoyed his job of running the nation's foreign affairs, was elected president in 1808, after Jefferson had stepped down after two terms, and held office for eight years himself. He retired and returned to Montpelier in 1816.

The three men had not only written *The Federalist* together and worked as a trio to ratify the Constitution during a tense winter of conventions in 1788, but also served their country well for years afterwards. Between them, Hamilton, Madison, and Jay worked in the army and the state and federal governments for a total of eighty-two years. The three, along with Washington, Adams, and Jefferson, created a new democracy.

As Madison put it so well, the government of the United States was "the best legacy ever left by lawgivers to their country and the best lesson ever given to the world."[658]

# ENDNOTES

## PRELUDE

1. William Peters, *A More Perfect Union* (New York: Crown Publishers, 1987), 2.

2. David O. Stewart, *The Summer of 1787* (New York: Simon & Schuster, 2007), 65–66.

3. Peters, *A More Perfect Union*, 149.

4. Ibid., 152.

5. Ibid., 147.

6. Ibid., 90.

7. Ibid., 151.

8. Ibid., 182–183.

9. Stewart, *The Summer of 1787*, 218–219.

## CHAPTER ONE

10. Ron Chernow, *Alexander Hamilton* (New York: Penguin Press, 2004), 187; Fisher Ames, *New York Mirror*, 1787, Hamilton Papers, reel 31, Library of Congress.

11. Alexander Hamilton, James Madison, and John Jay, *The Federalist*, with an introduction by Garry Wills (New York: Bantam Books, 1987), 2.

12. Peter Tappen to George Clinton, 29 September 1787. Clinton Papers, David Library of the American Revolution, New York Public Library; *Albany Gazette*, October 4, 1787; *New York Journal*, October 18, 1787; Jackson Turner Main, *The Antifederalists: Critics of the Constitution*,

*1781–1788* (Chapel Hill: University of North Carolina Press, 1961), 234–235.

13  F. Scott Fitzgerald, *The Great Gatsby* (New York: Charles Scribner's Sons, 1925), 182.

14  Richard Morris, *Witnesses at the Creation: Hamilton, Madison, Jay and the Constitution* (New York: Holt, Rinehart and Winston, 1985), 22–23.

15  Robert Hendrickson, *The Rise and Fall of Alexander Hamilton* (New York: Van Nostrand and Rheinhold Co., 1981), 228.

16  William Lee Miller, *The Business of May Next: James Madison and the Founding* (Charlottesville: University Press of Virginia, 1992), 156; George Washington to Alexander Hamilton, 28 August 1788, in George Washington, *The Writings of George Washington from the Original Manuscript Sources, 1745–1799*, ed. John C. Fitzpatrick, vol. 30 (Washington, DC: U.S. Government Printing Office, 1931–1944), 66. [*GWW* hereafter]

CHAPTER TWO

17  William Grayson to James Madison, 22 March 1786, in Edmund Burnett, ed., *Letters of the Members of the Continental Congress*, vol. 8, (Washington, DC: Carnegie Institution of Washington, 1936), 332–333.

18  Samuel Otis to James Warren, 6 February 1788, in Burnett, *Letters of the Members*, vol. 8, 788–789.

19  Benjamin Lincoln to Rufus King, 11 February 1786, in Charles R. King, ed., *The Life and Correspondence of Rufus King: Comprising His Letters, Private and Official, His Public Documents, and His Speeches* vol. 1, (New York: G. P. Putnam's Sons, 1894), 156–160.

20  Gordon Wood, *The Creation of the American Republic, 1776–1787* (New York: W. W. Norton & Co., 1972), 371, 464.

21  Richard Morris, *The Forging of the Union, 1781–1789* (New York: Harper and Row, 1987), 170–189.

22  Merrill Jensen, *The New Nation: A History of the United States During the Confederation, 1781–1789* (New York: Alfred A. Knopf, 1950), 184–190.

23  Rufus King to Elbridge Gerry, 29 March 1786, in Charles R. King, ed., *The Life and Correspondence of Rufus King*, 162.

24  James Madison to Edmund Pendleton, 24 February 1767, in Burnett, *Letters of the Members*, vol. 8, 547–548.

25  Miller, *The Business of May Next*, 17.

26  William B. Munro, *The Makers of the Unwritten Constitution* (New York, Macmillan Co., 1930), 4; Ralph Ketchum, *James Madison: A Biography* (Charlottesville: University Press of Virginia, 1990), 226.

27   James Madison to Thomas Jefferson, 9 December 1787, in Gaillard Hunt, ed., *The Writings of James Madison: Comprising His Public Papers and His Private Correspondence, Including Numerous Letters and Documents Now for the First Time Printed*, vol. 5, (New York: G. P. Putnam's Sons, 1900–1910), 62–69.

28   Thomas Jefferson to James Madison, 31 July 1788, in Thomas Jefferson, *The Life and Selected Writings of Thomas Jefferson*, ed. Adrienne Koch and William Peden, vol. 13 (New York: Modern Library, 1944), 440; Paul Smith, *Letters of Delegates to Congress, 1774–1789*, vol. 1, (Washington, DC: Library of Congress, 1976), 543–546; Jefferson to Madison, 18 November 1778, in Jefferson, *The Life and Selected Writings*, vol. 13, 452; Jefferson to Dr. Thomas Randolph, 30 May 1790, in Jefferson, *The Life and Selected Writings*, vol. 15, 486–497.

29   George Washington to the Marquis de Lafayette, 18 September 1787, in George Washington, *The Papers of George Washington*, ed. W. W. Abbot and Dorothy Twohig. Confederation series, vol. 5 (Charlottesville: University of Virginia Press, 1992–2000), 334.

30   *Federalist* No. 38.

31   Robert Goodloe Harper, "The Federalists as Realists," in *The Federalists: Realists or Ideologues?*, ed. George Athan Billias (Lexington, MA: D.C. Heath & Co., 1970), 45–47.

32   Samuel Eliot Morison, and Henry Steele Commager, *The Growth of the American Republic*, vol. 1, (New York: Oxford University Press, 1962), 290–292; James Madison to George Washington, 18 March 1787, in Hunt, *The Writings of James Madison*, vol. 2, 320–324; Edward Carrington to William Short, 25 October 1787, in Burnett, *Letters of the Members*, vol. 8, 665; Henry Knox to Rufus King, 19 June 1788, King, *The Life and Correspondence of Rufus King*, 335.

33   Bernard Schwartz, "Experience vs. Reason: Beautiful Books and Great Revolutions," in *The Bill of Rights: Government Proscribed*, ed. Ron Hoffman and Peter J. Albert (Charlottesville: University Press of Virginia for the U.S. Capitol Historical Society, 1997), 431; Fisher Ames, "The Federalists as Ideologues," in Billias, *The Federalists*, 48–62.

34   Ketchum, *James Madison*, 226.

35   Stewart, *The Summer of 1787*, 88.

36   Jeff Broadwater, *George Mason: Forgotten Founder* (Chapel Hill: University of North Carolina Press, 2006), 202.

37   Russell L. Caplan, *Constitutional Brinksmanship: Amending the Constitution by National Convention* (New York: Oxford University Press, 1988), 32; Richard Henry Lee to Samuel Adams, 5 October 1787, in Merrill Jensen, John Kaminski, and others, *The Documentary History of the Ratification of*

the Constitution, vol. 8, (Madison: State Historical Society of Wisconsin, 1988), 51–52. [Kaminski hereafter].

38   James Madison to Thomas Jefferson, 6 September 1787, in James Morton Smith, ed., *The Republic of Letters: The Correspondence Between Thomas Jefferson and James Madison, 1776–1826,* vol. 1 (New York: W. W. Norton & Co., 1995), 490–492.

39   Edward Carrington to James Madison, 23 September 1787, in Burnett, *Letters of the Members,* vol. 8, 647.

40   George Washington to Henry Knox, 15 October 1787, in Washington, *Papers of George Washington,* Confederation series, vol. 5, 375–376.

41   James Madison to Thomas Jefferson, 20 December 1787, in Smith, *The Republic of Letters,* vol. 1, 515–517; on Indian fears in Virginia and Georgia, Madison to Jefferson, 20 December 1787; Charles Thompson to Samuel Huntington, 27 December 1787, all in *Republic of Letters;* Robert McGuire and Robert Ohsfeldt, "Self-Interest Agency Theory and the Political Voting Behavior: The Ratification of the United States Constitution," *American Economic Journal,* March 1989, 220–224; Burnett, *Letters of the Members,* vol. 8, 690–691.

42   James Monroe to James Madison, 13 October 1787, in James Madison, *The Papers of James Madison,* ed. Robert Rutland, William Hutchinson, and William Rachal, vol. 10 (Chicago: University of Chicago Press, 1962–1981), 192–194.

43   *Pennsylvania Herald,* October 17, 1787.

44   Nathan Dane to Nathaniel Gorham, New York, 22 June 1787, 613–614; Cyrus Griffin to Thomas Fitzsimmons, 18 February 1788, 699–700; and Lord Dorchester to Lord Sydney, Quebec, 10 April 1787, 547; all in Burnett, *Letters of the Members,* vol. 8.

45   Gouverneur Morris to George Washington, 30 October 1787, in Washington, *Papers of George Washington,* Confederation series, vol. 5, 398–400.

46   James Madison to George Washington, 30 September 1787, in Burnett, *Letters of the Members,* vol. 8, 650.

47   Richard Henry Lee to William Shippen, 2 October 1787, in Burnett, *Letters of the Members,* vol. 8, 653.

48   Richard Henry Lee to George Mason, in Kaminski, *The Documentary History,* vol. 13, 281–282; Edward Carrington to James Madison, 23 September 1787, in Burnett, *Letters of the Members,* vol. 8, 647.

49   Richard Henry Lee to Edmund Randolph, 16 October 1787, in Burnett, *Letters of the Members,* vol. 8, 658.

50   George Mason to George Washington, 7 October 1787, in Madison, *The Papers of James Madison,* vol. 3, 1001–1002.

51　James Madison to George Washington, 30 September 30 1787, in Kaminski, *The Documentary History*, vol. 13, 375–276.

52　Irving Brant, *The Fourth President: A Life of James Madison*, (Indianapolis: Bobbs-Merrrill Co., 1970), 210; Ketchum, *James Madison*, 409.

53　Hoffman and Albert, *The Bill of Rights*, 436.

54　Morris, *Witnesses at the Creation*, 97–99.

55　Chernow, *Alexander Hamilton*, 174.

56　Ralph Ketcham, *James Madison: A Biography* (Charlottesville: University Press of Virginia, 1990), 112; J. P. Brissot de Warville, *New Travels in the United States of America, 1788* (Cambridge: Belknap Press, 1964), 147.

57　Richard Norton Smith, *Patriarch: George Washington and the New American Nation* (Boston: Houghton-Mifflin Co., 1993), 25–28.

58　Miller, *The Business of May Next*, 10–11.

59　James White to Governor Richard Carswell of North Carolina, 13 November 1787, 682; Nicholas Gilman to Governor John Sullivan of New Hampshire, 23 March 1787, 709; all in Burnett, *Letters of the Members*, vol. 8.

60　George Washington to Charles Carter, 14 December 1787, in Washington, *Papers of George Washington*, Confederation series, vol. 5, 489–492.

61　Sara Shumer, "New Jersey: Property and Price of Republican Politics," in *Ratifying the Constitution*, ed. Michael Allen Gillespie and Michael Lienesch (Lawrence: University Press of Kansas, 1989), 71.

62　James Madison to Archibald Stuart, 30 October 1787, in Hunt, *The Writings of James Madison*, vol 5, 47.

63　Charles Callan Tansill, *The Making of the American Republic: The Great Documents, 1774–1789* (New Rochelle, NY: Arlington House Press, 1972), 105.

64　Samuel Otis to Theodore Sedgwick, 15 June 1788, Sedgwick Papers, Massachusetts Historical Society.

65　Clinton Rossiter, *Alexander Hamilton and the Constitution* (New York: Harcourt, Brace and World, 1964), 72–73.

66　Thomas Paine, "The Rights of Man, Part One," in Kenneth M. Dolbeare and Michael S. Cummings, *American Political Thought*, 5th ed. (Washington, DC: CQ Press, 2004), 47; Morison, *The Growth of the American Republic*, vol. 1, 290.

67　Richard Henry Lee to George Mason, 1 October 1787, Richard Henry Lee Letters, vol. 2, 439.

68　David Redick to William Irvine, 24 September 1787, in Bernard Bailyn, ed., *The Debate on the Constitution: Federalist and Antifederalist Speeches,*

*Articles, and Letters During the Struggle Over Ratification*, (New York: Library of America, 1993), 15.

69 Fran Moran, "Iron Handed Despotism: Anti-Federalists and American Civil Liberties," *The Academic Forum,* New Jersey City University, 8.

70 Alexander Hamilton to James Madison, 19 May 1788, in Miller, *The Business of May Next*, 188.


CHAPTER THREE

71 Moran, "Iron Handed Despotism: Anti-Federalists and American Civil Liberties," 7.

72 Thomas Flexner, *George Washington in the American Revolution* (Boston: Little, Brown and Co., 1968), 412; Broadus Mitchell, *Alexander Hamilton: Youth to Maturity*, 2 vols. (New York: Thomas Crowell, 1980), 105–112.

73 Morris, *Witnesses at the Creation*, 27.

74 John C. Hamilton, *The Life of Alexander Hamilton*, vol. 1 (Boston: Houghton, Osgood, 1879), 137; Chernow, *Alexander Hamilton*, 83–84.

75 Alexander Hamilton to Nathanael Greene, 10 June 1783, in Harold C. Syrett, *The Papers of Alexander Hamilton*, vol. 3 (New York: Columbia University Press, 1961–1987), 310.

76 Ibid., 44–45; Chernow, *Alexander Hamilton*, 126–127; Alexander Hamilton to John Laurens, April 1779 in Syrett, *The Papers of Alexander Hamilton*, vol. 2, 37.

77 *Federalist* No. 72; Peter McNamara, *Alexander Hamilton, the Love of Fame and Modern Democratic Statesmanship* (New York: Rowman and Littlefield, 1999), 14.

78 Allan McLane Hamilton, *Intimate Life of Alexander Hamilton, Based Chiefly upon Original Family Letters and Other Documents* (New York: C. Scribner's Sons, 1911), 37.

79 Ibid., 36–37; Syrett, *The Papers of Alexander Hamilton*, vol. 2, 37.

80 John Jay to Robert Livingston, 1 January 1775, in Richard Morris, ed., *John Jay: The Making of a Revolutionary, Unpublished Papers, 1745–1780*, vol. 1 (New York: Harper and Brothers, 1975), 138–139.

81 Walter Stahr, *John Jay: Founding Father* (New York: Hambledon and London, 2005), 17.

82 John Jay to Robert Livingston, 1 January 1775, in Morris, *John Jay: The Making of a Revolutionary*, vol. 1, 138.

83 "Address of the Convention of the Representatives of the State of New York to their Constituents, 1777," in Stahr, *John Jay*, 72–73.

84 Manumission papers of Jay's slave Benoit, signed March 21, 1784, in Morris, *John Jay: The Making of a Revolutionary*, vol. 2, 705–706.

85 John Jay to Egbert Benson, 18 September 1780, in Morris, *John Jay: The*

*Making of a Revolutionary*, vol. 1, 822–823.

86 Stahr, *John Jay*, 236–237.

87 Ibid., 242.

88 Ibid., 222.

89 Miller, *The Business of May Next*, 8–9.

90 Fisher Ames to George Minot, 3 May 1789, in Fisher Ames, *The Works of Fisher Ames*, vol. 1, (Boston: Little, Brown and Company, 1854), 34–35.

91 Morris, *Witnesses at the Creation*, 224–225; Gillespie, *Ratifying the Constitution*, 10–12.

92 Gillespie and Lienesch, *Ratifying the Constitution*, 20–22.

93 Wood, *The Creation of the American Republic*, 462–465.

94 Staughton Lynd, *Anti-Federalism in Dutchess County, New York: A Study of Democracy and Class Conflict in the Revolutionary Era* (Chicago; Loyola University Press, 1962), 20; King, *The Life and Correspondence of Rufus King*, vol. 1, 63.

95 Jonathan Elliot, ed., *The Debates in the Several State Conventions on the Adoption of the Federal Constitution as Recommended by the General Convention at Philadelphia in 1787*, vol. 2 (New York: B. Franklin, 1968), 102.

96 Samuel Osgood to Stephen Higginson, 2 February 1784, in Burnett, *Letters of the Members*, vol. 7, 435. For a complete representation of Anti-Federalists' feelings on the rich, see Wood, *The Creation of the American Republic*, 484–490.

97 Lynd, *Anti-Federalism in Dutchess County*, 14; Linda Grant De Pauw, *The Eleventh Pillar: New York State and the Federal Constitution* (Ithaca, NY: Cornell University Press, 1966), 283–292.

98 Rufus King to James Madison, 20 January 1788 and a second, dated January 1788, both in Hunt, vol. 5, 92–93 and 96–97, respectively.

99 William Goddard, *The Prowess of the Whig Club, and the Manoeuvres of Legion* (Baltimore, March 17, 1777), 7, 12; *Philadelphia Gazette*, March 1, 1779; the "patch a shoe and patch a state" feeling runs through Wood's *The Creation of the American Republic*.

100 John Jay to Alexander Hamilton, 8 May 1778, in Syrett, *The Papers of Alexander Hamilton*, vol. 1; 483; Madison, *Federalist* No. 61.

101 Roger Alden notes in Burnett, *Letters of the Members*, vol. 8, 646.

102 Lynd, *Anti-Federalism in Dutchess County*, 20.

103 Henry Jackson to Henry Knox, 20 January 1778, Henry Knox Papers, Gilder Lehman collection, Pierpont Morgan Library, New York; Hugh Williamson to James Iredell, 26 July 1788, in Burnett, *Letters of the Members*, vol. 8, 768–769.

104 John Eliot to Jeremy Belknap, 12 January 1777, Belknap Papers, Massachusetts Historical Society, Boston, Massachusetts, 104.

105 *New York Journal*, March 18, 1788.

106 Lynd, *Anti-Federalism in Dutchess County*, 10; Main, *The Antifederalists*, 262–265.

107 "Letters From A Countryman From Dutchess County," *New York Journal*, November 21, 1787; "Letter from a Customer," *Cumberland (Maine) Gazette*, March 1788; "Address of the Albany Antifederal Committee," *New York Journal*, April 26, 1788; "Hon. Mr. Gerry's objections to signing the National Constitution," in Herbert J. Storing, *The Complete Anti-Federalist*, vol. 2 (Chicago: University of Chicago Press, 1982), 6–8; Hugh Grigsby, *The History of the Virginia Federal Convention of 1788*, vol. 1, (Richmond: Virginia Historical Society, 1890–1891), 48; Elliot, *The Debates in the Several State Conventions*, vol. 2, 551.

108 Samuel Adams to Elbridge Gerry, 23 April 1784, in Samuel Adams, *The Writings of Samuel Adams*, ed. Harry Alonzo Cushing, vol. 4, (New York: G. P. Putnam's Sons, 1908), 302; Samuel Adams to John Winthrop, 21 December 1778, in Burnett, *Letters of the Members*, vol. 3, 545; Hugh Hughes to Charles Tillinghast, 7 March 1787, Papers of John Lamb, New York Historical Society, New York, New York.

109 Wood, *The Creation of the American Republic*, 470.

110 Herbert J. Storing, *The Complete Anti-Federalist*, vol. 1, 67–68.

111 Ibid., vol. 2, 86; Leonard Levy, "The Bill of Rights," in *The American Founding*, eds. Jackson Barlow, Leonard Levy, and Kenneth Masugi (Westport, CT: Greenwood Press, 1988), 309–310.

112 Caplan, *Constitutional Brinksmanship*, 40.

113 Elliot, *The Debates in the Several State Conventions*, vol. 2, 556.

CHAPTER FOUR

114 Robert Kates, "Handgun Prohibition and the Original Understanding of the Second Amendment," *Michigan Law Review* 82 (1983), 229.

115 James Foley, ed., Thomas Jefferson, *The Jefferson Cyclopedia* (New York: Russell & Russell, 1967), 318.

116 Thomas Jefferson to George Washington, 9 June 1796, in Thomas Jefferson, *The Writings of Thomas Jefferson*, 20 vols., ed. Andrew Lipscomb, vol. 9 (Washington, DC: Thomas Jefferson Memorial Foundation, 1905), 341.

117 J. Foley, ed., *The Jefferson Cyclopedia*, 51.

118 "Weapons Possession in Massachusetts and Virginia," William Brigham, ed., *The Compact with the Charter and the Laws of the Colony of New*

*Plymouth* (Boston: Dutton and Wentworth, 1836), 31, 76; William Waller Hening, *The Statutes at Large: Being a Collection of All the Laws of Virginia, From the First Session of the Legislature in the Year 1619* (New York, 1823), 127, 173–174; The remarks from delegates to state conventions were compiled by the staff of the Senate Judiciary Committee in its report, *The Right to Keep and Bear Arms: Report of the Subcommittee on the Constitution*, 97th Cong., 2d sess., February 1982, (Washington, DC: U.S. Government Printing Office, 1982), 4–7.

119 "*The Federalist* No. 46," in Eugene W. Hickok Jr., ed., *The Bill of Rights: Original Meaning and Current Understanding* (Charlottesville: University Press of Virginia, 1991), 122.

120 Senate Judiciary Committee, *The Right to Keep*, 4–7.

121 Oscar and Mary Handlin, eds., *The Popular Sources of Political Authority: Documents on the Massachusetts Constitution of 1780* (Cambridge: Harvard University Press, 1966), 441–472.

122 Bernard Schwartz, ed., *The Bill of Rights: A Documentary History*, vol. 1 (New York: Chelsea House, 1971), 266.

123 Ibid., vol. 1, 278.

124 George Washington to John Hancock, 31 January 1777, in Washington, *GWW*, vol. 7, 80–81.

125 Washington to John Hancock, 23 February 1777, *GWW*, vol. 7, 193–195.

126 Washington to his stepson, Jack Custis, 22 January 1777, *GWW*, vol. 7, 52–54.

127 Diary of Sylvanus Seely, June 5, 1780, Morristown National Historical Park, New Jersey.

128 Washington to General Robert Howe, 10 June 1780, *GWW*, vol. 18, 494–496.

129 *Freeman's Journal*, March 5, 1788.

130 The Federalist No. 29, in Alexander Hamilton, James Madison, and John Jay, *The Federalist* (New York: Bantam House, 1982), 184–185.

131 Richard Henry Lee, *Letters from the Federal Farmer to the Republican (1787–1788)*, Birmingham, Alabama: University of Alabama Press, 305–306.

132 Moncure Daniel Conway, ed., *Writings of Thomas Paine*, vol. 1 (New York: G. P. Putnam's Sons, 1894), 56.

133 Joel Barlow, *Advice to the Privileged Orders in the Several States of Europe Resulting from the Necessity and Propriety of a General Revolution in the Principle of Government* (London: J. Johnson, 1792; repr., Ithaca, NY: Great Seal Books, Cornell University Press, 1956), 16–17.

134 Hickok, *The Bill of Rights*, 132–134.

135 James Madison to Edmund Pendleton, 21 February 1788, in Hunt, *The Writings of James Madison*, vol. 4, 107–110.

136 *The Federalist* No. 22 and 42.

137 Alexander Hamilton letter, September 1787, in Bernard Bailyn, ed., *The Debate on the Constitution*, 10–11.

138 Jay, *The Federalist* No. 2, in Stahr, *John Jay*, 248–249.

139 Gillespie, *Ratifying the Constitution*, 63.

140 James Madison to Thomas Jefferson, 19 February 1788, in Smith, *The Republic of Letters*, 531; Judge Thomas McKean, in Storing, *The Complete Anti-Federalist*, vol. 1, 68.

141 Thomas Jefferson to James Madison, 20 December 1787, in Jefferson, *The Life and Selected Writings of Thomas Jefferson*, vol. 12, 436–431; Thomas Jefferson to James Madison, in Hunt, *The Writings of James Madison*, vol. 12, 440.

142 James Madison, *The Complete Madison: His Basic Writings*, ed. Saul Padover, vol. 4 (New York: Harper, 1953), 253; Madison's notes on the federal convention, in Hunt, *Writings of James Madison*, vol. 4, 442.

143 John Adams to Joseph Hawley, 25 November 1775, in Burnett, *Letters of the Members*, vol. 1, 260. *Virginia Independent Chronicle*, August 8, 1778.

144 John Brown to David Howell, 23 October 1783, John Brown ms., XIV, no. 7, Rhode Island Historical Society.

145 Robert H. Webking, "Melancton Smith and the Letters from the Federal Farmer," *William and Mary Quarterly*, 3.44, no. 3 (July 1987), 485–509.

146 Morris, *Witnesses at the Creation*, 226–227; Ketcham, *James Madison*, 232–234; Michael G. Kammen, ed., *Origins of the American Constitution: A Documentary History* (New York: Penguin, 1986); Brutus complaints are registered, 301–360.

147 John McMaster and Frederick Stone, eds., *Pennsylvania and the Federal Constitution, 1787–1788*, vol. 1 (New York: De Capo Press, 1970), 780; Thomas Wait to George Thatcher, 27 November 1787, *History Magazine* 16 (1869), 258; Main, *The Antifederalists*, 126–128.

148 James Madison to George Washington, 18 October 1787, 11–15 and James Madison to Edmund Randolph, 21 October 1787, 15–17; both in Hunt, *The Writings of James Madison*, vol. 5.

149 Storing, *The Complete Anti-Federalist*, vol. 2, 105.

150 Nathan Dane to Nathaniel Gorham, 22 June 1787, in Burnett, *Letters of the Members*, vol. 8, 613.

151 Charles Cerami, *Young Patriots: The Remarkable Story of Two Men,*

*Their Impossible Plan, and the Revolution that Created the Constitution* (Naperville, IL: Sourcebooks, 2005), 264; letter from Madison's father, 30 January 1788, in Hunt, *The Writings of James Madison*, vol. 5, 105n.

152 James Madison to Thomas Jefferson, 24 October 1787, in Hunt, *The Writings of James Madison*, vol. 5, 17–44.

153 John Jay to Thomas Jefferson, 24 October 1787, in Thomas Jefferson, *The Papers of Thomas Jefferson*, ed. Julian Boyd, vol. 12 (Princeton: Princeton University Press, 1950), 265–266.

154 Alexander Hamilton to George Washington, 11–15 October 1787, in Syrett, *The Papers of Alexander Hamilton*, vol. 4, 280–281.

155 George Washington to Alexander Hamilton, 18 October 1787, in Syrett, *The Papers of Alexander Hamilton*, vol. 4, 284–285.

156 George Washington to James Madison, 10 October 1787, in Kaminski, *The Documentary History*, vol. 8, 49–50.

157 Alexander Hamilton to George Washington, 30 October 1787, 396–397; Henry Knox to George Washington, 11 December 1787, 485–486; both in Washington, *Papers of George Washington*, Confederation series, vol. 5.

158 Benjamin Lincoln to George Washington, 9 January 1788, in Washington, *Papers of George Washington*, Confederation series, vol. 6, 22–23.

159 George Washington to John Armstrong, 25 April 1788, *GWW*, vol. 29, 464–467.

160 George Washington to Benjamin Lincoln, 10 March 1788, *GWW*, vol. 29, 440–441.

161 *Philadelphia Independent Gazetteer*, October 5, 1787.

CHAPTER FIVE

162 Clinton Rossiter, *Alexander Hamilton and the Constitution* (New York: Harcourt, Brace, and World, 1964), 52–53.

163 Miller, *The Business of May Next*, 15.

164 George Washington to David Humphreys, 10 October 1787, *GWW*, vol. 29, 287–288.

165 Madison memo in *The Federalist: A Commentary on the Constitution of the United States, a Collection of Essays by Alexander Hamilton, Jay, and Madison, Also, The Continentalist and Other Papers*, J.C. Hamilton, ed., vol. 3 (Philadelphia, 1865), 85; Gouverneur Morris to W. H. Wells, 14 February 1815, in Jared Sparks, *Life of Gouverneur Morris*, vol. 3 (Boston: Gray Publishing, 1832), 339.

166 Ketcham, *James Madison*, 239–241; Madison to Jefferson, 10 August 1788, in Jefferson, *The Papers of Thomas Jefferson*, vol. 13, 497–499.

167  Kaminski, vol. 20, 581.

168  James Madison to Edmund Randolph, 2 December 1787, in Hunt, *The Writings of James Madison*, vol. 5, 60–61; Syrett, *The Papers of Alexander Hamilton*, vol. 4, 292n, 293n.

169  James Kent to Nathaniel Lawrence, 21 December 1787, in Kaminski, vol. 19, 453–454; *Philadelphia Freedman*, January 30, 1788.

170  George Washington to Chevalier de la Luzerne, 7 February 1788, *GWW*, vol. 29, 404–407.

171  Alexander Hamilton, John Jay, and James Madison, *The Federalist*, ix–x.

172  David Freeman, "Reflection on Human Nature: The Federalists and the Republican Tradition," in *The Federalists, the Anti-Federalists and the American Political Tradition*, ed. Wilson Carey McWilliams and Michael Gibbons (Westport, CT: Greenwood Press, 1992), 33.

173  David Humphreys to Alexander Hamilton, 1 September 1787, in Syrett, *The Papers of Alexander Hamilton*, vol. 4, 240–241.

174  Archibald Stuart to James Madison, 14 January 1788, in Hunt, *The Writings of James Madison*, vol. 5, 89n.

175  James Kent to Nathaniel Lawrence, 8 December 1787, in Kaminski, *The Documentary History*, vol. 19, 179–180.

176  Roger Alden to Samuel Johnson, 31 December 1787, in Burnett, *Letters of the Members*, vol. 8, 692n.

177  Alexander Hamilton to James Madison, 3 April 1788, in Hunt, *The Writings of James Madison*, vol. 5, 112n; George Washington to Henry Knox, 5 February 1788, *GWW*, vol. 29, 400–401.

178  *The Federalist* No. 6.

179  Chernow, *Alexander Hamilton*, 254.

180  *The Federalist* No. 66.

181  Neal Reimer, *James Madison: Creating the American Constitution* (Washington, DC: Congressional Quarterly Inc., 1986), 131.

182  Paul Finkelman, "Between Scylla and Charybdis: Anarchy, Tyranny and the Debate Over a Bill of Rights," in Hoffman and Albert, *The Bill of Rights*, 104.

183  *The Federalist* No. 14.

184  Thomas Jefferson to James Madison, 10 August 1815, in Lester Cappon, ed., *The Adams-Jefferson Letters: the Complete Correspondence between Thomas Jefferson and Abigail and John Adams* (Chapel Hill: University of North Carolina, 1988) vol. 2, 453; Thomas Jefferson to James Madison, 18 November 1778, in Cappon, vol. 2, 453.

185  George Washington to David Stuart, 30 November 1787, in Washington, *Papers of George Washington*, Confederation series, vol. 5, 467.

186 *New York Journal*, January 10, 1788.

187 Ibid.

188 De Pauw, *The Eleventh Pillar*, 114–115.

189 *New York Journal*, January 21, 1788; January 7, 1788.

190 Thomas Jefferson to James Madison, 18 November 1788, in Kaminski, *The Documentary History*, vol. 5, 120; John Horton, *James Kent: A Study in Conservatism, 1783–1847* (New York: D. Appleton-Century Company, Inc., 1939), 55.

191 Kaminski, *The Documentary History*, vol. 20, 563–564; 878–880.

192 De Pauw, *The Eleventh Pillar*, 110–111.

193 Lance Banning, *Sacred Fire of Liberty: James Madison and the Founding of the Federal Republic* (Ithaca: Cornell University, 1995), 232.

194 Charles Beard, *The Enduring Federalist* (New York: Frederick Ungar Publishing Co., 1948), 4.

CHAPTER SIX

195 *Middlesex (CT) Gazette*, July 21, 1788.

196 *Connecticut Courant*, June 25, 1787.

197 *Massachusetts Centinel*, November 17, 1787; *Independent Chronicle*, July 19, 1787.

198 *Massachusetts Centinel*, September 29, 1788; November 10, 1787.

199 *Connecticut Gazette*, October 26, 1787; for further assessment of newspaper coverage, see Carol Sue Humphrey, *The Press of the Young Republic, 1783–1833* (Westport, CT: Greenwood Press, 1996), 8–15.

200 *Independent Chronicle*, June 5, 1788.

201 *New Hampshire Gazette*, November 16, 1787.

202 *Exeter (NH) Freeman's Oracle*, September 5, 1786; House of Burgesses essay, reprinted in *Connecticut Gazette*, April 21, 1786.

203 Humphrey, *The Press of the Young Republic, 1783–1833*, 13–16.

204 *Providence Gazette*, September 30, 1786; *Salem (MA) Mercury*, March 3, 1789.

205 Humphrey, *The Press of the Young Republic, 1783–1833*, 14–16; Gillespie and Lienesch, *Ratifying the Constitution*, 127–128.

206 *Massachusetts Gazette*, January 29, 1788; Richard Henry Lee to George Mason, 15 May 1787, in Richard Henry Lee, *Letters of Richard Henry Lee, 1782–1794*, ed. James Ballagh, vol. 2 (New York: MacMillan, 1911), 419.

207 Gillespie, *Ratifying the Constitution*, 129–130.

208 Ibid., 68.

209 Thomas Jefferson to Edward Carrington, 16 January 1787, in Jefferson, *The Papers of Thomas Jefferson*, vol. 11, 49.

CHAPTER SEVEN

210 Ketcham, *James Madison*, 232–233.

211 Samuel Harding, *The Contest Over the Ratification of the Federal Constitution in the State of Massachusetts* (New York: Longmans, Green and Co., 1896), 49.

212 James Madison to Thomas Jefferson, 9 December 1787, in Hunt, *The Writings of James Madison*, vol. 5, 48–49, 66–67; James Madison to his father, 8 April 1787, also in Hunt, vol. 2, 226–338.

213 Wood, *The Creation of the American Republic*, 430.

214 James Madison to Edmund Pendleton, 21 February 1788, in Hunt, *The Writings of James Madison*, vol. 5, 107–110; Henry Lee to James Madison, December 1787, also in Hunt, vol. 5, 88n.

215 *Maryland Journal,* April 29, 1788; *Baltimore Advertiser,* April 29, 1788.

216 James Madison to Thomas Jefferson, 24 October 1787, in Hunt, *The Creation of the American Republic*, vol. 5, 35–37; Harrison's letter was mailed from Washington to Madison on October 22, 1787; the letter about mixed feelings was from Washington's son-in-law, David Stuart, to Washington and forwarded to Madison on November 5.

217 It is impossible to tell the total number of letters the Triumvirate wrote to Federalists around the country in their campaign. In a letter to Washington dated February 3, 1788, Madison recorded sixty letters just between he and King. See Hunt, *The Creation of the American Republic*, vol. 5, 95–97.

218 James Madison to Alexander Hamilton, note included in a letter from Madison to Washington, 11 February 1788, in Hunt, *The Creation of the American Republic*, vol. 5, 99–100; Rufus King to James Madison, 6 January 1788, in King, *The Life and Correspondence of Rufus King*, 312–313; Rufus King to J. Langdon, 10 June 1788 and Langdon to King, 30 June 1788, both also in King, 336.

219 Tench Coxe to James Madison, 11 June 1778, in Kaminski, *The Documentary History*, vol. 10, 1596.

220 James Madison to Thomas Jefferson, 19 February 1788, in Hunt, *The Creation of the American Republic*, vol. 5, 100–104.

221 George Nicholas to James Madison, 5 April 1788, in Hunt, *The Creation of the American Republic*, vol. 5, 114n; Madison to George Washington, 10 April 1788, also in Hunt, vol. 5, 116–118.

222 David Stuart to George Washington, 5 November 1787, in Washington, *Papers of George Washington*, Confederation series, vol. 5, 411–412.

223 Thomas Johnson to George Washington, 11 December 1787, in Washington, *Papers of George Washington*, Confederation series, vol. 5, 483–484.

224 Tench Coxe to James Madison, 21 October 1787, in Hunt, *The Creation of the American Republic*, vol. 5, 46n.

225 Joseph Jones to James Madison, 29 October 1787, in Hunt, *The Creation of the American Republic*, vol. 5, 47n; Joseph Jones Papers, Chicago Historical Society, Chicago, Illinois.

226 James McClurg to James Madison, 31 October 1787, in Hunt, *The Creation of the American Republic*, vol. 5, 48n.

227 Rufus King to James Madison, 16 January 1788, quoted in Madison's January 25 letter to Washington, in Hunt, *The Creation of the American Republic*, vol. 5, 91.

228 Morison, *The Growth of the American Republic*, 291; Rufus King to James Madison, 27 January 1788, later note quoted in February 3 letter from Madison to Washington, in Hunt *The Creation of the American Republic*, vol. 5, 95.

CHAPTER EIGHT

229 Charles Smith, *James Wilson: Founding Father, 1742–1798* (Chapel Hill: University of North Carolina Press, 1956), 321–322; Gillespie, *Ratifying the Constitution*, 56–57.

230 Gillespie, *Ratifying the Constitution*, 63–64.

231 Samuel Powel to George Washington, 12 December 1787, in Washington, *Papers of George Washington,* Confederation series, vol. 5, 488.

CHAPTER NINE

232 William Heath Diary, Massachusetts Historical Society; Merrill Jenson, John Kaminski, *The Documentary Histor of the Ratification of the Constitution*, vol. 7, 1522–1526; Dummer Sewall Diary in Pejepscot Papers, vol. 10, Maine Historical Society.

233 Harding, *The Contest Over the Ratification*, 50; Belknap Diary, (Massachusetts Historical Society Proceedings: Boston, Massachusetts, 1858) 296.

234 Sewall Diary.

235 *Massachusetts Gazette*, January 25, 1788.

236 *New York Morning Post*, March 21, 1788, in Kaminski, *The Documentary History*, vol. 7, 1522n.

237 *Massachusetts Gazette*, January 18, 1788.

238 Kaminski, *The Documentary History*, vol. 29, 1557n.

239 Wood, *The Creation of the American Republic*, 434.

240 Winthrop Sargent to Henry Knox, in Gillespie, *Ratifying the Constitution*, 148; James Madison to George Washington, 20 January

1788, in Washington, *Papers of George Washington*, Confederation series, vol. 6, 51–52.

241 Henry Knox to George Washington, 14 January 1788, in Washington, *Papers of George Washington*, Confederation series, vol. 6, 39–40.

242 Robert Ernst, *Rufus King: American Federalist* (Chapel Hill: University of North Carolina Press, 1968), 130; Harding, *The Contest Over the Ratification*, 67; James Madison to George Washington, 25 January 1788, in Washington, *Papers of George Washington*, Confederation series, vol. 6, 60–61; Ernst, *Rufus King*, 128.

243 Charles Tillinghast to Hugh Hughes, 28 January 1788, in Kaminski, *The Documentary History*, vol. 20, 667–670; Melancton Smith to Abraham Yates Jr., 28 January 1788, in Kaminski, vol. 29, 638–639 and vol. 20, 671–672; Staats Morris to Lewis Morris Jr., 29 January 1788, in Kaminski, vol. 20, 672.

244 Nathaniel Freeman Jr. to John Quincy Adams, 27 January 1788, Adams Family Papers, Massachusetts Historical Society, Boston, Massachusetts; Jeremy Belknap to Ebenezer Hazard, 20 January 1788, Belknap Papers, Massachusetts Historical Society, Boston, Massachusetts; Kaminski, vol. 7, 1533–1535.

245 George Benson to Nicholas Brown, 20 January 1788, Brown Papers, John Carter Brown Library, Providence, RI; Elliot, *The Debates in the Several State Conventions*, vol. 2, 133.

246 Joseph Crocker to George Thatcher, 26 January 1788, in Kaminski, *The Documentary History*, vol. 29, 1550–1551 Elliot, *The Debates in the Several State Conventions*, vol. 2, 133, 217.

247 Elliot, *The Debates in the Several State Conventions*, vol. 2, 219.

248 *Worcester Magazine*, January 31, 1788.

249 James Bowdoin, in Elliot, *The Debates in the Several State Conventions*, vol. 2, 130.

250 Wood, *The Creation of the American Republic*, 448–449.

251 Rufus King to James Madison, 23 January 1788, Papers of James Madison, Princeton University, 1745–1826; William Cranch to his cousin John Quincy Adams, 22 January 1788, Adams Family Papers.

252 James Madison to George Washington, in Kaminski, *The Documentary History*, vol. 29, 1546n.

253 Benjamin Lincoln to George Washington, 27 January 1788, in Kaminski, *The Documentary History*, vol. 29, 1555.

254 Melancton Smith to Abraham Yates Jr., RCS: Mass, 1091; Kaminski, *The Documentary History*, vol. 29, 1556.

255 James Madison to George Washington, 20 January 1788, in Kaminski,

*The Documentary History*, vol. 20, 696–697; *Albany Journal*, January 28, 1788.

256 Judge Sumner quoted in George Benson letter to Nicholas Brown, 30 January 1788, Brown Papers, John Carter Brown Library, Providence, RI.

257 Caplan, *Constitutional Brinksmanship*, 35.

258 C. Gore to Rufus King, 6 January 1788, in King, *The Life and Correspondence of Rufus King*, 311; Ralph Harlow, *Samuel Adams: Promoter of the American Revolution—A Study in Psychology and Politics* (New York: Octagon Books, 1971), 330–331.

259 Ernst, *Rufus King*, 129.

260 Harlow Unger, *John Hancock: Merchant King and American Patriot* (New York: John Wiley and Sons, 2005), 313–314; Harding, *The Contest Over the Ratification*, 86–87; William Fowler, *The Baron of Beacon Hill: A Biography of John Hancock* (Boston: Houghton-Mifflin Co., 1980), 270–273; Ernst, *Rufus King*, 131.

261 Morison, *The Growth of the American Republic*, 292; Fowler, *The Baron of Beacon Hill*, 273; Ernst, *Rufus King*, 130.

262 John Hancock speech to the Massachusetts Convention, February 6, 1788, in Bailyn, *The Debate on the Constitution*, 941–942.

263 Rufus King to George Washington, 6 February 1788, in Kaminski, *The Documentary History*, vol. 7, 1647–1648.

264 Sara Shumer, "New Jersey: Property and the Prince of Republican Politics," in Gillespie, *Ratifying the Constitution*, 84–88.

265 *Massachusetts Gazette*, February 7, 1788; *Massachusetts Centinel*, February 9 and 13, 1788; *Westminster (MA) Independent Chronicle*, March 3, 1788; *Boston Gazette*, February 11, 1788; *Essex Journal*, February 13, 1788; John Quincy Adams Diary, February 8 and 14, 1788, Adams Family Papers; Ernst, *Rufus King*, 137.

266 Henry Van Schaack to Theodore Sedgwick, 9 February 1788, in Kaminski, *The Documentary History*, vol. 7, 1689.

267 Ernst, *Rufus King*, 132.

268 James Madison to Thomas Jefferson, 19 February 1788, in Smith, *The Republic of Letters*, vol. 1, 530–532; Madison to George Washington, 15 February 1788, in Hunt, *The Writings of James Madison*, vol. 5, 100.

269 Francis H. Buffum, ed., *New Hampshire and the Federal Constitution: A Memorial of the Sesquicentennial Celebration of New Hampshire's Part in the Framing and Ratification of the Constitution of the United States*, 2nd ed. (Concord, NH: Granite State Press, 1942), 46.

270 George Washington to James Madison, January 1788, in Hunt, *The Writings of James Madison*, vol. 5, 88n.

271 James Madison to George Washington, 25 January 1788, in Hunt, *The Writings of James Madison*, vol. 5, 88–90.

272 Cyrus Griffin to James Madison, 24 March 1788, in Hunt, *The Writings of James Madison*, vol. 5, 110n.

273 James Madison to George Washington, 8 February 1788, in Hunt, *The Writings of James Madison*, vol. 5, 97–99; Madison to Thomas Jefferson, 17 October 1788, in Smith, *The Republic of Letters*, vol. 1, 562–566.

274 James Madison to Edmund Randolph, 3 March 1788, in Hunt, *The Writings of James Madison*, vol. 5, 113–114; Nicholas Gilman to John Sullivan, 23 March 1788, in Burnett, *Letters of the Members*, vol. 8, 709.

275 Cyrus Griffin to Thomas Fitzsimmons, March 1788, Gratz Collection, Historical Society of Pennsylvania.

CHAPTER TEN

276 *Pennsylvania Gazette*, August 22, 1787.

277 George Washington to David Stuart, 1 July 1787, in Washington, *Papers of George Washington*, Confederation series, vol. 5, 239–240.

278 George Washington to the Marquis de Lafayette, 18 September 1787, in Washington, *Papers of George Washington*, Confederation series, vol. 5, 334.

279 George Washington to David Humphreys, 10 October 1787, *GWW*, vol. 29, 287–288.

280 George Washington to the Marquis de Lafayette, 7 February 1788, *GWW*, vol. 28, 410.

281 George Washington to the Marquis de Lafayette, 28 January 1788, in Washington, *Papers of George Washington*, Presidential series, vol. 1, 262.

282 George Washington to Bushrod Washington, 10 November 1787, *GWW*, vol. 29, 309–313.

283 *Circular to the States*, 8 June 1783, *GWW*, vol. 26, 484–486; George Washington to Rev. William Gordon, 8 July 1783, *GWW*, vol. 27, 49.

284 George Washington to Benjamin Harrison, 18 January 1784, *GWW*, vol. 27, 305–306; George Washington to John Jay, 1 August 1786, *GWW*, vol. 28, 502.

285 George Washington to Henry Knox, 10 January 1788, *GWW*, vol. 29, 377–378.

286 George Washington to Benjamin Lincoln, 31 January 1788, *GWW*, vol. 29, 395–397.

287 George Washington to James McHenry, 31 July 1788, *GWW*, vol. 30, 28.

288 Stuart Leibiger, *Founding Friendship: George Washington, James Madison and the Creation of the American Republic* (Charlottesville: University of Virginia Press, 1999), 83.

289 George Washington to Bushrod Washington, 10 November 1787, in Washington, *Papers of George Washington*, Confederation series, vol. 5, 422–423.

290 Benjamin Lincoln to George Washington, 27 January 1788, in Washington, *Papers of George Washington*, Confederation series, vol. 6, 68–69.

291 George Washington to Bushrod Washington, 10 November 1787, *GWW*, vol. 29, 309–313.

292 John Fitzpatrick, *The Diaries of George Washington*, vol. 4 (Boston: Houghton-Mifflin Co. Mount Vernon Ladies Association of the Union, 1925), 313. Madison arrived on March 18 and remained for three days; he acknowledged that in several letters.

293 George Washington to James Madison, 5 February 1788, *GWW* vol. 29, 402–404.

294 George Washington to Benjamin Lincoln, in Washington, *Papers of George Washington*, Confederation series, vol. 5, 74; George Washington to Henry Knox, 3 March 1788, *GWW*, vol. 29, 434–435.

295 George Washington to Patrick Henry, 24 September 1787, *GWW*, vol. 29, 278.

296 George Washington to George Mason, 7 October 1787, *GWW*, vol. 29, 284.

297 James Madison to Edmund Pendleton, 22 April 1787, in Hunt, *The Writings of James Madison*, vol. 2, 353–357.

298 Numerous writers did this. One of the first was Noah Webster, who mailed Washington his pamphlet *Leading Principles of the Federal Constitution* the same week that it was published in October. Dozens of writers of newspaper essays mailed him editions of a newspaper in which they appeared. Washington had them copied and mailed to the Triumvirate and other friends; George Washington to Noah Webster, 4 November 1787, *GWW*, vol. 29, 301; George Washington to David Stuart, 5 November 1787, *GWW*, vol. 29, 302–303.

299 George Washington to Jonathan Trumbull, 5 February 1778, *GWW*, vol. 29, 399–400.

300 George Washington to James Madison, 10 October 1787, *GWW*, vol. 29, 285–287.

301 George Washington to Henry Knox, 15 October 1787, *GWW*, vol. 29, 288–290.

302 George Washington to Henry Knox, 15 October 1787, *GWW*, vol. 29, 287–289; Washington to Jonathan Trumbull, 5 February 1778, *GWW*, vol. 29, 399–400.

303 Kaminski, *The Documentary History*, vol. 8, 41.

304 George Washington to William Gordon, 1 January 1788, in Washington, *Papers of George Washington*, Confederation series, vol. 6, 1.

305 George Washington to Samuel Powel, 18 January 1788, in Washington, *Papers of George Washington*, Confederation series, vol. 6, 45–46.

306 George Washington to Samuel Powel, 18 January 1788, Washington, *Papers of George Washington*, Confederation series, vol. 6, 45-46.

307 Tobias Lear to William Prescott, 4 March 1788, in Kaminski, *The Documentary History*, vol. 8, 456; Leibiger, *Founding Friendship*, 88.

308 George Washington to James Madison, 7 December 1787, *GWW*, vol. 29, 331–334.

309 George Washington to Gouverneur Morris, 2 May 1788; to James Madison, 2 May 1778, both in Washington, *Papers of George Washington*, Confederation series, 258–260.

310 George Washington to Comte De Rochambeau, 8 January 1788, *GWW*, vol. 29, 359–360; George Washington to the Marquis de Chastellux, 25 April 1788, *GWW*, vol. 29, 483–486.

311 George Washington to Edmund Randolph, 8 January 1788, *GWW*, 17–18.

312 George Washington to David Stuart, 30 November 1787, *GWW*, vol. 29, 323–324; to James Madison, 7 December 1787, *GWW*, vol. 29, 331–334.

313 Olney Winsor to Mrs. Olney Winsor, 31 March 1788, Washington, *Papers of George Washington*, Confederation series, vol. 6, 523–524.

314 George Washington to Benjamin Lincoln, 10 March 1788, in Washington, *Papers of George Washington*, Confederation series, vol. 6, 478.

315 George Washington to James Madison, 7 December 1787, *GWW*, vol. 29, 331–334.

316 Archibald Stuart to James Madison, 14 January 1788, in Washington, *Papers of George Washington*, Confederation series, vol. 6, 302–303.

317 George Washington to Sir Edward Newenham, 25 December 1787, *GWW*, vol. 29, 345–346.

318 Richmond letter in stories reprinted in several newspapers within the next two weeks, including the *New York Daily Advertiser*, *Newport (RI) Mercury*, *Massachusetts Spy*, *Boston Gazette*, and the *Vermont Journal*.

319 George Washington to David Stuart, 30 November 1787, *GWW*, vol. 29, 323–324.

320 George Washington to Thomas Jefferson, 1 January 1788, in Washington, *Papers of George Washington*, Confederation series, vol. 6, 2–3; Washington to Henry Knox, 10 January 1788, also in Washington, *Papers*, Confederation series, vol. 6, 28–29.

321 George Washington to Thomas Johnson, 20 April 1788 and note from

Johnson to Washington, October 1788, both in Washington, *Papers of George Washington*, Presidential series, vol. 1, 43n.

322  *Connecticut Courant*, February 4, 1788.

323  Fayette County toasts in Smith, *The Republic of Letters*, 553.

CHAPTER ELEVEN

324  James Madison to Thomas Jefferson, 22 April 1788, in Smith, *The Republic of Letters*, 534-535.

325  Kaminski, *The Documentary History*, vol. 9, 574–575.

326  Ibid., 574.

327  Ibid., 577.

328  County stories, Ibid., 561–630.

329  James Madison to Thomas Jefferson, 22 April 1788, in Smith, *The Republic of Letters*, vol. 1, 534–535; Caplan, *Constitutional Brinksmanship*, 34.

330  Tobias Lear to John Langdon, 3 April 1788, in Kaminski, *The Documentary History*, vol. 9, 699; Banning, *Sacred Fire of Liberty*, 235.

331  Hugh Grigsby, *The History of the Virginia Federal Convention of 1788*, vol. 2, 8.

332  James Madison to Edmund Pendleton, 28 October 28, 1787, in Hunt, *The Writings of James Madison*, vol. 5, 44–45.

333  R. H. Lee to Edmund Randolph, 16 October 1787, in Richard Henry Lee, *The Letters of Richard Henry Lee*, ed. James Ballagh, vol. 2, 450.

334  Kent McGaughy, *Richard Henry Lee of Virginia: A Portrait of an American Revolutionary* (New York: Rowman and Littlefield, 2004), 196–197.

335  Lee general letter to friends, 27 September 1787, in Burnett, *Letters of the Members*, vol. 8, 648–649.

336  James Madison to George Washington, 30 September 1787, in Burnett, *Letters of the Members*, vol. 8, 650–652.

337  Lee to Washington, 11 October 1787, in Burnett, *Letters of the Members*, vol. 8, 656–657.

338  Richard Henry Lee to William Shippen Jr., 2 October 1787, in Kaminski, *The Documentary History*, vol. 13, 289.

339  Broadwater, *George Mason*, 205–209.

340  George Mason, "Objections to this Constitution of Government," September 16, 1787, in Robert Rutland, ed., *Papers of George Mason*, vol. 3 (Chapel Hill: University of North Carolina Press, 1970), 991–994.

341  Broadwater, *George Mason*, 213–214.

342  Ibid., 225.

343  Hugh Williamson to John Gray Blount, 3 June 1788, in Kaminski, *The*

*Documentary History*, vol. 10, 1572; Storing, *The Complete Anti-Federalist*, vol. 2, 9.

344 James Madison to Rufus King, 4 June 1788, and William Grayson to Nathan Dane, 4 June 1788, both in Kaminski, *The Documentary History*, vol. 10, 1573–1574 and 1572–1573, respectively.

345 Archibald Stuart to James Madison, 2 November 1787, and 14 January 1788, both in Hunt, *The Writings of James Madison*, vol. 5, 51–52n and 89n, respectively.

346 George Washington to James Madison, 2 March 1788, *GWW*, vol. 29, 430–432.

347 Thomas Jefferson to Edward Carrington, 27 May 1788, in Jefferson, *The Life and Selected Writings of Thomas Jefferson*, 46–47.

348 James Madison to Alexander Hamilton, 2 December 1787, in Hunt, *The Writings of James Madison*, vol. 5, 60–61.

349 James Madison to Edmund Randolph, 10 January 1788, in Hunt, *The Writings of James Madison*, vol. 5, 79–84.

350 James Madison to Thomas Jefferson, 9 December 1787, in Hunt, *The Writings of James Madison*, vol. 5, 63–67.

351 Caplan, *Constitutional Brinksmanship*, 36.

352 George Washington to Patrick Henry, 6 October 1787, *GWW*, vol. 29, 278; Patrick Henry to George Washington, 19 October 1787, Washington, *Papers of George Washington*, Confederation series, vol. 5, 387.

353 George Washington to Charles Carter, 14 December 1787, Washington, *Papers of George Washington*, Confederation series, vol. 5, 489–492.

354 Buffum, *New Hampshire and the Federal Constitution*, 7.

355 Robert Meade, *Patrick Henry*, (Philadelphia: Lippencott and Co., 1957), vol. 2, 342–343.

356 Henry Lee to James Madison, December 1787, in Hunt, *The Writings of James Madison*, vol. 5, 88n.

357 Ketcham, *James Madison*, 360.

### CHAPTER TWELVE

358 Imogene Brown, *American Aristedes: A Biography of George Wythe* (Rutherford, NJ: Fairleigh Dickinson University Press, 1981), 236–237.

359 Major William Pierce of Georgia, quoted in Tansill, *The Making of the American Republic*, 98.

360 Hugh Grigsby, *The History of the Virginia Federal Convention*, vol. 1, 75 and note.

361 Littleton Tazewell, *An Account and History of the Tazewell Family*, Tazewell Family Papers, Virginia State Library, 98–99.

362 Grigsby, *The History of the Virginia Federal Convention*, vol. 2, 57n.

363 William Wirt, *Sketches of Patrick Henry: Life, Correspondence and Speeches*, vol. 1 (New York, 1891), 280; Grigsby, *The History of the Virginia Federal Convention*, vol. 1, 4, 69, 151, 188.

364 Colin McGregor to Neil Jamieson, 4 June 1778, in Kaminski, *The Documentary History*, vol. 10, 1575; *Virginia Independent Chronicle*, June 4, 1788, also in Kaminski, vol. 10, 1579; John Brown to an anonymous delegate, 5 June 1788, also in Kaminski, vol. 10, 1579–1580; see also Kaminski, vol. 10, 1589n; Thomas Boyd, *Light-Horse Harry Lee* (New York: C. Scribner's Sons, 1931), 173.

365 Gouverneur Morris to Alexander Hamilton, 13 June 1788, in Syrett, *The Papers of Alexander Hamilton*, vol. 5, 7.

366 Tansill, *The Making of The American Republic*, 105.

367 Jefferson, *The Papers of Thomas Jefferson*, vol. 13, 98.

368 Grigsby, *The History of the Virginia Federal Convention*, vol. 2, 127.

369 *Pennsylvania Mercury*, June 17, 1788; *Pennsylvania Gazette*, June 11, 1788.

370 James Madison to Rufus King, 4 June 1788, in Kaminski, *The Documentary History*, vol. 10, 1573–1574.

371 James Monroe to Thomas Jefferson, in Jefferson, *The Papers of Thomas Jefferson*, vol. 13, 352.

372 William Grayson to Nathan Dane, 4 June 1788, in Kaminski, *The Documentary History*, vol. 10, 1572–1573.

373 James Madison to George Washington, 4 June 1788, in Kaminski, *The Documentary History*, vol. 10, 1574–1575.

374 George Washington to John Jay, 8 June 1788, in Kaminski, *The Documentary History*, vol. 10, 1587–1588.

375 Grigsby, *The History of the Virginia Federal Convention*, vol. 1, 95n; Ketchum, *James Madison*, 254–255.

376 Grigsby, *The History of the Virginia Federal Convention*, vol. 1, 99n.

377 Ibid., 100n.

378 George Mason to George Washington, 7 October 1787, and Mason June 11 speech, both in Gillespie, *Ratifying the Constitution*, 279 280; James Madison to Thomas Jefferson, 22 April 1788, in Jefferson, *The Papers of Thomas Jefferson*, vol. 13, 98.

379 *Federalist* No. 84 and No. 87; Jon Kukla, ed., *The Bill of Rights: A Lively Heritage* (Richmond: Virginia State Library and Archives, 1987), 10.

380 William C. Rives, *History of the Life and Times of James Madison*, vol. 2 (Boston: Little, Brown and Co., 1868), 535–538.

381 James Madison to Thomas Jefferson, in Jefferson, *The Papers of Thomas Jefferson*, vol. 12, 409–410 and 609.

382 Grigsby, *The History of the Virginia Federal Convention*, vol. 2, 76.

383 Wirt, *Patrick Henry*, vol. 2, 346–347.

384 St. Jean de Crevecoeur to William Short, 10 June 1788, in Kaminski, *The Documentary History*, vol. 10, 1592–1593.

385 Grigsby, *The History of the Virginia Federal Convention*, vol. 2, 32.

386 Ibid., 56.

387 James Madison to Edmund Randolph, 10 April 1788, Hunt, *The Writings of James Madison*, vol. 5, 117–120.

388 Campbell, *Patrick Henry*, 337–338.

389 Storing, *The Complete Anti-Federalist* vol. 5, 211.

390 Campbell, *Patrick Henry*, 345.

391 Ibid., 347.

392 Riemer, 136.

393 Irving Brant, *James Madison: the Virginia Revolutionist* (Indianapolis: Bobbs-Merrill Co., 1941), 397–398.

394 Grigsby, *The History of the Virginia Federal Convention*, vol. 2, 103; Gary Rosen, *American Compact: James Madison and the Problem of Founding* (Lawrence, Kansas: University Press of Kansas, 1999), 154.

395 Grigsby, *The History of the Virginia Federal Convention*, vol. 2, 83n.

396 Storing, *The Complete Anti-Federalist* vol. 5, 221.

397 Edmund Randolph, *History of Virginia*, ed. Arthur H. Shaffer (Charlottesville: University of Virginia Press, 1970), 179; Wirt, *Patrick Henry: Life, Correspondence and Speeches*, 13–16; Richard R. Beeman, *Patrick Henry, A Biography* (New York: McGraw-Hill, 1974), 110–116.

398 M.E. Bradford, *A Better Guide than Reason: Federalists and Anti-Federalists* (New Brunswick, NJ: Transaction Publishers, 1994), 101.

399 St. Jean de Crevecoeur to William Short, June 10, 1788, in Kaminski, *The Documentary History*, vol. 10, 1592–1593.

400 Robert Hilldrup, *The Life and Times of Edmund Pendleton* (Chapel Hill: The University of North Carolina Press, 1939), 289.

401 Campbell, *Patrick Henry*, 335.

402 Meade, *Patrick Henry*, vol. 2, 346.

403 Cyrus Griffin to James Madison, 14 April 1788, in Hunt, *The Writings of James Madison*, vol. 5, 120n.

404 Elliot, *The Debates in the Several State Conventions*, vol. 2, 317 and 335.

405 *Lansingburgh (NY) Northern Centinel*, November 20, 1787.

406 Kaminski, *The Documentary History*, vol. 10, 1624–1625.

407 James Madison to Rufus King, 9 June 1788, King Papers, New Hampshire Historical Society; Kaminski, *The Documentary History*, vol. 10, 1590.

408 Alexander White to Mary Wood, 10–11 June 1788, in Kaminski, *The Documentary History*, vol. 10, 1591–1592.

409 Morris, *Witnesses at the Creation*, 233.

410 Ibid., 237.

411 Storing, *The Complete Anti-Federalist*, vol. 5, 239.

412 Grigsby, *The History of the Virginia Federal Convention*, vol. 2, 178n.

413 Ibid., 227n.

414 Robert Morris to Horatio Gates, 12 June 1788, in Kaminski, *The Documentary History*, vol. 10, 1613.

415 James Madison to Tench Coxe, 11 June 1788, in Kaminski, *The Documentary History*, vol. 10, 1595–1596; Madison to George Washington, 18 June 1788, in Hunt, *The Writings of James Madison*, vol. 5, 211n.

416 James Madison to Rufus King, 13 June 1788, King Papers, New Hampshire Historical Society; James Madison to Alexander Hamilton and Madison to George Washington, in Kaminski, *The Documentary History*, vol. 10, 1630 and 1619–1620, respectively; George Nicholas to James Madison, 10 April 1788, in Hunt, *The Writings of James Madison*, 115n.

417 Gouverneur Morris to Alexander Hamilton, 13 June 1788, Kaminski, 10: 1622-1623.

418 Peter Singleton to Charles Pettigrew, 10 June 1788, in Sarah Lemmon, ed., *The Pettigrew Papers*, vol. 1 (Raleigh: North Carolina State University Press, 1971), 57–58; James Madison Jr. to James Madison Sr., 20 June 1788, in Hunt, *The Writings of James Madison*, vol. 5, 216n.

419 Grigsby, *The History of the Virginia Federal Convention*, vol. 2, 151.

420 *Baltimore Gazette*, June 20, 1788; *Charleston City (S.C.) Gazette*, July 9, 1788.

421 William Grayson to Nathan Dane, 18 June 1778, in Kaminski, *The Documentary History*, vol. 10, 1636.

422 Kaminski, *The Documentary History*, vol. 8, xxxvii.

423 Madison speech, June 11, 1788, in Hunt, *The Writings of James Madison*, vol. 5, 160.

424 Morris, *Witnesses at the Creation*, 238.

425 *Pennsylvania Mercury*, June 26, 1788; poem in *Massachusetts Centinel*, June 25, 1788.

426 Irving Brant, *The Fourth President*, 218–219.

427 James Madison to George Washington, 18 June 1788, in Hunt, *The Writings of James Madison*, vol. 5, 212n.

428 William Heth diary, June 13, 1788.

429 Elliot, *Debates*, vol. 2, 652 and 666.

430 Each member of the Triumvirate and his friends, such as Gouverneur Morris, had been writing people about Washington as the chief executive since the Philadelphia Convention had ended the previous September. See

Morris to George Washington, 30 October 1787, in Washington, *Papers of George Washington*, Confederation series, vol. 5, 398–401. Washington denied it throughout the winter of the ratification process, told all that he did not want to be president, did not campaign, and only accepted the presidency after the Electoral College elected him unanimously. He began to dissuade people from thinking that he wanted to be President in an October 26, 1787, letter to General Benjamin Lincoln; see Washington, vol. 5, 70–73.

431 Broadwater, *George Mason*, 232–234.

432 Ibid., 236–237.

433 James Madison to Rufus King, 22 June 1788, in King, *The Life and Correspondence of Rufus King*, 336–337.

434 Madison's June 25 speech in Hunt, *The Writings of James Madison*, vol. 11, 177.

435 James Madison to Thomas Jefferson, 17 October 1788, in Lester Cappon, Jr., *The Adams-Jefferson Letters: The Complete Correspondence Between Thomas Jefferson, Abigail and John Adams,* (Chapel Hill: University of North Carolina Press, 1988) vol. 2, 453.

436 James Madison to Rufus King, 22 June 1788, in King, *The Life and Correspondence of Rufus King*, vol. 1, 336–337.

437 Tench Coxe to Timothy Pickering, 25 June 1788, Pickering Papers, Massachusetts Historical Society, Boston, Massachusetts; James Madison to George Washington, 24 June 1788, in Hunt, *The Writings of James Madison*, vol. 5, 226n.

438 Selections from the Ezra Stiles Diary, June 25, 1788, in Kaminski, *The Documentary History*, vol. 10, 194; Philippe Andre Joseph de Letombe to Comte de la Luzerne, 26 June 1788, in Kaminski, *The Documentary History*, vol. 10, 194.

439 George Washington to Marquis de Lafayette, 18 June 1788, *GWW*, vol. 29, 522–526.

440 Elliot, *The Debates in the Several State Conventions*, vol. 3, 587; Brown, *American Aristedes*, 239–241.

441 David Jay Mays, "The Address of David Mays in the Old House of Delegates of the Capitol of Virginia on the Occasion of the Unveiling of the Bust of George Wythe" (Richmond: National Society of the Colonial Dames of America in the Commonwealth of Virginia, 1964), 8.

442 Kukla, *The Bill of Rights*, 11.

443 George Mason, "Objections to the Constitution of Government Formed by the Convention (1787)," in Storing, *The Complete Anti-Federalist*, vol. 2, 11–13.

444 James Madison to Rufus King, 25 June 1788, in King, *The Life and Correspondence of Rufus King*, vol. 1, 337–338.

445 George Washington to Benjamin Lincoln, 29 June 1788, *GWW*, vol. 30, 11–12.

CHAPTER THIRTEEN

446 De Pauw, *Eleventh Pillar*, 5–7.

447 Thomas Cochran, *New York in the Confederation* (Columbus, OH, 1931), 49; Cecil Eubanks, "New York: Federalism and the Political Economy of Union," in Gillespie, *Ratifying the Constitution*, 300–307.

448 Samuel Webb to Joseph Barrell, 1 July 1788, in W. C. Ford, ed., *Correspondence and Journals of Samuel Blanchley Webb*, vol. 3 (New York, 1893–1894), 108; Kaminski, "Reluctant Pillar," in Stephen Schecter, *The Reluctant Pillar: New York and the Adoption of the Federal Constitution* (Troy, NY: Russell Sage College Press, 1985), 50.

449 George Washington to George Clinton, June 1780, *GWW*, vol. 19, 84.

450 De Pauw, *Eleventh Pillar*, 15–17; Kaminski, "Reluctant Pillar," in Schecter, 52–53 and 55–57.

451 *New York Daily Advertiser*, February 13, 1787, in De Pauw, *Eleventh Pillar*, 43.

452 Bayard Tuckerman, *Life of General Philip Schuyler, 1733–1804* (New York: Dodd, Mead and Company, 1903), 252.

453 De Pauw, *Eleventh Pillar*, 19–22; Kaminski, "New York: The Reluctant Pillar," in Schechter, *The Reluctant Pillar*, 49.

454 Philip Schuyler to John Jay, 30 June 1777, in Johnston, *The Correspondence and Public Papers of John Jay*, vol. 1, 144.

455 John Vaughan to John Dickinson, *Charleston (NY) Columbian Herald*, June 19, 1788.

456 Abigail Adams Smith to Abigail Adams, 13 June 1788, in Kaminski, *The Documentary History*, vol. 20, 1173.

457 Carl Lotus Becker, *The History of Political Parties in the Province of New York, 1760–1776* (Ph.D. diss., published by the Bulletin of the University of Wisconsin, Madison, 1909), 260–261.

458 *Pennsylvania Herald*, February 9, 1788, in Schecter, *The Reluctant Pillar*, 60–61, 64–65.

459 Becker, *The History of Political Parties*, 274–275.

460 *New York Journal*, December 14, 1786.

461 *New York Journal*, June 28, 1787; June 9, 1787.

462 De Pauw, *Eleventh Pillar*, 73–74.

463 Max Farrand, ed., *The Records of the Federal Convention of 1787*, vol. 3 (New Haven: Yale University Press, 1937), 89.

464 Rossiter, *Alexander Hamilton and the Constitution*, 46–47; Kaminski, in Schecter, *The Reluctant Pillar*, 62–63; Morris, *Witnesses at the Creation*, 230.

465 Ibid., p. 74.

466 J. C. Hamilton, *Works,* (New York, 1851) vol. 1, 444.

467 Hamilton, notes to himself, in Syrett, *The Papers of Alexander Hamilton*, vol. 4, 275–277.

468 Paul Ford, *Essays on the Constitution of the United States Published During its Discussion by the People, 1787-1788* (Brooklyn, 1888), 249; Kaminski, "Reluctant Pillar," in Schecter, *The Reluctant Pillar*, 69.

469 Ford, *Essays on the Constitution*, 254; Rossiter, *Alexander Hamilton and the Constitution*, 60–61.

470 Hamilton writing as "H. G." February 21, 1789, in Syrett, *The Papers of Alexander Hamilton*, vol. 4, 265.

471 George Washington to Alexander Hamilton, 28 August 1788, in Syrett, *The Papers of Alexander Hamilton*, vol. 5, 196–198.

472 *New York Daily Advertiser*, July 26, 1788.

473 Ibid., November 23, 1787.

474 Eubanks, in Gillespie, *Ratifying the Constitution*, 316.

475 *New York Journal*, September 13 and 20, 1787.

476 George Washington to Alexander Hamilton, 18 October 1787, in Syrett, *The Papers of Alexander Hamilton*, vol. 4, 284.

477 De Pauw, *Eleventh Pillar*, 83.

478 Clarence Miner, *The Ratification of the Federal Constitution by the State of New York* (New York: Columbia University Press, 1921), 30–31.

479 James Madison to Edmund Pendleton, 28 October 1787, in Hunt, *The Writings of James Madison*, vol. 5, 46.

480 George Washington to James Madison, 31 March 1787, *GWW,* vol. 29, 191.

481 *New York Daily Advertiser*, January 28, 1788; Elliot, *The Debates in the Several State Conventions,* vol. 2, 246; Murray Dry, "The Case Against Ratification: Anti-Federalist Constitutional Thought," in Leonard Levy and Dennis Mahoney, *The Framing and Ratification of the Constitution* (New York: Macmillan Publishing, 1987), 277.

482 Kaminski, "Reluctant Pillar," in Schecter, *The Reluctant Pillar*, 71.

483 *Daily Advertiser*, February 23, 1788.

484 *New York Journal*, December 18, 1787.

485 Ibid., December 24, 1787.

486 Ibid., December 12, 1787.

487 Ibid.

488 Ibid., December 19 and 20, 1787; *Lansingburg (N.Y.) Northern Centinal*, December 25, 1787.

489  De Pauw, *Eleventh Pillar*, 101–102.

490  *New York Packet*, January 1, 1788.

491  *Poughkeepsie Country Journal*, December 12, 1787.

492  Kaminski, *The Documentary History*, vol. 19, 429–430.

493  Hannah Thompson to John Mifflin, 2 March 1788, in Kaminski, *The Documentary History*, vol. 20, 837.

494  Major North to Henry Knox, 13 February 1788, Knox Papers, vol. 21, 143.

495  Abraham Yates to Abraham Lansing, 28 February 1788, in Yates Papers, New York Public Library, New York, N.Y.

496  Journal of Dewitt Clinton, New York Historical Society.

497  Henry Gilpin, Papers of James Madison, vol. 2 (New York: J. & H. G. Langley, 1841), 670; John Jay to George Washington, 20 April 1788, in Morris; Jay Papers, Columbia University; Henry Knox to George Washington, U.S. Bureau of Rolls and Library *U.S. Department of State Bulletin* (Washington, 1893), vol. 11, 537.

498  De Pauw, *Eleventh Pillar*, 132–133.

499  *Albany Gazette*, January 17, 1788.

500  De Pauw, *Eleventh Pillar*, 137.

501  Ibid., 139.

502  Ibid., 154–155.

503  Hugh Hughes, "Countryman" series, February 28, 1788, *Philadelphia Independent Gazetteer* and others.

504  Elliot, *The Debates in the Several State Conventions*, vol. 2, 397.

505  John Jay to Thomas Jefferson, 8 September 1787, U.S. Bureau of Rolls and Library (Washington, DC, 1894–1903), vol. 4, 276; De Pauw, *Eleventh Pillar*, 147.

506  *New York Journal*, June 25, 1788.

507  Henrietta Maria Colden to Francis Bland Tucket, 28 December 1787, in Kaminski, *The Documentary History*, vol. 19, 478–479.

508  *New York Journal*, April 2, 1788.

509  John Jay to George Washington, 20 April 1788, in Morris, Jay Papers.

510  Thomas Jefferson to William Carmichael, 27 May 1788, in Stahr, *John Jay*, 251 and 253–254; Paul Gilje, *The Road to Mobocracy: Popular Disorder in New York City, 1763–1834* (Chapel Hill: University of North Carolina Press, 1987), 78–81; Nicholas Gilman to John Sullivan, 19 April 1788, in Burnett, *Letters of the Members*, vol. 8, 722; William Heth to Edmund Randolph, April 1788, in Burnett, *Letters of the Members*, 722n; various newspaper accounts.

511  Kaminski, "Reluctant Pillar," in Schecter, 72, Morris, Jay Papers.

512  Stahr, *John Jay*, 15; George Washington to John Jay, 15 May 1788, in

Washington, *Papers of George Washington*, Confederation series, vol. 6, 275–276.

513 John Jay to George Washington, 3 February 1788, in Kaminski, *The Documentary History*, vol. 20, 746.

514 Ibid., notes on the New York elections can be found in vol. 21, 1536-1541, with Thomas Treadwell's campaign.

515 Ibid., 98.

516 *Albany Anti-Federal Committee Circular*, April 10, 1778.

517 "W.M." note, in *Albany Journal*, March 10, 1788.

518 Lynd, *Anti-Federalism in Dutchess County*, 18–19.

519 Kaminski, "Reluctant Pillar," in Schecter, *The Reluctant Pillar*, 80.

520 Ibid., 85.

521 Ibid., 92.

522 Ibid., 94.

523 Kaminski, *The Documentary History*, vol. 8, 1536 and 1542–1543.

524 Kaminski, "Reluctant Pillar," in Schecter, *The Reluctant Pillar*, 79; Alexander Hamilton to James Madison, 8 June 1788, in Syrett, *The Papers of Alexander Hamilton*, vol. 5, 3.

525 *Virginia Independent Chronicle*, May 9, 1788.

526 Kaminski, *The Documentary History*, vol. 10, 1598–1599.

527 Hendrickson, *The Rise and Fall of Alexander Hamilton*, 235.

528 Abigail Adams to John Quincy Adams, 8 June 1788, in Kaminski, *The Documentary History*, vol. 20, 1136–1137.

529 James Hughes to John Lamb, 17 June 1788, Papers of John Lamb, New York Historical Society, New York, N.Y.

530 Hamilton to anonymous friend, J. C. Hamilton, Works *of Alexander Hamilton, Comprising His Correspondence and His Political and Official Writings, Exclusive of The Federalist, Civil and Military.* 7 vols. (C. S. Francis Co., 1851) vol. 1, 452.

531 Rossiter, *Alexander Hamilton and the Constitution*, 63; Miner, *The Ratification of the Federal Constitution*, 95; Storing, *The Complete Anti-Federalist*, vol. 1, 75n.

532 Storing, *The Complete Anti-Federalist*, vol. 1, 73.

533 Tench Coxe to James Madison, 11 June 1788, in Kaminski, *The Documentary History*, vol. 20, 1138–1139.

534 Chernow, *Alexander Hamilton*, 263.

535 *New York Packet*, November 16, 1787.

536 Cato, in *New York Journal*, December 13, 1787.

537 Don Diego de Gardoqui to Conde de Floridablanca, Spain's Secretary of State, 6 December 1787, in Kaminski, *The Documentary History*, vol. 19, 360–361.

538 Hugh Hughes to John Lamb, 8 June 1788, Papers of John Lamb, New York Historical Society, New York, N.Y.

539 Elliot, *The Debates in the Several State Conventions*, vol. 2, 246.

540 De Pauw, *Eleventh Pillar*, 185.

541 Alexander Hamilton to James Madison, 19 June 1788, in Syrett, *The Papers of Alexander Hamilton*, vol. 5, 12–13.

542 Elliot, *The Debates in the Several State Conventions*, vol. 2, 209.

543 Tench Coxe, "To the New York Convention," *Pennsylvania Gazette*, June 11, 1788; Abraham Yates Jr., "To the Citizens of the State of New York," June 13 and 14, 1788, *Albany Gazette*, in Kaminski, *The Documentary History*, vol. 20, 1153–1168.

544 Richard Platt to Winthrop Sargent, 14 June 1788, in Kaminski, *The Documentary History*, vol. 20, 1169.

545 Francis Newton Thorpe, *Constitutional History of the United States* (Chicago: Callaghan & Company, 1901), 238.

546 *New York Packet*, October 30, 1787.

CHAPTER FOURTEEN

547 De Pauw, *Eleventh Pillar,* 188–189.

548 Miner, *The Ratification of the Federal Constitution*, 100–104; De Pauw, *Eleventh Pillar*, 192–193; Alexander Hamilton to James Madison, 19 June 1788, in Madison, *The Papers of James Madison*, vol. 2, 156.

549 Elliot, *The Debates in the Several State Conventions*, vol. 2, 210.

550 Dry, in Levy, 275.

551 Charles Tillinghast to John Lamb, 21 June 1788, Papers of John Lamb, New York Historical Society, New York, N.Y.

552 Isaac Roosevelt to Richard Varick, 1 July 1788, in Edmund Platt, *Eagle's History of Poughkeepsie from Earliest Settlements, 1683 to 1905* (Poughkeepsie, NY: Platt & Platt, 1905), 58.

553 Alexander Hamilton to John Sullivan, 6 June 1788, in Syrett, *The Papers of Alexander Hamilton*, vol. 5, 2.

554 Smith to delegates in New Hampshire and Virginia, June 1788, in Papers of John Lamb, New York Historical Association, New York, N.Y.

555 William Kent, ed., *Memoirs and Letters of James Kent, Late Chancellor of the State of New York* (Boston: Little, Brown and Co., 1898), 305; William Paterson to William Duane, September 22, 1788, Duane Papers, New York Historical Society.

556 Melancton Smith to Nathan Dane, 28 June 1788, in Burnett, *Letters of the Members*, vol. 8, 757n.

557 Kent, *Memoirs and Letters of James Kent*, 306, 309.

558 Elliot, *The Debates in the Several State Conventions*, vol. 2, 222.

559 Ibid, 217.

560 Ibid., 296.

561 Ibid., 375.

562 Ibid., 301 and 307.

563 Ibid., 223–224.

564 Ibid., 334.

565 Morris, *Witnesses at the Creation*, 240.

566 Alexander Hamilton letter, September 1787, in Bailyn, *The Debate on The Constitution*, 10–11.

567 Elliot, *The Debates in the Several State Conventions* vol. 2, 263.

568 Ibid., 356.

569 Ibid., 257.

570 Ibid., 257.

571 Ibid., 296; Rossiter, *Alexander Hamilton and the Constitution*, 66; *Maryland Gazette*, July 17, 1788; Syrett, *The Papers of Alexander Hamilton*, vol. 5, 138–141.

572 Elliot, *The Debates in the Several State Conventions*, vol. 2, 285.

573 *New York Journal*, June 26, 1788.

574 Elliot, *The Debates in the Several State Conventions*, vol. 2, 234–235.

575 Ibid., 239.

576 J. C. Hamilton, U.S. Bureau of Rolls and Library, vol. 1, 459 and vol. 9, 748.

577 Clason, "Convention of New York, 1788," *Magazine of American History* 16, 158.

578 *New York Daily Advertiser*, June 28, 1788.

579 Morris, *Witnesses at the Creation*, 243.

580 De Pauw, *Eleventh Pillar*, 209.

581 Elliot, *The Debates in the Several State Conventions*, vol. 2, 324–325.

582 George Clinton to John Lamb, June 1788, Papers of John Lamb; Elliot, *The Debates in the Several State Conventions*, vol. 2, 276.

583 Elliot, *The Debates in the Several State Conventions*, vol. 2, 276.

584 Alexander Hamilton to James Madison, 2 July 1788, in Syrett, *The Papers of Alexander Hamilton*, vol. 5, 140–141; "H.G." *New York Daily Advertiser*, March 14, 1789.

585 Alexander Hamilton, "To the Electors of the City and County of New York," *New York Daily Gazette*, April 28, 1789.

586 *New York Daily Advertiser*, July 16, 1788.

587 Ibid.

588 Alexander Hamilton to James Madison, 8 June 1778, in Syrett, *The Papers of Alexander Hamilton*, vol. 5, 2–4.

589 John Pintard to Elisha Boudinot, June 10, 1788, Boudinot-Pintard Papers, New Hampshire Historical Society.

590 Henry Knox to Otho Williams, 11 June 1788, Williams Papers, Maryland Historical Society.

591 Elliot, *The Debates in the Several State Conventions*, vol. 2, 405.

592 *New York Journal*, November 21, 1787.

593 Elliot, *The Debates in the Several State Conventions*, vol. 2, 366–367.

594 *New York Independent Journal*, July 2, 1788.

595 U.S. Bureau of Rolls and Library, vol. 11, 767.

596 *New York Daily Advertiser*, July 7, 1788.

597 Kaminski, *The Documentary History*, vol. 18, 260–268.

598 Morris, *Witnesses at the Creation*, 246.

599 *New York Daily Advertiser*, July 5, 1788.

600 Miner, *The Ratification of the Federal Constitution*, 129.

601 *New York Morning Post*, March 11, 1788.

602 *Federalist* No. 84, in Jacob E. Cooke, ed., *The Federalist* (Middletown, CT: Wesleyan University Press, 1961), 579.

603 Elliot, *The Debates in the Several State Conventions*, vol. 2, 370–371; Cecil Eubanks, "New York: Federalism and the Political Economy of Union," in Gillespie, *Ratifying the Constitution*, 329.

604 Chernow, *Alexander Hamilton*, 264.

605 Clinton speech, July 17, 1788, Papers of George Clinton, Library of the American Revolution, Washington's Crossing, PA.

606 *New York Journal*, July 21, 1788.

607 Elbridge Gerry to James Warren, 28 June 1788, in Kaminski, *The Documentary History*, vol. 28, 206.

608 Alexander Hamilton to James Madison, 22 July 1788, in Syrett, *The Papers of Alexander Hamilton*, vol. 5, 187.

609 *Pennsylvania Gazette*, May 14, 1788; Stahr, *John Jay*, 260.

610 John Jay to George Washington, 8 July 1788, *GWW*, vol. 30, 18n.

611 De Pauw, *Eleventh Pillar*, 230–241; Kaminski, *The Documentary History*, vol. 21, 1630–1666; Burnett, *Letters of the Members*, vol. 8, 765n.

612 James Madison to Edmund Randolph, 16 July 1788, in Burnett, *Letters of the Members*, vol. 8, 761–762.

613 Samuel Otis to George Thatcher, 17 July 1788, in Burnett, *Letters of the Members*, vol. 8, 763.

614 Comte Moustier to Comte Montmorin, 25 June 1787, in Kaminski, *The Documentary History*, vol. 18, 189–193.

615 James Madison to Alexander Hamilton, July 1788, in Syrett, *The Papers of Alexander Hamilton*, vol. 5, 193.

616 Rossiter, *Alexander Hamilton and the Constitution*, 70; Melancton Smith,

"The Movement Toward a Second Constitutional Convention," in J. Franklin Jameson, *Essays in the Constitutional History of the United States in the Formative Period* (Boston: Houghton-Mifflin, 1889), 88.

617 Kaminski, *The Documentary History*, vol. 18, 162; Miner, *The Ratification of the Federal Constitution*, 123.

618 Eubanks, in Gillespie, *Ratifying the Constitution*, 328–330; Robin Brooks, "Alexander Hamilton, Melancton Smith and the Ratification of the Constitution in New York," *William and Mary Quarterly*, 3.24, no. 3 (July 1967), 339–341.

619 Rev. John Mason oration at Hamilton's funeral, in Rossiter, *Alexander Hamilton and the Constitution*, 67n.

620 Joshua Atherton to John Lamb, 29 February 1789, Papers of John Lamb, New York Historical Society, New York, N.Y.; De Pauw, *Eleventh Pillar*, ix.

621 Miner, *The Ratification of the Federal Constitution*, 120.

622 George Washington to Sir Edward Newenham, 29 August 1788, in Kaminski, *The Documentary History*, vol. 18, 358–360.

623 Andrew Allen to Tench Coxe, 8 September 1788, in Kaminski, *The Documentary History*, vol. 18, 361–362.

624 John Page to James Madison, 6 August 1788, in Miller, *The Business of May Next*, 238–239.

AFTERMATH

625 Hardin Burnley to James Madison, 16 December 1788, in Hunt, *The Writings of James Madison*, vol. 11, 398.

626 James Madison to George Eve, 2 January 1789, in Hunt, *The Writings of James Madison*, vol. 11, 404–405.

627 Reimer, *James Madison*, 139.

628 Lance Banning, *Sacred Fire of Liberty*, 281–286.

629 James Madison to Thomas Jefferson, 15 October 1788, in Miller, *The Business of May Next*, 239; Smith, *The Republic of Letters*, vol 1, 590–591.

630 Humphrey, *The Press of the Young Republic*, 30–31; Jack Rakove, *James Madison and the Creation of the American Republic* (Glenview, IL: Scott, Foresman and Company, 1990), 82–84.

631 Fisher Ames to George Minot, 29 May 1789, in Ames, *The Works of Fisher Ames*, vol. 1, 49.

632 Rakove, *James Madison*, 92–94.

633 Ketcham, *James Madison*, 376–381.

634 Sydney Gay, *James Madison* (New Rochelle, NY: Arlington House, 1970), 216–222.

635 Ibid., 243.

636 Ketcham, *James Madison*, 408.

637 Ibid., 409.

638 Rakove, *James Madison*, 93.

639 Ibid., 134–138.

640 Ibid., 258–259.

641 Stahr, *John Jay*, 271–273.

642 George Washington to John Jay, 5 October 1789, in Washington, *Papers of George Washington*, Confederation series, vol. 4, 137.

643 Morris, *Witnesses at the Creation*, 260.

644 Elbert Hubbard, *John Jay: Chief Justice of the United States* (New York: Hartford Lunch Co., 1918), 24–25

645 Ibid., 27.

646 John Miller, *Alexander Hamilton, Portrait in Paradox* (New York: Harper and Row, 1959), 226.

647 Richard Brookhiser, *Alexander Hamilton, American* (New York: Free Press, 1999), 83–97.

648 Brookhiser, *Alexander Hamilton*, 88–89.

649 Louis Hacker, *Alexander Hamilton in the American Tradition* (New York: McGraw Hill, 1957), 149–155; Henry Cabot Lodge, *Alexander Hamilton* (New Rochelle, NY: Arlington House, 1970), 130–133.

650 Ibid. Lodge, 228.

651 Hendrickson, *The Rise and Fall of Alexander Hamilton*, 285.

652 Ibid., 251.

653 Morris, *Alexander Hamilton and the Founding of the Nation* (New York: Dial Press, 1957), vii–xiv.

654 Ford, *Correspondence and Journals*, vol. 1, 115 and 165.

655 Hendrickson, *The Rise and Fall of Alexander Hamilton*, 547.

656 Hacker, *Alexander Hamilton*, 242–246.

657 Milton Canton, *Alexander Hamilton* (Englewood Cliffs, N.J.: Prentice Hall, 1971), 122; Hendrickson, *The Rise and Fall of Alexander Hamilton*, x.

658 Banning, *Sacred Fire of Liberty*, 288.

# BIBLIOGRAPHY

## Archival Sources

Diary of Sylvanus Seely, Morristown National Historical Park

Papers of John Adams Family, Massachusetts Historical Society

Papers of John Quincy Adams, Massachusetts Historical Society

Papers of Jeremy Belknap, Harvard University

Papers of Elisha Boudinot—John Pintard, New Hampshire Historical Society

Papers of John Brown, Rhode Island Historical Society

Papers of George Clinton, New York Public Library, Princeton University

Papers of Alexander Hamilton, Library of Congress

Papers of Rufus King, New Hampshire Historical Society

Papers of Henry Knox, David Library of the American Revolution

Papers of John Lamb, New York Historical Society

Papers of James Madison, Princeton University, 1745–1826

Papers of James Maury, University of Virginia

Papers of Timothy Pickering, Massachusetts Historical Society

Papers of Thomas Sedgwick, Massachusetts Historical Society

# Newspaper Sources

*Albany Gazette,* 1787

*Albany Journal,* 1787–1788

*Baltimore Gazette,* 1787–1788

*Boston Gazette,* 1786–1789

*Charleston (NY) Columbian Herald,* 1787–1788

*Connecticut Courant,* 1786–1789

*Connecticut Gazette,* 1787–1788

*Cumberland (ME) Gazette,* 1787–1788

*Exeter (NH) Freeman's Oracle,* 1787–1788

*Landsingburgh Northern Centinel,* 1787–1788

*Maryland Journal and Baltimore Advertiser,* 1787–1788

*Massachusetts Centinel,* 1786–1789

*Massachusetts Gazette,* 1787–1788

*Massachusetts Spy,* 1787–1788

*Middlesex (CT) Gazette,* 1787–1788

*New Hampshire Gazette,* 1787–1788

*Newport Mercury,* 1787–1788

*New York Journal,* 1787–1788

*New York Morning Post,* 1787–1788

*New York Packet,* 1787–1788

*Pennsylvania Gazette,* 1787–1789

*Pennsylvania Herald,* 1787

*Pennsylvania Mercury,* 1788

*Philadelphia Gazette,* 1787–1788

*Poughkeepsie (NY) Country Journal,* 1788

*Providence (RI) Gazette,* 1787–1788

*Salem (MA) Mercury,* 1787–1788

*Vermont Journal,* 1787-1788

*Virginia Independent Chronicle,* 1787–1788

*Westminster Independent Chronicle,* 1787–1788

*Worcester Magazine,* 1787–1788

# Journal Articles and Book Chapters

Ames, Fisher. "The Federalists as Ideologues." In *The Federalists: Realists in I deologues*, edited by George Billias. Lexington, MA: D. C. Heath and Co., 1970.

Brooks, Robin. "Alexander Hamilton, Melancton Smith and the Ratification of the Constitution in New York." *William and Mary Quarterly*, 3.24, no. 3, (July 1967).

Dry, Murray. "The Case Against Ratification: Anti-Federalist Constitutional Thought." In *The Framing and Ratification of the Constitution*, edited by Leonard Levy and Dennis Mahoney. New York: Macmillan Publishing, 1987.

Eubanks, Cecil. "New York: Federalism and the Political Economy of Union." *Ratifying the Constitution*, edited by Michael Allen Gillespie and Michael Lienesch. Lawrence: University Press of Kansas, 1989.

Finkelman, Paul. "Between Scylla and Charybdis: Anarchy, Tyranny and the Debate Over a Bill of Rights." In *The Bill of Rights: Government Proscribed*, edited by Ron Hoffman and Peter Albert. Charlottesville: University of Virginia Press, 1997.

Freeman, David. "Reflections on Human Nature: The Federalists and the Republican Tradition." In *The Federalists, the Anti-Federalists and the American Political Tradition*, edited by Wilson Carey McWilliams and Michael Gibbons. Westport, CT: Greenwood Press, 1992.

Harper, Robert Goodloe. "The Federalists as Realists." In *The Federalists: Realists or Ideologues?*, edited by George Billias. Lexington, MA: D. C. Heath and Co., 1970.

Kates, Robert. "Handgun Prohibition and the Original Understanding of the Second Amendment." *Michigan Law Review* (1983).

Levy, Leonard. "The Bill of Rights." In *The American Founding*, edited by Jackson Barlow, Leonard Levy, and Kenneth Masugi. Westport, CT: Greenwood Press, 1988.

McGuire, Robert, and Robert Ohsfeldt, "Self-Interest Agency Theory and the Political Voting Behavior." In "The Ratification of the United States Constitution." Special issue, *American Economic Journal* (March 1989).

Moran, Fran. "Iron Handed Despotism: Anti-Federalist and American Civil Liberties." In New Jersey City University's *Academic Forum,* vol. 14, no. 1, Spring, 2005.

Schwartz, Bernard. "Experience vs. Reason: Beautiful Books and Great

Revolutions." In *The Bill of Rights: Government Proscribed*, edited by Ron Hoffman and Peter Albert. Charlottesville: U.S. Capitol History Society and University Press of Virginia, 1997.

Shumer, Sara. "New Jersey: Property and Price of Republican Politics." In *Ratifying the Constitution*, edited by Michael Gillespie and Michael Lienesch, Lawrence: University Press of Kansas, 1989.

Smith, Melancton. "The Movement Toward a Second Constitutional Convention." In *Essays in the Constitutional History of the United States in the Formative Years*, edited by J. Franklin Jameson. Boston: Houghton-Mifflin Co., 1889.

U.S. Congress, Subcommittee on the Constitution, "The Right to Keep and Bear Arms," 97th Cong., 2nd sess., February 1982. Washington, DC: U.S. Government Printing Office, 1982.

# Books

Adams, Samuel. *The Writings of Samuel Adams*. Edited by Harry Alonzo Cushing. 4 vols. New York: G. P. Putnam's Sons, 1904–1908.

Ames, Fisher. *The Works of Fisher Ames*. 2 vols. Boston: Little, Brown and Company, 1854.

Bailyn, Barnard, ed. *The Debate on the Constitution: Federalist and Anti-Federalist Speeches, Articles and Letters During the Struggle Over Ratification*. New York: Library of America, 1993.

Banning, Lance. *Sacred Fire of Liberty: James Madison and the Founding of the Federal Republic*. Ithaca: Cornell University Press, 1995.

Barlow, Joel. *Advice to the Privileged Orders of the Several States of Europe Resulting from the Necessity and Propriety of a General Revolution in the Principle of Government*. London: J. Johnson, 1792, reprint, Ithaca, NY: Great Seal Books, Cornell University Press, 1956.

Beard, Charles. *The Enduring Federalist*. New York: Frederick Ungar Publishing Co., 1948.

Beeman, Richard. *Patrick Henry: A Biography*. New York, McGraw-Hill, 1974.

Boyd, Thomas. *Light Horse Harry Lee*. New York: C. Scribner's Sons, 1931.

Bradford, M. E. *A Better Guide Than Reason: Federalists and Anti-Federalists*. New Brunswick, NJ: Transaction Publishers, 1994.

Brant, Irving. *James Madison: The Virginia Revolutionist*. Indianapolis: Bobbs-Merrill Co., 1941.

————. *The Fourth President: A Life of James Madison.* Indianapolis: Bobbs-Merrill Co., 1970.

Brigham, William, ed. *The Compact with the Charter and the Laws of the Colony of New Plymouth.* Boston: Dutton and Wentworth, 1836.

Broadwater, Jeff. *George Mason: Forgotten Founder.* Chapel Hill: University of North Carolina Press, 2006.

Brookhiser, Richard. *Alexander Hamilton, American.* New York: Free Press, 1999.

Brown, Imogene. *American Aristides: A Biography of George Wythe.* Rutherford, NJ: Fairleigh Dickinson University Press, 1981.

Buffum, Francis, H., ed. *New Hampshire and the Federal Constitution: A Memorial of the Sesquicentennial Celebration of New Hampshire's Part in the Framing and Ratification of the Constitution of the United States,* 2nd ed. Concord, NH: Granite State Press, 1942.

Burnett, Edmund. *Letters of the Members of the Continental Congress.* 8 vols. Washington, DC: Carnegie Institution of Washington, 1921–1936.

Campbell, Norine. *Patrick Henry: Patriot and Statesman.* New York: Devin-Adair Co., 1969.

Canton, Milton. *Alexander Hamilton.* Englewood Cliffs: Prentice Hall, 1971.

Caplan, Russell. *Constitutional Brinksmanship: Amending the Constitution by National Convention.* New York: Oxford University Press, 1988.

Cappon, Lester, ed. *The Adams-Jefferson Letters: the Complete Correspondence between Thomas Jefferson and Abigail and John Adams.* Chapel Hill: University of North Carolina Press, 1988.

Cerami, Charles. *Young Patriots: The Remarkable Story of Two Men, Their Impossible Plan and the Revolution that Created the Constitution.* Naperville, IL: Sourcebooks, 2005.

Chernow, Ron. *Alexander Hamilton.* New York: Penguin Press, 2004.

Cochran, Thomas. *New York in the Confederation.* Clifton, NJ: A. M. Kelley, 1972.

Conway, Moncure Daniel, ed. *Writings of Thomas Paine,* New York: G. P. Putnam's Sons, 1894.

Cooke, Jacob E. *The Federalist.* Middlebury, Conn.: Wesleyan University Press, 1961.

De Pauw, Linda. *Eleventh Pillar: New York State and the Federal Constitution.* Ithaca: Cornell University Press, 1966.

De Warville, J. P. Brissot. *New Travels in the United States of America, 1788.* Cambridge: Belknap Press, 1964.

Elliot, Jonathan, ed. *The Debates in the Several State Conventions on the Adoption of the Federal Constitution as Recommended by the General Convention at Philadelphia in 1787.* 5 vols. New York: B. Franklin, 1968.

Ernst, Robert. *Rufus King: American Federalist.* Chapel Hill: University of North Carolina Press, 1968.

Farand, Max, ed. *The Records of the Federal Constitution of 1787.* 4 vols. New Haven: Yale University Press, 1937.

Fitzgerald, F. Scott. *The Great Gatsby.* New York: Charles Scribner's Sons, 1925.

Fitzpatrick, John, ed. *Diaries of George Washington.* 4 vols. Boston: Houghton-Mifflin Co., Mount Vernon Ladies Association of the Union, 1925.

———. The Writings of George Washington. 38 vols. Washington, D.C.: United States Government Printing Office, 1932.

Flexner, Thomas. *George Washington in the American Revolution.* Boston: Little, Brown and Co., 1968.

Foley, James. Ed. Thomas Jefferson. *The Jefferson Cyclopedia.* New York: Russell & Russell, 1967.

Ford, Paul, ed. *Essays on the Constitution of the United States, Published During Its Discussion by the People, 1787–1788.* Brooklyn, NY: 1888.

Ford, W. C., ed. *Correspondence and Journals of Samuel Blanchley Webb.* New York, 3 vols., 1893–1894.

Gay, Sydney. *James Madison.* New Rochelle: Arlington House, 1970.

Gilje, Paul. *Road to Mobocracy: Popular Disorder in New York City, 1763–1834.* Chapel Hill: University of North Carolina Press, 1987.

Gillespie, Michael, and Michael Lienesch, eds. *Ratifying the Constitution.* Lawrence: University Press of Kansas, 1989.

Goddard, William. *The Prowess of the Whig Club, and the Manoeuvres of Legion.* Baltimore, March 17, 1777.

Grigsby, Hugh. *History of the Virginia Federal Convention of 1788.* 2 vols. Richmond: Virginia Historical Society, 1890–1891.

Hacker, Louis. *Alexander Hamilton in the American Tradition.* New York: McGraw-Hill, 1957.

Hamilton, Alexander, James Madison, and John Jay. *The Federalist.* New York: Bantam Books, 1987.

Hamilton, Allan McLane. *Intimate Life of Alexander Hamilton, Based Chiefly upon Original Family Letters and Other Documents.* New York: Charles Scribner's Sons, 1911.

Hamilton, J. C., ed. *The Federalist: A Commentary on the Constitution of the United States, a Collection of Essays by Alexander Hamilton, Jay and Madison. Also, the Continentalist and Other Papers by Hamilton.* 3 vols. Philadelphia, 1865.

Hamilton, John C. *The Life of Alexander Hamilton.* 7 vols. Boston: Houghton, Osgood, 1879.

———. *The Works of Alexander Hamilton, Comprising His Correspondence and His Political and Official Writings, Exclusive of The Federalist, Civil and Military.* 7 vols. New York: C.S. Francis Co., 1851.

Handlin, Oscar, and Mary Handlin, eds. *The Popular Sources of Political Authority: Documents on the Massachusetts Constitution of 1780.* Boston: Harvard University Press, 1966.

Harding, Samuel. *The Contest over the Ratification of the Federal Constitution in the State of Massachusetts.* New York: Longmans, Green and Co., 1896.

Harlow, Ralph. *Samuel Adams: Promoter of the American Revolution–A Study in Psychology and Politics.* New York: Octagon Books, 1971.

Hendrickson, Robert. *The Rise and Fall of Alexander Hamilton.* New York: Van Nostrand and Rheinhold Co., 1981.

Hening, William Waller. *The Statutes at Large: Being a Collection of All the Laws of Virginia, From the First Session of the Legislature in the Year 1619.* New York, 1823.

Hickok, Eugene W. Jr., ed. *The Bill of Rights: Original Meaning and Current Understanding.* Charlottesville: University Press of Virginia, 1991.

Hilldrup, Robert. *The Life and Times of Edmund Pendleton.* Chapel Hill: University of North Carolina Press, 1939.

Horton, John. *James Kent: A Study in Conservatism, 1783–1847.* New York, D. Appleton-Century Company, Inc., 1939.

Hubbard, Elbert. *John Jay: Chief Justice of the United States.* New York: Hartford Lunch Co., 1918.

Humphrey, Carol Sue. *The Press of the Young Republic, 1783–1833.* Westport, CT: Greenwood Press, 1966.

Hunt, Gaillard. Ed. *The Writings of James Madison, Comprising His Public Papers and His Private Correspondence, Including Numerous Letters and Documents, Now for the First Time Printed.* 5 vols. New York: G. P. Putnam's Sons, 1900–1910.

Jefferson, Thomas. *The Life and Selected Writings of Thomas Jefferson.* Edited by Adrienne Koch and William Peden. New York: Modern Library, 1944.

———. *The Papers of Thomas Jefferson.* Edited by Julian Boyd. 29 vols. Princeton: Princeton University Press, 1950.

———. *The Writings of Thomas Jefferson.* Edited by Andrew Lipscomb. Washington, DC: Thomas Jefferson Memorial Association of the United States, 1903–1904.

Johnston, Henry P., ed. *The Correspondence and Public Papers of John Jay, 1763–1826.* 4 vols. New York: B. Franklin Co., 1970.

———. *The Correspondence and Public Papers of John Jay.* 4 vols. New York, G. P. Putnam's Sons, 1890–1893.

Kaminski, John. *The Documentary History of the Ratification of the Constitution.* Edited by Merrill Jensen. 16 vols. Madison: Wisconsin State Historical Society, 1988.

Kent, William, ed. *Memoirs and Letters of James Kent, Late Chancellor of the State of New York.* Boston: Little, Brown and Co., 1898.

Ketcham, Ralph. *James Madison: A Biography.* Charlottesville: University Press of Virginia, 1990.

King, Charles R. *The Life and Correspondence of Rufus King: Comprising His Letters, Private and Official, His Public Documents and His Speeches.* 6 vols. New York: G. P. Putnam's Sons, 1894.

Kukla, Jon, ed. *The Bill of Rights: A Lively Heritage.* Richmond: Virginia State Library and Archives, 1987.

Lee, Richard Henry. *The Letters of Richard Henry Lee, 1782–1794.* Edited by James Ballagh. 2 vols. New York: MacMillan, 1911.

———. *Letters of a Federal Farmer.* Chicago: Quadrangle Press, 1962.

Leibiger, Stuart. *Founding Friendship: George Washington, James Madison and the Creation of the American Republic.* Charlottesville: University of Virginia Press, 1999.

Lemmon, Sarah, ed. *The Pettigrew Papers.* 2 vols. Raleigh: North Carolina State University Press, 1971.

Lodge, Henry Cabot. *Alexander Hamilton.* New Rochelle, NY: Arlington House, 1980. First published 1898 by Houghton-Mifflin, Boston.

Madison, James. *The Papers of James Madison.* Edited by Robert Rutland, William Hutchinson, and William Rachal. 17 vols. Chicago: University of Chicago Press, 1962–1991.

———. *The Papers of James Madison: Presidential Series.* Edited by Robert A. Rutland. 5 vols. Charlottesville: University of Virginia Press, 1984.

Main, Jackson Turner. *The Anti-Federalists: Critics of the Constitution, 1781–1788.* Chapel Hill: University of North Carolina Press, 1961.

Martin, Joseph Plumb. *Private Yankee Doodle, Being a Narrative of Some of the*

*Adventures, Dangers and Sufferings of a Revolutionary Soldier.* Boston: Little, Brown and Co., 1962.

Mason, George. *Papers of George Mason.* Edited by Robert A. Rutland. 3 vols. Chapel Hill: University of North Carolina Press, 1970.

Mays, David. *The Address of David Mays in the Old House of Delegates in the Capitol of Virginia on the Occasion of the Unveiling of the Bust of George Wythe.* Richmond: National Society of the Colonial Dames of America in the Commonwealth of Virginia, 1964.

McCoy, Drew. *The Last of the Fathers: James Madison and the Republican Legacy.* New York: Cambridge University Press, 1989.

McGaughy, Kent. *Richard Henry Lee of Virginia: A Portrait of an American Revolutionary.* New York: Rowman and Littlefield, 2004.

McNamara, Peter. *Alexander Hamilton, the Love of Fame and Modern Democratic Statesmanship.* New York: Rowman and Littlefield, 1999.

Meade, Robert. *Patrick Henry.* 2 vols. Philadelphia: Lippencott and Co., 1957–1969.

Miller, William Lee. *The Business of May Next: James Madison and the Founding.* Charlottesville: University Press of Virginia, 1992.

Miner, Clarence. *The Ratification of the Federal Constitution by the State of New York.* New York: Columbia University Press, 1921.

Mitchell, Broadus. *Alexander Hamilton, Youth to Maturity.* 2 vols. New York: Thomas Crowell, 1980.

Morison, Samuel, and Henry Steele Commager. *The Growth of the American Republic.* 2 vols. New York: Oxford University Press, 1962.

Morris, Richard, ed. *John Jay: The Making of a Revolutionary, Unpublished Papers, 1745–1780.* 2 vols. New York: Harper and Brothers, 1975.

——. *John Jay.* New York: Harper and Row, 1975.

——. *Witnesses at the Creation: Hamilton, Madison, Jay and the Constitution.* New York: Holt, Rinehart and Winston, 1985.

Munro, William B. *The Makers of the Unwritten Constitution.* New York: Macmillan Co., 1930.

Padover, Saul, ed. *James Madison: The Complete Madison: His Basic Writings.* New York: Harper, 1953.

Paine, Thomas. "The Rights of Man." In *American Political Thought*, 5th ed, edited by Kenneth Dolbeare and Michael Cummings. Washington, DC: Congressional Quarterly Press, 2004.

Platt, Edmund. *Eagle's History of Poughkeepsie from Earliest Settlements, 1683 to 1905*. Poughkeepsie, NY: Platt & Platt, 1905.

Rakove, Jack. *James Madison and the Creation of the American Republic*. Glenview, IL: Scott, Foresman and Co., 1990.

Randolph, Edmund. *History of Virginia*. Edited, with an introducion by Arthur H. Shaffer. Charlottesville: University of Virginia Press, 1970.

Reimer, Neal. *James Madison: Creating the American Constitution*. Washington, DC: Congressional Quarterly Inc., 1986.

Rives, William. *History of the Life and Times of James Madison*. 2 vols. Boston: Little, Brown and Company, 1870–1881.

Rosen, Gary. *American Compact: James Madison and the Problem of Founding*. Lawrence: University Press of Kansas, 1999.

Rossiter, Clinton. *Alexander Hamilton and the Constitution*. New York: Harcourt, Brace and World, 1964.

Rutland, Robert Allen. *George Mason: Reluctant Statesman*. Williamsburg, VA: Colonial Williamsburg, distributed by Holt, Rinehart and Winston, New York, 1961.

Rutland, Robert. *Ordeal of the Constitution: The Anti-Federalists and the Ratification Struggle of 1787–1788*. Norman: University of Oklahoma Press, 1966.

Schechter, Stephen. *The Reluctant Pillar: New York and the Adoption of the Federal Constitution*. Troy, NY: Russell Sage College Press, 1985.

Schwartz, Bernard, ed. *The Bill of Rights: A Documentary History*. New York: Chelsea House, 1971.

Smith, Charles. *James Wilson: Founding Father, 1742–1798*. Chapel Hill: University of North Carolina Press, 1956.

Smith, James Morton, ed. *The Republic of Letters: The Correspondence Between Thomas Jefferson and James Madison, 1776–1826*. 3 vols. New York: W. W. Norton & Co., 1995.

Smith, Richard Norton. *Patriarch: George Washington and the New American Nation*, Boston: Houghton-Mifflin Co., 1993.

Sparks, Jared. *The Life of Gouverneur Morris*. 3 vols. Boston: Gray Publishing, 1832.

Stahr, Walter. *John Jay: Founding Father*. New York: Hambledon and London, 2005.

Stewart, David. *The Summer of 1787*. New York: Simon & Schuster, 2007.

Syrett, Harold, ed. *The Papers of Alexander Hamilton*. 27 vols. New York: Columbia University Press, 1962–1987.

Tansill, Charles Callan. *The Making of the American Republic: The Great Documents, 1774–1789.* New Rochelle, NY: Arlington House Press, 1972.

Tazewell, Littleton. *An Account and History of the Tazewell Family.* Virginia State Library. Tazewell Family papers, 1782–1844, MSS2 T21986b.

Thatcher, James. *Military Journal of the American Revolution, from the Commencement to the Disbanding of the American Army, Comprising a Detailed Account of the Principal Events and Battles of the American Revolution with Their Exact Dates and a Biographical Sketch of the Most Prominent Generals.* Hartford: Hurlbut, Williams and Co., 1862.

Thayer, Theodore. *Colonial and Revolutionary Morris County.* Morris County Heritage Commission, 1975.

Thorpe, Francis Newton. *Constitutional History of the United States.* Chicago: Callaghan & Company, 1901.

Tuckerman, Bayard. *Life of General Philip Schuyler, 1733–1804.* New York: Dodd, Mead and Company, 1903.

Unger, Harlow. *John Hancock: Merchant King and American Patriot.* New York: John Wiley and Sons, 2005.

Washington, George. *Papers of George Washington.* Edited by W. W. Abbot and Dorothy Twohig. Confederation series. 33 vols. Charlottesville: University Press of Virginia, 1992–2008.

Washington, George. *The Writings of George Washington from the Original Manuscript Sources, 1745–1799.* Edited by John C. Fitzpatrick. 39 vols. Washington, D.C.: U.S. Government Printing Office, 1931–1944. [GWW]

Wirt, William. *Patrick Henry: Life, Correspondence and Speeches.* Philadelphia: E. Claxton, 1881.

Wood, Gordon. *The Creation of the American Republic, 1776–1783.* New York: W. W. Norton & Co., 1972.

# INDEX